2. 9. '95

Thomas

Happy 18th Birthday
v best wishes for the future.
with love
Mollie

This collection of essays by a group of leading authorities is addressed primarily to a non-specialist readership, with the aim of introducing people and achievements associated with the University of Cambridge over the past 150 years. It explains, in simple terms, what has been done in a wide variety of fields – including philosophy (Ray Monk on Russell, Peter Hacker on Wittgenstein, Robert Grant on Oakeshott); economics (Geoffrey Harcourt on Keynes); anthropology (Ernest Gellner on Frazer); the study of English (Stephen Heath on Richards and Leavis). Some who have made important contributions to Cambridge science describe their own work and discoveries – Max Perutz in molecular biology ; Antony Hewish in radioastronomy; Simon Conway Morris in palaeontology. As a whole, the book offers an intellectual portrait of many of modern Cambridge's most notable achievements which will be appreciated by a broad range of readers within the University and far beyond.

CAMBRIDGE MINDS

CAMBRIDGE
MINDS

Edited by

RICHARD MASON

CAMBRIDGE
UNIVERSITY PRESS

Published by the Press Syndicate of the University of Cambridge
The Pitt Building, Trumpington Street, Cambridge CB2 1RP
40 West 20th Street, New York, NY 10011–4211, USA
10 Stamford Road, Oakleigh, Melbourne 3166, Australia

© Cambridge University Press 1994

First published 1994

Printed in Great Britain at the University Press, Cambridge

A catalogue record for this book is available from the British Library

Library of Congress cataloguing in publication data

ISBN 0 521 45405 0 hardback
ISBN 0 521 45625 8 paperback

Contents

Contents

Contributors

RAY MONK is at the University of Southampton.

STEPHEN HEATH is Reader in Cultural Studies and Fellow of Jesus College, Cambridge.

GILLIAN SUTHERLAND is Vice-Principal of Newnham College, Cambridge.

ANTONY HEWISH is Emeritus Professor of Radioastronomy and Fellow of Churchill College, Cambridge. He was Director of the Mullard Radioastronomy Observatory from 1982 to 1987. He was awarded the Nobel Prize for Physics in 1974.

LORD RENFREW is Disney Professor of Archaeology and Master of Jesus College, Cambridge.

GEOFFREY HARCOURT is Reader in the History of Economic Theory, Fellow of Jesus College, Cambridge, and Emeritus Professor of Economics at the University of Adelaide.

JEREMY GRAY is a Lecturer in Mathematics at the Open University.

PAUL MCHUGH is a Principal Lecturer in History at Anglia Polytechnic University.

RICHARD KEYNES is Emeritus Professor of Physiology and Fellow of Churchill College, Cambridge.

SIMON CONWAY MORRIS is Reader in Evolutionary Palaeobiology and Fellow of St John's College, Cambridge.

P. M. S. HACKER is a Fellow of St John's College, Oxford.

JEFFREY HUGHES until recently was a Fellow of Corpus Christi College, Cambridge, and is now a Lecturer in the History of Science at the University of Manchester.

Contributors

MARK GOLDIE is a University Lecturer in History and Vice-Master of Churchill College, Cambridge.

M. F. PERUTZ is former Director of the Medical Research Council Laboratory of Molecular Biology in Cambridge. He was awarded the Nobel Prize for Chemistry in 1962.

ERNEST GELLNER is Emeritus Professor of Social Anthropology and Fellow of King's College, Cambridge. He is now a Research Professor at the Central European University, Prague.

ROBERT GRANT is Senior Lecturer in English at the University of Glasgow.

Preface

The chapters in this book are based on a series of lectures given to the Cambridge University International Summer School in July 1993. The Summer School was attended by about 350 people from over thirty countries, studying a variety of subjects. Summer School students spend a month in Cambridge and can appreciate for themselves the visible splendours of its college and university buildings. Its intellectual achievements are rather less visible. As director of the Summer School, I invited the contributors to this series to explain the importance of what had been achieved in each of their subjects, for a completely non-specialised audience.

Many of the resulting studies concentrate on individual figures. This is not intended as an endorsement of history through the Great Names of the Past, but only to provide some focus of interest for subjects that may be alarmingly abstract to grasp. And the subjects here are almost absurdly varied: radioastronomy, economics, anthropology, molecular biology, philosophy, palaeontology, and many more. There is an equal variety in the fame of the characters whose work is discussed: from Keynes and Wittgenstein at one end of the scale to James Stuart and John Neville Figgis at the other.

The series goes back only about 150 years, partly because of a need to draw the line somewhere, and partly because this has been a period when whole careers – rather than only short years as students – were spent in Cambridge by some of its most well-known products. So Byron, Bacon, Milton, Wordsworth and Cromwell can wait, perhaps for another occasion.

One limitation in the contents calls for an embarrassed apology. Gillian Sutherland's chapter explains some of the reasons why this book might almost have been called *Cambridge Men*. The story of the acceptance of women in Cambridge is far from concluded. It has contained some shameful episodes which Gillian Sutherland relates with telling restraint. Although Dorothy Garrod in archaeology, Charlotte Angas Scott in mathematics and Dorothy Hodgkin in molecular biology do receive recognition in these pages, it will be many years before women could take up a just proportion of a collection equivalent to this. A collection entitled *Cambridge Women*, cited by Carmen Blacker and Edward Shils, is, however, planned for publication in 1995.

In 1970, the editors of an anthology of articles from *The Cambridge Review* – Eric Homberger, William Janeway and Simon Schama – seemed to feel a more than normally English diffidence about bottling the spirit of Cambridge into a volume which they called *The Cambridge Mind* (Cape). Maybe we are less modest today, or perhaps in today's climate we *have* to be less modest. It is doubtful whether anyone in 1970 could have foreseen a day when our University would have produced a prospectus for applicants carrying advertising from commercial sponsors, or a day when it would employ a fund-raising director with a salary higher than those of its professors; but these days are now with us. In any event, there are some good reasons for a lack of modesty, as well as less good ones. This collection, for example, could contain several other, wholly different sets of Cambridge figures from the same period, with no loss of eminence: Turing or Ramanujan in mathematics; Moore, McTaggart or Ramsey in philosophy; Dirac or Clerk Maxwell in theoretical physics; Acton, Maitland, Knowles or Trevelyan in history; Housman or Forster in literature; William Whewell or Joseph Needham in many fields; and so on. And this still leaves untouched whole areas where there is much to be said: theology, espionage, classics, law . . .

The chapters in this book present almost as much variety in genre or style as in their subject-matter. They include biographical portraits, critical appraisals, family history, personal accounts of scientific discovery, philosophical exposition and advocacy on behalf of the nearly forgotten. Reading through them leaves their editor reluctant to speculate on whether they display any unifying attitude or mentality. I would only add one episode that seems to me to represent what Cambridge has been able to offer. It includes two of the characters in this book: on 18 October 1911, Bertrand Russell received an unannounced visitor in his rooms in Trinity: 'a man who had learned engineering at Charlottenburg, but during his course had acquired, by himself, a passion for the philosophy of maths . . . ' This was Wittgenstein, at that time with no status whatever in the College or in the University, not even as an undergraduate, and with no qualifications or formal background in philosophy. He had arrived to study logic, and he believed that Russell, as the greatest authority, should be his teacher. Russell could have ignored him, thrown him out or sent him to whoever dealt with college admissions at that time. Instead he listened, talked and argued late into the nights and gave Wittgenstein, intellectually, all he had. By April 1913 he was writing: 'I find I no longer talk to him about *my* work, but only about his . . . '

As an instance of openness and generosity this could hardly be bettered, although not everyone would have been so impressed by Russell. A few years later, D. H. Lawrence wrote of a day's visit to Russell and Keynes in Cambridge: 'it sent me mad with misery and hostility and rage', and he dreamt afterwards of 'black beetles'. Not long after that, Russell was removed from Trinity for his activities in the First World War.

I am grateful for advice and help from my colleagues Sarah Ormrod, Jem Poster, Maggie Jones and Piers Bursill-Hall; and for guidance from Jeremy Mynott, William Davies and Simon Mitton at Cambridge University Press. The lectures on which the chapters are based were supported by the University of Cambridge Board of Continuing Education.

Richard Mason
Madingley Hall

CHAPTER 1

The effects of a broken home: Bertrand Russell and Cambridge

RAY MONK

Bertrand Russell once described Cambridge as: 'the only place on earth that I could regard as home'.[1] It is a remark that says as much about his attitude to his family home as it does about his attitude to Cambridge, but it also indicates something of the kind of relationship he had with Cambridge. Like that of a prodigal son to his family, it was occasionally stormy and difficult but ultimately supportive.

His first experience of Cambridge was in December 1889, when he came to Trinity to sit a scholarship exam. On that occasion, it has to be said, he felt anything but at home. He stayed in rooms in New Court and was so shy that he did not dare to ask directions to a lavatory. And so, every morning before his exam, he walked to the railway station to use the public lavatory there.

Having won his scholarship, Russell went up to Trinity in October 1890. From that moment, he writes in his *Autobiography*, 'everything went well with me'.[2] The discovery, he says, 'that I could say things that I thought, and be answered with neither horror nor derision, but as if I had said something quite sensible, was intoxication'.[3]

It was perhaps the first instance in Russell's life in which he made some sort of breakthrough from the intense loneliness that had characterised the first years of his life. One does not have to be especially Freudian to see in this deep-seated loneliness the effects of the tragic events of his first few years. His mother and his sister died when he was two years old and his father when he was four. After that he was brought up by his grandparents in Pembroke Lodge, the house in Richmond Park given to his grandfather, the great Whig

Prime Minister, Lord John Russell, by Queen Victoria. His grand-father then died when Russell was six. After that, he used to lie in bed wondering when his grandmother too was going to be taken away from him. This sense of loss and loneliness seems somehow linked to the wellspring of his philosophical work. His earliest intellectual adventure came at the age of eleven when he was introduced to the axiomatic system of geometry contained in Euclid's *Elements*. He describes the experience as being like the rhapsody of first love. In a world in which everything had seemed alarmingly unstable, uncer-tain and impermanent, it was a delight to discover the iron certainty with which mathematical theorems could be demonstrated from within an axiomatic system. The only thing that spoiled his enjoy-ment was the realisation that, although the theorems could be deduced rigorously from the axioms, the axioms themselves had to be taken on trust. One might regard his later work on the philosophy of mathematics as an attempt to solve this problem.

Russell came from one of the most notable families in English history and he was brought up to be acutely conscious of the fact. His grandmother taught him to respect the achievements, not only of his grandfather, Lord John Russell, but also of his more distant ancestors: his great-grandfather the sixth Duke of Bedford, for example, who had been one of the few Whigs to support Charles James Fox in his opposition to the war against the French, and his great-great-grandfather the fourth Duke of Bedford, who was one of the most powerful of the Whig magnates of the eighteenth century.

He was taught to regard the history of England as inseparable from the destiny of his family, and, like Lord John Russell, he came to look upon his family history as part and parcel of the march of progress of liberty and intelligence. A key role in this powerful family mythology was allotted to Lord William Russell, the son of the fifth Earl of Bedford, who for his part in the Rye House Plot during the reign of Charles II became one of the very first Whig martyrs. At the root of the family tree was John Russell, the first Earl of Bedford and the founder of the family fortunes, who, at the beginning of Henry VIII's reign, was a minor courtier, but who, by the time of Henry's death, having amassed massive amounts of monastic property, was one of the richest and most powerful noblemen in the country.

The weight of this tradition was brought to bear with all its force on the young Bertrand Russell, who for about the first eighteen years of his life was known to most people as 'Lord John Russell's grand-son'. It was assumed by his grandmother that he would follow in his grandfather's footsteps and become in time a great Liberal Prime Minister. Absorption in philosophical questions, therefore, was severely discouraged. Whenever the subject of metaphysics was broached, Granny Russell would laugh derisively and say? 'What is mind? No matter. What is matter? Never mind.'

In the face of such ridicule, the teenage Bertrand Russell pursued his philosophical thinking furtively and alone. His first philosophical work is in the form of a journal discussing day by day his attempts to wrestle with his loss of religious faith and with the question of whether we do or do not have free will. To avoid detection, it was written in Greek characters and has come to be known as the 'Greek Exercises'.

To go from such furtiveness to the open discussion of ideas he experienced at Cambridge was, for Russell, like stepping out of the shadows and into the light. The joy was, however, not entirely unalloyed. Though he revelled in the opportunity to discuss his philosophical ideas, he quickly became disillusioned with the way mathematics was then taught at Cambridge. Owing, he came to think, to the obligation imposed by the Wrangler system of making very fine distinctions between candidates, mathematics was taught as a succession of tricks and hurdles, and the foundations of the subject – which is what had interested him from the age of eleven – were ignored altogether. In his fourth year, therefore, Russell switched to philosophy, or moral sciences as it was then known in Cambridge.

Russell's reputation as a philosopher is that of the last of the great British empiricists. But arguably his best work in philosophy was done within a fervently anti-empiricist framework. Indeed, for a while, he even embraced the neo-Hegelian Idealism that was fashionable at Cambridge during his undergraduate days. Before he went to Cambridge, the only philosopher he had really studied was John Stuart Mill, but even as a fifteen-year-old he had found Mill's philosophy of mathematics inadequate. Mill had argued that mathematical truths were generalisations of everyday, empirically established facts. We see that two apples plus two apples make four apples, and that two oranges plus two oranges make four oranges, and we infer that, in general, two plus two is always equal to four.

To the teenage Russell, infatuated as he was with the sublime certainty of Euclid's demonstrations, such a doctrine seemed not only obviously false but also positively repulsive. It seemed to ignore altogether what was peculiar to mathematics and what was so wonderful about it: namely, the *necessity* of its truths. Two plus two did not just *happen* to equal four, it couldn't possibly be equal to anything else. An adequate philosophy of mathematics, he felt, would have to do justice to this necessity.

As it happened, this innate revulsion of his against an empiricist philosophy of mathematics chimed perfectly with the philosophical climate of Cambridge in the 1890s, the general mood of which was characterised by a disillusionment with the British tradition of empiricism and a willingness to embrace the German tradition of Hegelian Idealism. The only empiricist philosopher among those who taught Russell as an undergraduate was the utilitarian Henry Sidgwick, who was nicknamed 'Old Sig' and thought to be impossibly old-fashioned. The tutors who had the most to do with Russell during his undergraduate days were James Ward and G. F. Stout, respectively a Kantian and a Hegelian. But the dominant figure of Cambridge philosophy during this period and the man to whom Russell looked up to most was Ellis McTaggart. McTaggart was to Cambridge what Bradley was to Oxford: the leading figure of the British wave of neo-Hegelian Idealists. He was especially notorious for arguing strongly for the unreality of space and time and all their phenomena.

It is doubtful, I think, whether Russell ever took this doctrine quite seriously. Certainly he was always alive to its comic aspects. Philosophy at this time seemed to him, as he says in his *Autobiography*, 'great fun'. 'I enjoyed', he writes there, 'the curious ways of conceiving the world that the great philosophers offer to the imagination'.[4] Cambridge neo-Hegelianism is, in this respect, one of the most curious, and Russell was not alone in finding it also the greatest fun. The Apostles, the famous Cambridge debating society to which Russell was elected in 1892, embraced the jargon of McTaggart's Hegelianism with an obvious relish for its comic absurdity. On the model of McTaggart's metaphysics, they described their own Society as The World of Reality, and everything else mere 'appearance'. People who were not in the Society were 'phenomena' while those who were in it were assumed, like McTaggart's reality, to lie outside Space and Time.

The greatest happiness of his time at Cambridge, Russell says in his *Autobiography*, was connected with the Apostles. The Society seemed to epitomise for him the quality he most admired and liked about Cambridge life: its intellectual honesty and willingness to discuss anything, no matter how intimate or controversial.

'In general,' he writes, 'I felt happy and comparatively calm while at Cambridge, but on moonlit nights I used to career round the country in a state of temporary lunacy. The reason, of course, was sexual desire, though at the time I did not know this'.[5]

Prompted no doubt at least in part by the strength of this sexual desire, Russell married early. In the summer of 1893, when he was twenty-one and just after he had been placed Seventh Wrangler in the Mathematics Tripos, he proposed to Alys Pearsall Smith, the youngest daughter of an American Quaker family that lived close to Russell's Uncle Rollo in Haslemere. His grandmother disapproved strongly of the match and so the year in which Russell took the second part of the Moral Sciences Tripos was one fraught with domestic strife. Russell, however, claimed that: 'I never found that love, either when it prospered or when it did not, interfered in the slightest with my intellectual concentration'.[6]

Alys took most of that year to consider Russell's proposal and only finally consented to it about the time that Russell finished the Moral Sciences Tripos (and true to what he says about not being distracted, he got a First with distinction). Upon Alys's acceptance, Russell's family – and particularly his grandmother – massively increased the pressure on him not to marry her. The tactic they eventually hit upon was one which, whether they knew it or not (and they most possibly did), played into the hands of Russell's deepest fear: the fear of madness. They told him that he must not marry because if he had children they would almost certainly be insane. They had not told him the truth about his family hitherto, they said, but in fact there was a strong streak of hereditary madness: his Uncle Willy, for example, lived permanently in a mental asylum, having gone insane while serving in the army and having tried to murder one of his fellow officers; his maiden Aunt Agatha too, suffered from mental disturbances, and that was why she had never married. And his father also had been epileptic.

These revelations chimed with a fear that Russell had already had. The previous summer he had dreamt that his mother was not dead, but mad, locked away in secrecy somewhere. Now, he wrote in a diary of the time, he felt 'haunted by the fear of the family ghost, which seems to seize on me with clammy invisible hands'. Pembroke Lodge, his family home, began to seem like a vault 'haunted by the ghosts of maniacs'. He began to have a recurring dream in which he was being murdered by a lunatic. The fear of madness transformed his personality. It caused him, he says, 'to avoid all deep emotion, and live, as nearly as I could, a life of intellect tempered by flippancy'. In the short term, however, Russell and Alys, determined to marry whatever, declared that in the light of Grandmother Russell's revelations they would not have children. Upon this, Grandmother Russell produced an expert to testify that contraception was invariably harmful – it was, it turned out, what had caused Russell's father to become epileptic in the first place. After receiving independent medical advice, Russell and Alys decided to ignore this particular piece of nonsense and announced that they were going ahead with the marriage regardless.

Countess Russell's last strategy was to find Russell a temporary post of honorary attaché to Lord Dufferin, the British Ambassador in Paris and a family friend. Out of loyalty to his grandmother, Russell spent three months in diplomatic service, during which, he later said, his chief task was to persuade the French that a lobster is not a fish. Despite his success in this endeavour, Russell felt no sense of achievement or even of involvement in his work at the Embassy. He loathed his job, denounced Paris and the French generally as degenerate and spent the whole time counting the days until he could be back in England with his fiancée. As soon as he did return, he and Alys got married. Granny Russell's battle was lost.

The family ghost she had raised, however, continued to haunt Russell, not only in the sense that he continued to be haunted by a deep-seated terror of insanity, but also, most cruelly of all, in the fact that Granny Russell turned out to be right: Russell's eldest son *was* schizophrenic, as were two of his granddaughters, the suffering that was caused to all three of them being massively increased by Russell's terror of their condition.

After his marriage, Russell had little to do with his grandmother and spent as little time as he could in Pembroke Lodge. On their honeymoon in Berlin, Russell resolved during a walk in the Tiergarten not to adopt a profession (it was in those days, still considered possible – by, for example, his grandmother – that he would enter politics) but to devote himself to writing. His grand scheme was to write two series of books: one on the philosophy of the sciences from mathematics to physiology, and the other on social and political questions. The result would be a great system of philosophy analogous to Hegel's.

On his return to Haslemere, where he and Alys had decided to live close to her family, Russell made the first step on this impossibly ambitious project, when he wrote his Fellowship dissertation on the foundations of geometry. Supervised by James Ward, this was an essentially Kantian piece of work, an attempt to answer the question 'How is geometry possible?' with reference to the necessary features of space, features which we can know (*à la* Kant) *a priori*. Where it differed from Kant was in taking consideration of non-Euclidean geometries and admitting at least the prima facie possibility that physical space might not be as Euclid describes it but as, for example, Riemannian geometry describes it. Whether physical space actually was Euclidean or Riemannian was held by Russell to be an empirical matter, the concern not of geometry but of physics.

Despite his later scorn for it, Russell's Fellowship dissertation is a serious contribution to its subject. It was, in any case, much admired by his examiners, James Ward and Alfred North Whitehead, who had no hesitation in awarding him a prize Fellowship, tenable for five years, on the strength of it. The following year it was published in an amended version as a book entitled *The Foundations of Geometry*. Because of his later repudiation of its view, this book was never reprinted, so that copies of this first and only printing are rare and valued items.

Though it was his first published work of philosophy, *The Foundations of Geometry* was not Russell's first published book. That honour goes to a book called *German Social Democracy*, a study of Marxist theory and practice as exemplified by the German Social Democratic Party, based on Russell's first-hand study of the German socialism during a three-month stay in Berlin in the autumn of 1895. The book is based on a course of lectures Russell gave on the subject at the newly founded London School of Economics in February and March 1896.

The book is something of an anomaly in Russell's development at the time, his study of German social democracy being a residue of the idea cherished by his family that he might pursue a career in politics. Even before beginning the book, Russell had decided that, instead, he would take up his Fellowship at Trinity and pursue an academic career – or, what practically amounted to the same thing, given the terms of his Fellowship – to adopt no career at all and to concentrate on writing. For in those days a prize Fellowship at Trinity carried few obligations. Russell was not required to teach or to research, or even to live during term-time in Cambridge.

Accordingly, most of his first period as a Fellow of Trinity was spent living, not at Cambridge, but in the Sussex countryside, in a small cottage called 'The Millhanger' that Russell and Alys bought at Fernhurst, near her family's home in Haslemere. 'In this cottage', Russell says, 'many of the happiest times of my life were passed'.[7] During the first few years of his marriage, Russell developed a close friendship with Whitehead and his wife Evelyn, the Whiteheads coming often to stay with the Russells in the country and the Russells staying with the Whiteheads in Cambridge.

During the last three months of 1896, Russell and Alys went to America to meet her family, many of whom were in academic life. Her cousin Carey Thomas, for example, was President of Bryn Mawr, and through this contact Russell was invited to lecture not only at Bryn Mawr but also at Johns Hopkins University. He lectured on non-Euclidean geometry and so came into contact with the mathematicians at these universities. These contacts, he said, led him gradually to abandon the belief that everything worth knowing was known in Cambridge and to realise the superiority of Germany over England in almost all academic matters.

It was not until 1898, three years into his marriage and two years into his Fellowship of Trinity, that Russell and Alys began a practice of spending part of each year in Cambridge. By this time, the most important intellectual influence at Cambridge on Russell was neither Ward nor McTaggart, nor even Whitehead, but G. E. Moore. Moore's conversations and his seminal paper, 'On the Nature of Judgment', were to lead Russell to abandon the neo-Hegelianism he had acquired from the philosophy tutors at Cambridge and to embrace a strident and, for him, refreshing realism. It was, he writes in *My Philosophical Development*, a profound relief to believe once more that grass really was green.[8]

Of more consequence for his work on the foundations of

mathematics, however, was the parallel belief in the reality of relations. Under the influence of the Oxford philosopher F. H. Bradley, British Idealist philosophers had come to believe that there cannot really be such things as relations. This was a consequence of their belief that there was in reality only one thing, which was the Absolute, of which everything else was a part. There cannot be relations between things because that would imply the opposite: i.e., that there was more than one thing. So, in the light of this doctrine, the relations established by inference in, say, logic and mathematics, were held to be 'internal', that is to say, they were not relations between two or more things, but connections between aspects of the Absolute.

Connected with this doctrine was the assumption, held by traditional Aristotelian logic, that all propositions are of the subject–predicate form. Russell's realisation of the importance of this did not strike him with full force until he began a detailed study of the work of Leibniz. The occasion for this was that when McTaggart left Trinity to spend a year in New Zealand, the College asked Russell to take his place lecturing on Leibniz. The result was *The Philosophy of Leibniz*, published in 1900, Russell's first philosophical book since his abandonment of Idealism.

Russell's realisation that not quite everything worth knowing was known at Cambridge received a new and powerful impetus in the summer of 1900 when he attended the International Congress of Philosophy in Paris. With this, he writes, 'a new chapter of my life began'.[9]

Intellectually the road he had travelled was this: having been enraptured by his first experience at eleven of Euclid's geometry, he became entranced by the suggestive possibility that all in life might not be transient and impermanent, that there might be some genuinely certain knowledge to be acquired. This was what he hoped to acquire from his study of mathematics, but his experience of mathematics at Cambridge disillusioned him and he turned to philosophy instead. Initially attracted to the then fashionable view that everything in the world of the senses was mere appearance and that the only reality was the one, indivisible Absolute, Russell, led by Moore, came to rebel against this view. In reaction to it, he swung completely the other way: from denying the reality of everything, he came to assert the reality of anything and everything, including – to

9

quote a list he was to give in *Principles of Mathematics* – numbers, chimeras, four-dimensional spaces and Homeric gods.

Thus, in the philosophy of mathematics, he had gone from the Kantian view that mathematics studies the necessary features of our experience, the structure of our appearance, to the view associated with Plato that the objects of mathematics have an objective existence not dependent upon our perception or knowledge.

What Russell desired more than anything by the summer of 1900, was a way of *proving* the Kantian view of mathematics to be false and of showing how the theorems of mathematics can (a) be derived within an axiomatic system analogous to Euclid's and (b) be understood in a non-Kantian way as objective matters of fact concerning, not our perceptions, but reality.

At the Congress, he discovered – to his almost unbounded delight – what he took to be a way of attaining both these ends in the mathematical logic of the Italian mathematician Guiseppe Peano. Immediately he returned from the Congress he set about reading everything by Peano and his disciples. In the months that followed, at his home in Fernhurst Russell underwent a period of philosophical activity and creativity that – if it has any parallel in twentieth-century British philosophy – matches that of Wittgenstein in his year in Norway in 1913/14. 'The time was one of intellectual intoxication,' he writes in his *Autobiography*:

> My sensations resembled those one has after climbing a mountain in the mist, when, on reaching the summit, the mist suddenly clears, and the country becomes visible for forty miles in every direction. For years I had been endeavouring to analyse the fundamental notions of mathematics, such as order and cardinal numbers. Suddenly, in the space of a few weeks, I discovered what appeared to be definitive answers to the problems which had baffled me for years. And in the course of discovering these answers, I was introducing a new mathematical technique, by which regions formerly abandoned in the vaguenesses of philosophers were conquered for the precision of exact formulae. Intellectually, the month of September 1900 was the highest point of my life. I went about saying to myself that now at last I had done something worth doing, and I had the feeling that I must be careful not to be run over in the street before I had written it down.[10]

Becoming acquainted with Peano's system was the greatest intellectual adventure in Russell's life since his introduction to

Euclid. In the first flush of excitement, he wrote a popular article called 'Mathematics and the Metaphysicians' that is unrestrainedly rhapsodic in its enthusiasm. 'One of the chief triumphs of modern mathematics', he writes in this article, 'consists in having discovered what mathematics really is'.[11] And what is it? It is no more and no less than logic. The axioms of Euclidean geometry that had been troubling him since he was eleven do not, he now realised, have to be taken on trust after all, for they are not the true foundation of their subject:

> All pure mathematics – Arithmetic, Analysis, and Geometry – is built up by combinations of the primitive ideas of logic, and its propositions are deduced from the general axioms of logic, such as the syllogism and the other rules of inference. And this is no longer a dream or an aspiration. On the contrary, over the greater and more difficult part of the domain of mathematics, it has already been accomplished; in the few remaining cases, there is no special difficulty, and it is now being rapidly achieved. Philosophers have disputed for ages whether such deduction was possible; mathematicians have sat down and made the deduction. For the philosophers there is now nothing left but graceful acknowledgment.[12]

'What is now required', he concluded:

> is to give the greatest possible development to mathematical logic, to allow to the full the importance of relations, and then to found upon this secure basis a new philosophical logic, which may hope to borrow some of the exactitude and certainty of its mathematical foundation. If this can be successfully accomplished, there is every reason to hope that the near future will be as great an epoch in pure philosophy as the immediate past has been in the principles of mathematics. Great triumphs inspire great hopes; and pure thought may achieve, within our generation, such results as will place our time, in this respect, on a level with the greatest age of Greece.[13]

It was the fact that it all seemed so clear to Russell that enabled him to work so astonishingly quickly on the first draft of *Principles of Mathematics*. He knew what he had to do: he had to show that our knowledge of mathematical truths can be shown to be logically sound, because it can be shown that, fundamentally, mathematical truths *are* logical truths. And he knew *how* he was to achieve this: by embedding Peano's axioms within the logic of classes and relations. The prize for doing both these things would be that of demonstrating from first principles the indisputable truth of mathematics.

By the spring of 1901, however, Russell's honeymoon period with mathematical logic came to a crashing halt when he discovered a contradiction in the notion of a class. This has since become famous as Russell's Paradox and is drilled into all undergraduate students of logic. When it is first encountered, it seems trivial. Indeed, Russell thought that it was a minor problem that could be dealt with very quickly. When he communicated the problem to Whitehead, however, Whitehead knew better. Quoting from Browning's poem 'The Lost Leader', Whitehead remarked gravely: 'Never glad confident morning again.' And when, after a year of struggling with the contradiction himself, Russell wrote to tell Frege about it, Frege – who had, Russell had belatedly discovered, been working on the same project of founding mathematics on the theory of classes – replied:

> Your discovery of the contradiction has surprised me beyond words and, I should almost like to say, left me thunderstruck, because it has rocked the ground on which I meant to build arithmetic. It is all the more serious as [it] seems to undermine not only the foundations of my arithmetic but the only possible foundations of arithmetic as such.[14]

The contradiction arises from considering the difference between classes that are members of themselves and classes that are not: the class of tables is not itself a table and so is not a member of itself; the class of all classes is itself a class and so *is* a member of itself. Now, suppose we define the class of all classes that are not members of themselves. Such a definition does not immediately seem to pose any difficulties, but, in fact, on further consideration, it leads to a contradiction and thus shows that there is something wrong with the simple notion of a class, the very notion that both Frege and Russell wanted to use as a foundation for the whole of mathematics. For, take the class of all classes that do not belong to themselves and ask of it: is *it* a member of itself or not? However we answer this question, we end up contradicting ourselves. It is rather like defining the barber in a village as the man who shaves all men who do not shave themselves: does *he* shave himself or not?

Shortly after writing to Frege, Russell published *Principles of Mathematics*. Far from being, as he had hoped only two years previously it would be, the final, definitive statement on the nature of mathematical knowledge, it was, though still a great book, rather provisional. Its tone is not one of triumph but rather one of bafflement and defeat. Having recommended that the notion of class be regarded as fundamental to the nature of mathematics, he is forced to recognise that the notion is itself problematic. 'I must confess', he writes in the preface, 'I have failed to perceive any concept fulfilling the conditions requisite for the notion of *class*. And the contradiction . . . proves that something is amiss, but what this is I have hitherto failed to discover.'

By the time he published *Principles of Mathematics*, Russell was no longer a Fellow of Trinity. His five-year Fellowship expired in October 1901, and though he continued to lecture on logic and mathematics during the following year, by 1903 he had given up teaching altogether. Officially, he had at this time no more con- nection with Trinity than any other graduate of the College, but unofficially, of course, during the years that he wrestled with the problems of the Paradox, he was in close touch with members of the College, especially Whitehead.

The Principles of Mathematics was originally intended to be the first volume in a two-volume work demonstrating the logical foundation of mathematics. Specifically, it was intended to present the philo- sophical arguments for thinking mathematics to be essentially logic; the second volume had the formidable task of actually proving mathematically, theorem by theorem, how the whole of mathematics could be derived from a few logical axioms. The amount of work involved in this was prodigious and Russell was only too pleased to accept the offer of Whitehead to co-write the book. In the end it turned out to be itself a massive three-volume work that took ten years for the two of them to complete. Publishing it as the second volume of the *Principles* would have been ludicrous, so it was given its own name and called *Principia Mathematica*.

Between the publication of *Principles of Mathematics* in 1903 and the completion of the first volume of *Principia Mathematica* in 1910, Russell's philosophical views, in successive attempts to deal with the Paradox, underwent a radical and fundamental change. In the process, his world became greyer and sadder. When he began his project of founding mathematics in logic, he understood math- ematics to be the establishing of indubitable truths about eternal objects; when he finished he understood it to be the establishing of trivialities about language.

The change came about in this way: he began with specifically mathematical notions like primes and squares, multiplication and exponentiation, then he saw how all these could be simplified down to the three basic notions at the heart of Peano's system. Then he, like Frege, thought he saw how these notions in turn could be simplified down to the basic notion of a class.

But the notion of a class proved to be contradictory, so Russell came, during the interval between the *Principles* and *Principia* to believe that there *were* no classes, there were only linguistic expressions that gave the *appearance* of referring to classes. These expressions of convenience Russell called propositional functions: 'x is a man', for example, is a propositional function. In the light of the contradiction, Russell came to see mathematics as the science of propositional functions. It was a view which seemed to strip mathematics of the sublime significance it had had for him until then. Mathematics was not the gateway to a Platonic realm of abstract objects and timeless certainties; it was simply a way of manipulating linguistic symbols.

The period between the discovery of the Paradox in 1901 and the completion of *Principia* in 1910 was one of great disillusionment in Russell's personal life too. During a bicycle ride in 1902 – or so he claims in his *Autobiography* – he suddenly realised that he no longer loved Alys. Actually, the diary he kept during that period, suggests that the realisation was more gradual than this, but, whether suddenly or slowly, Russell fell out of love with Alys completely during this period. Just as Cambridge had previously been a home from Pembroke Lodge, so it now became a home from Fernhurst, and, after 1905, from the home in Bagley Wood near Oxford that he and Alys had built for them.

When, in 1910, he was offered a lectureship by Trinity, therefore, he had personal as well as intellectual reasons for accepting it – financial ones too, for by this time his inheritance had all been used up. It is perhaps in the way of these things that by the time he had been offered a lectureship, his best work in philosophy was behind him. He himself was acutely conscious of this, and his years as a lecturer at Trinity from 1910 until the outbreak of the First World War in 1914 are marked less by progress in philosophy than by progress in his personal development, specifically his meetings with a succession of remarkable characters who would have a permanent effect upon his character and outlook: Ottoline Morrell, Ludwig Wittgenstein and Joseph Conrad.

When Wittgenstein came into his life in 1911, Russell soon came to think that he had found the successor he had been looking for. The price to pay for this was that Wittgenstein stripped him of what confidence he had left in his own capacity to continue making fundamental contributions to philosophy. Wittgenstein's criticism of the theory of judgement contained in *The Theory of Knowledge*, a large work on epistemology that Russell began in 1913, caused Russell to abandon not only that book but also any idea that he might have anything left to contribute to technical philosophy.

His perspective on the value of abstract work in general had in any case undergone a dramatic transformation during this time. In the same year that he discovered the Paradox, Russell experienced a sort of religious conversion. The immediate cause of this experience was the sight of Evelyn Whitehead in pain, apparently suffering from an angina attack. The passage which describes the experience is among the most extraordinary in Russell's *Autobiography*:

> Suddenly the ground seemed to give way beneath me, and I found myself in quite another region. Within five minutes I went through some such reflections as the following: the loneliness of the human soul is unendurable; nothing can penetrate it except the highest intensity of the sort of love that religious teachers have preached; whatever does not spring from this motive is harmful, or at best useless; it follows that war is wrong, that a public school education is abominable, that the use of force is to be deprecated, and that in human relations one should penetrate to the core of loneliness in each person and speak to that.[15]

In other words, perhaps, the retreat into the 'life of intellect tempered by flippancy' that he had earlier described as a result of the fear of insanity instilled into him by his grandmother was now being halted. Faced by the suffering of Evelyn Whitehead, he felt compelled to overcome his fear of emotion and to give way, at last, to feelings of empathy for another human being. In the days immediately after this experience, indeed, he began to feel that he knew the inmost thoughts of everybody he met in the street. 'Though this was no doubt an illusion,' he writes, 'I did in actual fact find myself in far closer touch than previously with all my friends, and many of my acquaintances'.[16]

The consequences of this experience were profound and were to affect all parts of Russell's life. For example: 'Having for years cared only for exactness and analysis, I found myself filled with semi-mystical feelings about beauty, with an intense interest in children, and with a desire almost as profound as that of the Buddha to find some philosophy as which should make human life endurable'.[17] The immediate consequence of this last was the so-called 'religion of sorrow' outlined in his essay, 'The Free Man's Worship', first published in 1903 and still today his best-known essay. But there were longer term consequences as well. Russell himself lists four: 'my attitude during the first war, my interest in children, my indifference to minor misfortunes, and a certain emotional tone in all my human relations'.[18]

One he does not mention, but which is implicit in what he does say, is the subversive effect this experience had on his love for mathematics. The Platonic certainties of mathematics were no longer for him the ultimate goal of life; neither did the Platonic realm of mathematical truth represent for him the best escape from a life of loneliness: now he saw that the only real way to overcome loneliness was to engage with other people. There is thus an emotional investment in his abandonment of Platonism, which helps to explain, I think, why, even when – in the wake of Gödel's Theorem – there were good mathematical and philosophical reasons for adopting a Platonic conception of mathematics, Russell refused to return to his earlier view.

One other long-term consequence of the transformation in him wrought by this conversion experience and the desire for a deeper connection with people is his recognition that his marriage to Alys could never satisfy him and his search for a deeper level of human relations. That is ultimately what is at stake in his famous love affair with Ottoline Morrell, which raged from 1911 to 1916.

Russell mentions his attitude to the First World War as a consequence of his conversion. This attitude led ultimately to a breach between himself and Trinity College that was to drive him out of his self-appointed 'home' for the next thirty years.

As part of his work for the pacifist movement against the war, Russell published in 1916 a leaflet defending a conscientious objector called Everett. In Liverpool three men were arrested for distributing the leaflet, whereupon Russell wrote to *The Times* saying that, as he was its author, he too should be prosecuted. This rather forced the hands of the authorities and Russell was accordingly tried and fined £100. This gave the older members of Trinity – including, much to Russell's disgust, Ellis McTaggart – the chance they had been waiting for to distance themselves from Russell's pacifist activities. Russell's five-year lectureship expired in October 1915. In the summer of 1915, some of the Fellows friendly to Russell put forward the suggestion that when his lectureship expired, he should be made a Fellow. A Fellowship was duly offered to him, but on the condition that any leave of absence from the post could only be for academic research not for political campaigning. This condition he refused, so the offer was changed to a lectureship, thus making it easier when the time came to get rid of him altogether. The time came in the summer of 1916 after his fine. The Council of the College – by this stage dominated by those too old to fight in the war – met to decide to dismiss Russell from his post. Upon hearing the news Russell wrote to the College insisting that his name be scratched from the book. For the second half of the war, then, Russell was not in any way attached to Trinity, being not even a member of College.

After the war, the younger Fellows of Trinity, led by the mathematician, G. H. Hardy, insisted that Russell be offered his post back. Thus, in 1920, he was offered a lectureship beginning that October. With certain misgivings, he accepted, but on condition that he would be away on leave during the first year of his appointment, 1920/1. He was to spend this year in China, as a visiting lecturer in Peking. He took with him to China his lover Dora Black and, while there, took delight in living openly 'in sin' (as he liked to put it). Realising, however, that the authorities of Trinity would look askance at one of their lecturers living in sin with one woman while remaining still married to another, Russell wrote to Trinity in January 1921, resigning from the lectureship he had never really taken up.

From 1921, then, Russell having left his 'home', was forced to make his own way in the world. Apart from returning to give the Tarner lectures in 1925 (which he turned into the book, *The Analysis of Matter*), Russell had nothing more to do with Trinity until 1944. During this period, it was Trinity's turn to reject him. In the mid-1930s, after his second marriage had ended in divorce and he had abandoned his attempts to run a progressive school, Russell wanted nothing more than to return to philosophy, and, particularly, to his 'home' in Trinity. To this end he solicited Moore to see if there was any chance of a lecturing post. The answer was an emphatic 'no', so, in 1938, Russell took the best offer he had and went over to America to take up a post at the University of Chicago. He was to remain in America for most of the war, in a succession of unsatisfactory jobs which ended with his disastrous employment and eventual sacking by Albert Barnes in Philadelphia.

Fortunately for him, Hardy had been reviving, during 1942, the issue of Trinity's treatment of one of its most famous sons. His book about the dispute in the First World War, *Bertrand Russell and Trinity*, was published as part of a campaign to make Trinity feel ashamed of itself. It worked. In 1943, Russell was invited to take up a five-year Fellowship beginning in October 1944. Although he was no longer at the height of his powers, the Fellowship did enable him to complete in peace his very last work of philosophy, *Human Knowledge*, by no means his greatest contribution to philosophy, but a substantial work nevertheless and a much better book than its reputation would suggest.

In the autumn of 1949, Russell – by now thoroughly respectable, a peer of the realm, the holder of the Order of Merit and shortly to become a Nobel Prize winner – was awarded the highest honour Trinity could bestow when he was granted a lifetime Fellowship. Coming as it did when he was in his seventy-eighth year, the honour was somewhat belated, and certainly too late to allow Russell to make any further contribution to philosophy. But it was at the very least an acknowledgement that, at last, he was welcome back home.

NOTES

1 Bertrand Russell, *Autobiography*, London: Allen and Unwin 1967–9, p. 71.
2 Ibid., p. 53.
3 Ibid., p. 60.
4 Ibid., p. 65.
5 Ibid., p. 70.
6 Ibid., p. 80.
7 Ibid., p. 129.

8 Bertrand Russell, *My Philosophical Development*, London: Allen and Unwin 1959, p. 48.
9 Russell, *Autobiography*, p. 138.
10 Ibid., p. 148.
11 Bertrand Russell, *Mysticism and Logic*, London: George Allen and Unwin 1963, p. 60.
12 Ibid.
13 Ibid., p. 74.
14 Frege to Russell, 16 June 1902, quoted in, e.g., Jean van Heijenoort (ed.), *From Frege to Gödel: A Sourcebook in Mathematical Logic*, ed. Jean van Heijenoort, Cambridge, Mass.: Harvard University Press 1967, p. 124.
15 Russell, *Autobiography*, p. 149.
16 Ibid.
17 Ibid.
18 Ibid.

CHAPTER 2

I. A. Richards, F. R. Leavis and Cambridge English

STEPHEN HEATH

The phrase 'Cambridge English' comes with a weight that is more than that of simple reference to the possibility of studying English in the University. It is taken as pointing to something more substantial, a particular way of thinking about and doing English, of what that represents. In this substantial sense, Cambridge English has a particular historical development in the years between the two World Wars and a powerful social influence through the extension of its version of 'English' into schools and universities both in Britain and in other English-speaking countries. It can be seen, in fact, as about an intense crisis in culture and society and, as such, part of a process of critical engagement with modern civilisation that had been developed throughout the nineteenth century (the tradition so well described by the Cambridge-English-educated Raymond Williams in his book *Culture and Society*). To understand Cambridge English in these terms is to consider the work of two men, I. A. Richards and F. R. Leavis; it is from them that Cambridge English derived its definition, they who made it more than just English at Cambridge.

English came late to Cambridge, decisively established as an independent subject for study only in the years following the First World War. Initially, it was an optional language in the new Medieval and Modern Languages Tripos set up in 1884, with the focus linguistic and philological. In 1891 the various languages were separately organised into sections; for English, this gave one section devoted to Anglo-Saxon, Norse, English historical grammar and related topics, and another with papers on Chaucer, Shakespeare, and literature after, as well as before, 1500 (Old English figured in this section too). Numbers were small and most of the lecturing was done by the Professor of Anglo-Saxon, with help from a few freelance lecturers. Despite opposition, a lectureship to meet the lack of teaching in 'the middle and later English subjects' was created in 1896, but proposals in 1909 to shift the balance between language and literature in favour of the latter, meeting with similar opposition, were not carried through. The next year, however, an offer was accepted from the press magnate Sir Harold Harmsworth to endow a professorship in memory of the late King for the study of 'English Literature from the age of Chaucer onwards . . . on literary and critical rather than on philological and linguistic lines' and on 10 May 1911 the first King Edward VII Professor of English Literature – the now-forgotten Arthur Verrall, previously a lecturer in classics – delivered his inaugural lecture.

The war forced the decisive development, giving urgency to the need for educational change, for response to the reality of what was perceived as a confused and complex new world. In 1917 a report insisted that languages be taught with a much stronger modern relevance (the medieval and modern became the Modern and Medieval Languages Tripos) and that there be 'an independent Tripos for English'. This was agreed and in 1919 the first examination for the English Tripos took place (it was intended to be taken after a Part I in another subject, usually classics). It was quickly felt desirable that there should be a complete and distinct two-part course and this was achieved in 1926 (the number of students taking English was then nearly 250) by the creation of a fully independent Board of English and an English Tripos allowing a unique separation of literary from linguistic studies – a degree could be obtained at Cambridge in English with no requirements in Old English or philology (the separation was made the easier by post-war anti-German feeling, philology being seen as 'Germanic'). Part I comprised papers in English literature, life and thought from Chaucer on, plus passages for critical discussion and some critical set books; Part II, more comparative and more specialised, had papers on tragedy, history and theory of criticism, English moralists, special periods and topics in English literature, practical criticism, and foreign language and literature. This was to be the basic framework for the study and examination of English in the University for the

next forty or more years; indeed, it is still in many respects recognisably there today.

This late appearance of English in Cambridge falls, of course,
within the very much wider history of the educational emergence of
English, its validation as a subject for schools and universities.
'Englishe matter in the Englishe tongue, for Englishe men', wrote
the humanist Roger Ascham in the mid-sixteenth century and we
could take the history back to that Renaissance interest in a cultural
literacy in the vernacular. The interest includes recognition of the
need to bring this 'Englishe tongue' into some kind of identity, to fix
and improve it, and of literature as having a role in this inasmuch as
its achievement of a perfection matching that of writings in other
'tongues' – Greek and Latin above all – would raise English to the
status of a worthy language. An awareness of English authors and
English literature as such thus became important, even while the
grammar schools and the universities – Oxford and Cambridge –
pursued the classical curriculum. What gave English an important
educational reality was the pressure from the new scientific thinking
on the one hand and anti-classical non-conformism on the other (the
two running together at so many points in the economically and
politically developing middle class): where Milton (1608–74) went to
St Paul's School and Christ's College, Cambridge, and received a
classical education, Defoe (1660–1757) studied at the Revd Charles
Morton's Newington Green Academy – one of the non-conformist
Dissenting Academies – where emphasis was on 'practical' subjects,
including modern languages and science, and, breaking with
tradition, instruction was given in English, which was then also a
matter for study. Literature figured in this teaching as a source of
instances of the good exercise of language (the eighteenth-century
chemist Joseph Priestley, who taught for a while in a Dissenting
Academy, wrote a *Rudiments of English Grammar* for schools that
draws – for 'exemplification' – on passages from Pope and Addison
and other of 'our most celebrated writers'). Increasingly too, it could
figure as a source of 'politeness' in language and manners: through
acquaintance with literature the mercantile classes might be
instructed in taste, given social ease – *Rudiments of English Grammar*
now coupled with *Elegant Extracts*. The author of a school anthology
of that title, published in 1824, stressed the benefits to be derived
by those classes from 'the pleasures of polite literature': 'Nothing

perhaps contributes more to liberalize their minds, and prevent that narrowness which is too often the consequence of a life attached . . . to the pursuit of lucre.'

What we have, therefore, is English gaining an educational place but in class and indeed gender terms (the need to provide for the education of middle-class women who, of course, had no access to the classical education). A major development was then the extension from the relatively superficial idea of literature as a schooling in taste into the more socially pressing one of its effectiveness as a liberalising force. In the context of the spread of literacy and the movement to democracy in the rapidly expanding and changing urban-industrial society, appeal was made to literature as a crucial cultural pedagogy, something that could offer the values and truths on which the maintenance of social unity was felt to depend – a unity, significantly enough in an age of Empire, that it could give too as a strength of national identity (literature seen as 'the autobiography of a nation'). English, in fact, was to be a new classics: the key subject for the moral and intellectual culture of all those outside the public school/ancient university ambit (a falling off of classical studies in the grammar schools in the course of the nineteenth century was simultaneous with the creation of a large number of new public schools). Speaking to a Parliamentary Commission in 1868, the headmaster of Marlborough urged that 'unusual weight' be given to English language and literature in lower social status schools: 'to attempt to humanize and refine a boy's mind by trying to familiarize him with English poetry'. Nor was it a question only of a *boy*'s mind: English in these terms gained a central place in colleges for working men and for women, in university extension courses, in the new university foundations in London and the industrial cities.

Though most often taken for granted, the idea of humanising and refining by familiarisation with literature could also raise problems as to quite how literature was to be taught. In a post-Romantic equation, literature was writing rooted in moral feelings and the power of the imagination, in the deep primary emotions. To familiarise was to expose people to it, make them read it. What else did one do? What kind of subject was English? The answer – the opposition – in the ancient universities was that it was no kind at all, that it lacked discipline, mere matter for women and children: 'learning English', as a member of the Cambridge Senate put it in the debate on the proposal for an English Lectureship, 'should be kept within the first ten years of one's life ... literary attainments should be acquired through erudition in the Greek and Latin languages.' To make it a fit subject was to firm it up with linguistic and philological difficulty, to link it with Anglo-Saxon or indeed with classics itself (both part of the earlier establishment of English at Oxford). Cambridge's belatedness, allowing for a modern development, also allowed for questioning and experimentation; the new subject could be – had to be – worked out precisely as such, its very nature defined, along with its teaching and aims. That this was contemporary with modernism, with radical experimentation in literature itself, only increased – was very much part of – the sense of innovation felt in the beginnings of English in Cambridge (the poetry of T. S. Eliot was particularly present). The possibility was there for something that would be more than the repetition of the study of English as it had elsewhere been assumed. It was this possibility that was taken up in the shaping work of Richards and Leavis.

I. A. Richards (1893–1979) had studied moral sciences, the version of what Cambridge now calls philosophy and which at the time was empiricist, analytical and mathematical, with a strong interest in psychology. Somewhat by chance, he was invited in 1919 to lecture for the newly developing School and gave as his first courses 'The Novel' and 'Criticism'. The latter for him necessarily involved the *theory* of criticism and this became his major concern: the development of a systematic understanding of literary criticism, far removed from aestheticism and existing belletristic notions of 'appreciation'. The very titles of the books Richards produced at Cambridge in the 1920s are indicative of his purpose: *The Foundations of Aesthetics* (with C. K. Ogden and James Wood, 1922), *The Meaning of Meaning* (with Ogden, 1923), *Principles of Literary Criticism* (1924), *Science and Poetry* (1926), *Practical Criticism* (1929). As a student, he had been influenced by the Cambridge philosopher G. E. Moore with his attempt to get free of forms of metaphysical speculation, to start afresh with clear principles, and the working title of *Principles of Literary Criticism* was *Principia Critica*, modelled on that of Moore's important treatise on ethics, *Principia Ethica*: Richards's aim similarly was to cut through previous argumentation, all the 'chaos of critical theories'.

For Richards, the First World War had been the catastrophic

demonstration of the necessity for ensuring good understanding and so for curbing the effects of dogmatism and propaganda, the widespread misuses of language. Linguistic discrimination had given way to 'the stereotyping and standardizing both our utterances and our interpretation', with the commercially controlled modern media largely responsible for this continuing degeneration – 'we have not yet fathomed the more sinister potentialities of the cinema and the loudspeaker'. To investigate meaning – the meaning of language – was imperative: the need was for precision, for clear-cut separations of kinds of language-use and awareness of their different grounds of legitimacy. Elaborating his critical principles, Richards was thus engaged in diagnosis and disinfection: 'as closely occupied with the health of the mind as the doctor with the health of the body'.

Crucial for mental health was the recognition of two distinct uses of language: *scientific*, producing factual statements, with truth a matter of verification; *emotive*, producing pseudo-statements, forms of words justified entirely by their effect 'in releasing or organizing our impulses [sensations, images, feelings] or attitudes [tendencies to action that result from the connection of impulses into some idea of an end to be reached]'. The emotive deals with experiences – combines impulses – in a manner free from logical relations and reference; the modern mind's 'insidious perversion' is its common confusion of scientific and emotive and the intermingling of knowledge and beliefs, taking and acting on the latter as though they had some verifiable referential truth.

This might suggest that Richards would proceed only to set the scientific over the emotive, trying as far as possible to cut back the extension of the latter, to pare away pseudo-statements as meaningless. The emotive, however, is not just some fount of pathological illusion: it is also the domain of religion and poetry; and while Richards's procedure itself is proposed as resolutely scientific, his argument asserts an essential role for poetry: it will help us through momentous change. The change in question is the transformation from a religious 'magical' – view of the world to, precisely, a scientific one, in which knowledge and belief have necessarily come apart, this being the condition of the progress of science, but in which there has then been a dangerous 'collapse of beliefs' (dangerous not least because the attendant disarray allows the confusions of thoughts and feelings that the media produce and exploit). If science transforms human life, it nevertheless cannot provide any basis for wholeness of mind, for the *direction* of experience. To counter current mental anarchy, order must be found (Richards talks – his image so much of its time – of the need for 'a League of Nations for the moral ordering of the impulses'). Religion, the magical world-view in which belief and knowledge are one, is no longer viable, poetry, 'the supreme form of emotive language', *is*: 'It is capable of saving us; it is a perfectly possible means of overcoming chaos.'

This may seem extravagant but it must be noted that Richards is here continuing the nineteenth-century tradition of socio-cultural criticism mentioned earlier which sought to propose sources of order and value – of 'culture' – in the face of the secularised society of science, democracy, capital, the society of what is then identified as 'mass civilization'. Within this tradition, Richards is, in fact, directly echoing Matthew Arnold, who had made the same claim almost fifty years before in an essay on 'The Study of Poetry':

> More and more mankind will discover that we have to turn to poetry to interpret life for us, to console us, to sustain us. Without poetry, our science will appear incomplete; and most of what now passes with us for religion and philosophy will be replaced by poetry.

Where Richards innovates is in his ambition to give a precise account of what poetry is, showing exactly how and why it can fulfil this salvatory role, and it is the analysis of poetry and reading this account brings with it that then becomes important for the development of Cambridge English.

Richards approaches poetry with regard to a psychological theory of value. The theory depends on the notion of 'the integrative action of the nervous system' (the title of a book published in 1906 by the distinguished biologist Charles Scott Sherrington, whose work was seminal for Richards). Conducting our lives is a matter of organising impulses: 'appetencies' and 'aversions' – the two kinds of impulse – need to be reconciled, integrated in such a way as to allow for the greatest satisfaction possible: 'the highest degree of organization of the satisfaction of impulses'. Though Richards's focus is on the individual mind, there is a direct social point inasmuch as what counts are the widest and most comprehensive orderings, judged not in terms of 'the wishes of majorities' but rather in those of 'the actual range and degree of satisfaction which different systematizations of impulse yield'. What poetry offers is a lesson in maximising organ-isation: where the ordinary man 'suppresses nine-tenths of his impulses, because he is incapable of managing them without confusion', the poet represents 'the point at which the growth of the mind shows itself'; this by virtue of achieving 'a completeness of response', ordering what in most minds stays suppressed or dis-ordered. The poem reflects this mental work; its words on the page are there to communicate the recognition of a range of different elements of experience delicately and freely interconnected. Thus the proper reading of good poetry – getting perfectly *the mental condition* relevant to the poem – is literally a matter of health of mind, indi-vidual and social.

Proper reading, good poetry . . . Poetry can be assessed according to degree of organisation, marshalling of adequate impulses (as opposed to conventional attitudes), and resolution of opposed impulses (lesser poems are built out of sets of impulses that run parallel, suppressing oppositions). Richards's attention, however, is directed not so much to particular evaluations as to the question of reading. The critical need is for disengagement from the stock responses that remove us from experience – acquired fixations of attitude in which we come to dwell and which are utilised by popular writing and the commercial media in their appeal to and creation of an average reader. Above all, we have to sever our reading of poetry from beliefs. 'It is when we introduce illicit beliefs into poetry that danger arises.' We must not, in other words, read poetry as though it were truth or knowledge, bringing it into line with some ready-made idea or reference; on the contrary, it is pure pseudo-statement, unlike religion demanding no belief as true and valuable precisely for its plasticity, the suppleness with which it can balance heterogeneous impulses. Literature does not tell you anything; it models this balancing, frees up capacity for organisation, disconcerts stock responses.

Beginning in 1925, Richards gave courses on 'practical criticism' in which he distributed short poems for written comment; the poems were provided with no indication of author or date and mixed good with bad. His 1929 volume *Practical Criticism* was based on this 'field-work' and sought to document the – parlous – state of culture. The reports received were presented as evidence of a general inability to read literature, successfully to possess the experience of poems. Ten kinds of failure were discussed at length, ranging from failure to grasp plain sense to failure resulting from stock responses, doctrinal inhibitions, and general critical preconceptions, and Richards ended by advocating reform in the teaching of English: a central place should be assigned to learning how language works, studying kinds of meaning, looking at the causes of misunderstanding – 'in brief, the psychology of the speech-situation'.

The direct educational effect of Richards's investigations in the 1920s was, in fact, the establishment of practical criticism itself as the nub of the study of English both in Cambridge and more generally. Close textual analysis with attention to the complex interrelations of the various elements of the poem treated as a specifically autonomous object ('the well-wrought urn' of American New Criticism, much influenced by Richards) became a standard of teaching and assessment (practical criticism provided English with something that was readily *examinable*). Richards's own prime interest in reading and the reception of meaning, however, was not such as to lead to any particular study of literature and he himself turned away from literary criticism to larger tasks in the improvement of communication, devoting himself to the theory and practice of language teaching and the propagation of Basic English, the 850-word version of English developed by his initial Cambridge collaborator C. K. Ogden to serve as an international language.

F. R. Leavis (1895–1978) took the English Tripos in 1921 and went on to do a Ph.D., supervised by Sir Arthur Quiller-Couch, Verrall's successor, on the relationship of journalism to literature with reference to the early development of the press in England. He was appointed as a probationary lecturer in English in 1927 and in 1929 married a Girton student, Queenie Roth, who wrote a Ph.D. thesis under Richards on fiction and the reading public that was prompted by his concern with standards of reading and the effects of the propagation of stock responses. Leavis himself, who attended Richards's lectures (a report by him is cited in *Practical Criticism*) and shared the concern, published a pamphlet in 1930 entitled *Mass Civilization and Minority Culture* and in 1932 was involved in the founding of an influential journal of English and cultural criticism of which he quickly became the principal editor, with his wife a major collaborator. At Leavis's suggestion, it was called *Scrutiny*.

Leavis continued much of Richards's critique, expressing it in the overall terms of a loss of integral connection between society and culture. Economic and social change has led to standardisation at the cost of standards, to a materialistic civilisation characterised by philistinism and 'the cheap response'. As in Richards, the media are regarded as both symptom and cause, with Leavis developing a powerful indictment of their hold over the production and regulation of available meanings, this seen as a constitutive feature of modern capitalism. The vision of contemporary crisis goes along with a narrative of decline in which Richards's shift from religion to science becomes that from organic *community* to modern *society*, the damaging transition from a coherent wholeness of living, based on a natural order of relations developed over long periods of continuous experience, to an artificial agglomeration of atomised individuals caught up in a process of accelerated change. The key moment here for Leavis is the seventeenth century with the start of the scientific revolution, the rise of capitalism, the articulation of opposed class interests, the movement towards new definitions of Church and State, spiritual and secular – in short, all the factors in the trans-formation that ends in the present disintegration. Cultural coherence has gone: Shakespeare had an audience embracing all classes; the poetry of T. S. Eliot – whose own idea of 'a dissociation of sensibility' in the seventeenth century is there in Leavis's account – can now be only for a small minority.

It is not that culture had not always been in minority hands (Shakespeare's plays were at once popular drama *and* poetry 'that could be appreciated only by an educated minority'), it is that the contemporary civilisation (always a savagely ironic word) is actively hostile to it: 'the prospects for culture are very dark'. What 'culture' means essentially to Leavis is a literary tradition that represents fineness of consciousness and provides currency for values of authentic living. This literary tradition, moreover, is fundamentally a development of the language it belongs to, at the same time that it is through the tradition that the language is produced and sustained. Culture indeed is the realisation of language that the literature of the tradition offers: 'the language, the changing idiom, upon which fine living depends, and without which distinction of spirit is thwarted and incoherent'. Far from Richards's single poems, individual readers and mental experiences, Leavis is involved with community and culture and language as the embodiment of the community's assumptions and aspirations, as the bearer of its culture – an 'essential Englishness'. Value is in the realised continuity of the tradition, not in some organisation of impulses; strictly speaking, there are no *literary* values: the critic deals in 'judgements about life'. Where for Richards language was largely the medium of an exchange between two subjectivities or 'minds', for Leavis, in the literature of the tradition, it is thick with this 'life', sensuously enacting its richness of meaning, its organic wholeness. Naturally enough, he could have nothing but scorn for Richards's turn to Basic English: what has the propagation of such a reductive linguistic tool to do – other than negatively – with concern for 'the future of Shakespeare's language'?

Leavis's response to that concern offered forceful directions for English, not least in the emphasis it put on English as an education demanding not just the study of literature but also attention to the reality of contemporary society and its media environment. This for Leavis was a matter of resistance, of an oppositional understanding which it was important to get developed, including in schools. *Culture and Environment*, produced with a former student Denys Thompson in 1933, was intended as a school text in critical awareness (it concentrated on advertising) and the influence of *Scrutiny* and the commitment of Leavis's many pupils who became teachers did much to substantiate this cultural work. Its corollary, of course, was the task of maintaining the vital tradition and Leavis involved English in a particular kind of critical literary history, mapping out the true English tradition, identifying the writing in which it 'lives'. The point is not knowledge about authors and periods but exactly those 'judgements about life': full recognition of and response to the significant writings of the culture; sharp assessment of those which betray its intrinsic nature (Milton, who 'forgot the English language', or Joyce, whose 'liberties with English' are those of an inorganic cosmopolitanism). The mapping out – offering *Revaluation*, providing *New Bearings in English Poetry*, defining *The Great Tradition* (titles of major books in 1936, 1932 and 1948 respectively) – more than anything else set the syllabus of what would and should be read, and showed how, on what evaluative terms.

Leavis's stress overall, therefore, was on the imperative need to create a critical readership able to maintain standards, to preserve and protect the values of the tradition. Richards's vision was in principle egalitarian, that of a general training in reading; Leavis's was of a minority trained to withstand the majority's cultural poverty. What was needed were centres of authority capable of fostering the requisite critical understanding. As to where they might be located, the only hope, given the existing social context, lay in the universities and, within them, in the English School – 'the educational centre of the university'. English is not a specialist subject – nothing to do with 'scholarly industry and academic method' – but the humane core – 'a discipline of intelligence and sensibility'. Thus Leavis comes back to the idea of English as the new classics but from the perspective of his acutely defensive analysis of culture and society, tying it to this conception of the necessary minority. English, indeed, must *make* the centre, sustain a consensus of values through training in perception, judgement and analytic skill. Practical criticism is again of prime importance; close verbal analysis but now taken up with intense moral argument in an education in maturity of response and evaluation. The exchange of judgements in critical co-operation – 'This is so, isn't it?' / 'Yes, but', in Leavis's famous formulation – is to produce 'the consensus as to what English Literature, the truly living reality, is – for us' (for 'us' the crucial minority).

Cambridge English developed an identity as such from the work of Richards and Leavis, from the former's analytic procedures and from the latter's development of an evaluative literary-critical practice wedded to a powerfully adduced literary history. The result was a decisive representation of English – what it was, what studying it was about – that made it a matter of extreme socio-cultural import, this giving that oft-recorded feeling of excitement to English at Cambridge in those initial years. While Richards moved away in the early 1930s, Leavis stayed for the duration of his life, a central presence. Not that he felt himself central in the Faculty, which settled into an academic routine that he disturbed and disparaged ('utter defeat at Cambridge', he would bitterly say), but his English nevertheless came largely to dominate, and far beyond Cambridge. His was the vision of the role of English and of Cambridge – an ideal Cambridge – as the place in which that English – the vital humanity – could be secured. 'We *were*, in fact, that Cambridge,' he later wrote of himself and his *Scrutiny* collaborators.

By the 1970s, it was common to find statements to the effect that, as the *Times Higher Education Supplement* put it in 1976, 'the traditional notion of English studies equated with the Cambridge school of criticism and imbued with the philosophy of F. R. Leavis is dying fast'. A few years later, in 1981, the Cambridge English Faculty itself exploded into a widely reported controversy – 'the MacCabe affair' – over just what English should involve and the intellectual issues at stake in its teaching. Leavis, in fact, had very much resisted any relation of his work to a 'philosophy' (aiming 'to deal in doctrine, theory and general terms as little as possible', another point of divergence from Richards), this in defence of English as bound up with a specificity of literary experience, a particularity of language and response that demands concrete critical engagement not abstract theoretical construction. Increasingly, however, respect for this and the lessons it had to offer could not be at the expense of consideration of the questions it raised, questions that new circumstances – the expansion and diversification of the student body in higher education, to cite only one – were making it hard to avoid.

Those questions bore, for example, on the relations between literature and other forms of writing and representation, asking for new kinds of attention that would not simply separate literature off as some declared area of value and ignore or dismiss other forms of cultural production (the actual effect of Leavis's negative critique of the media was to remove them *in toto* from English); on the very idea of 'literature', seeking to understand its socio-historical constructions and assumptions and also to realign English studies with writing current today (in the 1920s, Richards and Leavis had been directly concerned with some of the key modernist writing of the time, but Leavis's tradition then served as an embattled standard that excluded contemporary creative work, and his influence generally fed into an academic establishment of canonical texts, of what counted in and as 'doing English'); on the understanding of language in literary studies (seeking to raise issues of language in history as social production and of the materiality of language as constitutive – not merely reflective – of subjectivity, to end the separation from language studies that practical criticism in its development from Richards through Leavis to exercise and examination had actually become: the words on the page for the assumed 'close' reading and 'direct' response); on matters of evaluation (how do we, can we find bases for assessment, make necessary judgements, avoiding appeals to 'life' but equally avoiding the indifference of relativism or of the academicist severance of study and analysis from any matter of values?). The various questions turn precisely on *English* – the term for a language, a people, a tradition, an academic subject, and then more; with a felt need to think about the implications of our given ideas of the things held together under that one term, about the possibilities and presumptions of identity that English – 'English' – can bring, and the exclusions it can mean.

Engaged with just that problem of English as it was posed in the particular context of their time, Richards and Leavis were committed in their different and difficult ways to an urgently *modern* subject, *Cambridge* English as that; which is their lesson, still, for today.

READING

For accounts of the overall development of English studies, see: D. J. Palmer, *The Rise of English Studies*, London: Oxford University Press 1965; Chris Baldick, *The Social Mission of English Criticism*, Oxford: Clarendon Press 1987. The coming of English to Cambridge is described, by a participant in its arrival, in E. M. W. Tillyard, *The Muse Unchained*, London: Bowes and Bowes 1958. John Paul Russo's *I. A. Richards*, London: Routledge 1989, provides an extensive account of Richards's life and work, while Francis Mulhern's *The Moment of Scrutiny*, London: NLB 1979, gives a detailed history of Leavis's intellectual career and influence.

CHAPTER 3

Emily Davies, the Sidgwicks and the education of women in Cambridge

GILLIAN SUTHERLAND

I am the token woman in this collection, both as contributor and in having the explicit mention of women in my title. It is not entirely fanciful to treat this as a metaphor for relations between the University of Cambridge and women students and scholars for much of the last century and a quarter. Cambridge was initially hostile towards women with academic ambitions, deeply reluctant even to tolerate their presence and for a long time treated them as marginal figures.

The first women with aspirations to be students arrived in 1871. In 1881 they were admitted to University examinations; but thereafter they were held at arm's length. The University of London admitted women to full membership in 1878; the University of Oxford managed it in 1918. But Cambridge only admitted women to full membership of the University after the Second World War in 1948.[1]

Throughout this time the proportion of women in the University remained tiny. For nearly a century from the 1870s there were only two women's colleges, Girton and Newnham. In 1954 they were joined by a third college, New Hall, and then in 1966 by a fourth, Lucy Cavendish, which has come to concentrate its efforts on mature women returning to study. In the 1970s, too, men's colleges began to open their doors to women students.

Even now, women remain in a clear minority. After a quarter-century which has seen a dramatic increase in the numbers of women amongst university students in the UK as a whole, Cambridge still has one of the lowest proportions in the country. Just over 40 per cent of Cambridge undergraduates are women, compared to not quite 50 per cent nationally. The gaps is nearly as striking if we look at graduate students: nationally women represent just over 40 per cent of the graduate student population; in Cambridge they have just reached 34 per cent. And the gap is at its most dramatic if we look at university teachers: nationally women represent about 16 per cent; in Cambridge they are just over 8 per cent of the total.[2]

The days of marginality are not entirely behind us. However, this chapter is concerned with the earliest campaigners for a place for women in the University; what animated, what motivated them. It attempts to explore the concerns that drove them to campaign as they did; concerns which have more than ephemeral interest and continue to have resonance in the contemporary world. Its title – 'Emily Davies, the Sidgwicks and the education of women' may sound a slightly cumbersome one, but it was chosen deliberately, for two reasons. First, it seems important to stress the collective, group activity, the involvement of men as well as women. In studying any campaign it is limiting to treat campaigners as isolated heroic figures out of time; we need their context to help make sense of what they did. Second, in looking at the key figures in the founding of both the first two women's colleges, Newnham and Girton, we can explore some of their differences over both strategies and tactics, an enquiry which will illuminate both the enduring issues and the difficulties they faced.[3]

Emily Davies was born in 1830, into the family of an Anglican clergyman.[4] The family was a reasonably affluent one; but both parents were essentially conventional in their approach to gender roles: the female supported and attended upon the males in the family. Emily was educated with her brothers, but only up to a certain point; once they went away to school, she was expected to spend her time on home duties and parish visiting, both making demands well below the level of her considerable energies and abilities and breeding intense frustration. She wrote long afterwards of the development of a 'feeling of resentment at the subjection of women' well before she had read any explicitly feminist writing or met women of like mind.[5]

Two events allowed Emily Davies to break out of this constraining situation: a fortunate friendship, begun in 1858, and her father's death in 1861. The friendship was begun in Algiers, whither she had travelled to care for one of her brothers dying of consumption, with Annie Leigh Smith and her sister, Barbara Bodichon. The daughters of the extreme Radical MP for Norwich, both were themselves radical and somewhat exotic creatures, Barbara, the model for Romola in George Eliot's novel, even more so than Annie. Most important, they were key members of a group of middle-class women based in London, concerned to improve the position of women on all fronts. The address of their offices led Miss Davies to christen them the Langham Place circle.

Emily Davies corresponded with and visited her new friends on her return to England; and her father's death in 1861 allowed her and her mother to move from Gateshead, where her father had had a parish, to London, ostensibly to be near her one surviving brother, likewise a clergyman. It also allowed her to put her considerable talents as a campaigner and organiser fully to work at last.

Her earliest successes were concerned with secondary education for girls. She secured the admission of girls to the Local Examinations run by Cambridge. These, recently started, were seen as a key means of raising standards in secondary schools of all kinds. She also secured the inclusion of girls' schools in the agenda of the Royal Commission, chaired by Lord Taunton, which investigated the state of secondary schooling nationally between 1865 and 1867. When legislation enabling the remodelling of endowments for secondary schooling eventually followed its report, this allowed provision for girls as well as for boys.[6]

Emily Davies's central preoccupation, however, was the provision of higher education for women. She published a small book on the subject in 1866.[7] Then in 1869, supported by a committee of well-wishers and fund-raisers, she welcomed the first five students to Benslow House, Hitchin, close enough, it was hoped, to Cambridge and to London for teachers at those Universities to come to them. The impracticality of this hope and the constraints of the site soon became apparent. Land at Girton, then two miles from Cambridge, was purchased, Alfred Waterhouse appointed as architect, and building began. The College moved to Girton in 1873; but by then they were not the only aspiring women students on the Cambridge scene.

In 1871 the moral philosopher, Henry Sidgwick, a key figure in the group organising a series of lectures for women in Cambridge, had leased a house in which women coming from a distance to these lectures could reside. He invited Anne Jemima Clough, sister of the poet Arthur Hugh Clough, to take charge of it. By 1875, Sidgwick, Eleanor Balfour (whom he was shortly to marry), Anne Jemima Clough, and their friends and supporters had bought land in what was then the village of Newnham on the western edge of Cambridge, appointed Basil Champneys architect, and commenced building likewise.

These years, 1869–75, therefore saw the creation of two very distinct institutions. There was from the first a fundamental difference between them: how to construe equality for women. Emily Davies could not see how to construe equality except as 'sameness'; to be sure women were equal to men, they had to be seen to do exactly the same things, within the same timetable, as men. Thus Girton students had to commit themselves to full Tripos – Cambridge degree – courses, to be followed at the same pace as that set for the men students in the University.

This strategy had high costs, in a number of ways. In the 1860s no serious structure of girls' secondary schooling existed – schools there were, but too many of them resembled Miss Pinkerton's Academy for Young Ladies, attended by Becky Sharp and Amelia Sedley, at the beginning of Thackeray's *Vanity Fair*. It is worth remembering that Emily Davies had begun her career as an activist with schemes for the improvement of secondary education for girls. The first women's college of the University of London, Bedford College, which had opened its doors in 1849, nearly succumbed to pressures to become a girls' school rather than a higher educational establishment and in the end split into two. The Girls' Public Day School Company was founded only in 1872; and the work of the Endowed Schools Commission in remodelling endowments to create schools for girls, got under way likewise in the 1870s.

Thus the key decades in the first creation of a systematic network of girls' secondary schools were the 1870s and 1880s. Young women wanting to attempt a programme of *higher* education in those decades were likely to lack a systematic preparatory training. They might be widely read, but often what they had done had little rigour about it. Characteristic was the experience of Mrs Humphry Ward, best-selling novelist, granddaughter of Dr Arnold of Rugby and niece of Matthew Arnold, the poet:

How little those who are schoolgirls of today [1918] can realise what it was to be a schoolgirl in the fifties or the early sixties of the last century! . . . As far as intellectual training was concerned, my nine years from seven to sixteen were practically wasted. I learnt nothing thoroughly or accurately, and the German, French and Latin, which I soon discovered after my marriage to be essential to the kind of literary work I wanted to do, had all to be re-learnt before they could be of any real use to me; nor was it ever possible for me . . . to get that firm hold on the structure and literary history of any language, ancient or modern, which my brother William, only fifteen months my junior, got from his six years at Rugby, and his training there in Latin and Greek.[8]

To insist on girls with this kind of background taking a full Tripos, to the same timetable as their brothers and cousins, was to exclude sizeable numbers. Even those educationally equipped to cope, with parents prepared to commit themselves to three years' worth of fees straight off, did not always choose to fit Miss Davies's scheme of things. The entry in the *Girton Register* for Agnes Amy Bulley reads: 'The College, Hitchin and Girton L. 1871–3; Newnham 1873–4; Moral Sciences Tripos Class 1, 1874 from Newnham, whither she had migrated because Miss Emily Davies would not consent to her postponing her Tripos for a 4th year.'

As this suggests, the Newnham philosophy was different. In its earliest years, the College was prepared to admit women to work at a variety of levels, for periods as short as one term. There was even a handful of students who came for one term, then came back some time later for a further term or terms. Did they work, perhaps as governesses or teachers, and save to pay a further set of fees in the interval? What biographical data there are on the earliest students make it plain that Newnham students were less affluent and socially secure than Girton students; and oral tradition has it that, at first, Newnham was for governesses and Girton for ladies.[9]

This difference was in part a recognition of the practical reality of many women's lives and resources in the period, something about which Miss Clough, who had run a school and was active in the North of England Council for the Higher Education of Women, knew a great deal. In part also it was rooted in a difference of principle. Henry Sidgwick was less interested in formal equalities and more interested in improving access to the best in education. Throughout his life, work to improve the lot of women was inextricably intertwined with battles on other issues. Forced to choose, he might have described himself as an educational reformer first and a supporter of women second. When he took up their cause he already had a distinguished record as a campaigner for reform in general and university reform in particular, one of those whom Matthew Arnold was to satirise as the 'lights of Liberalism'.[10]

Born in 1838, and, like Emily Davies, the child of an Anglican clergyman, Sidgwick became a Fellow of Trinity College, Cambridge, in 1859. One of his earliest and most dramatic challenges was to the retention of religious tests for members of the University. In 1869 he resigned his Fellowship, as one no longer able to subscribe to or defend such tests and was a key figure in the campaign which secured their abolition by legislation in 1871. Newnham was the first and remains the only undergraduate college not to have a chapel; and its statutes commit its members to further simply the ideals of 'education, learning and research', rather than the traditional Cambridge formula 'religion, education, learning and research'.

On Sidgwick's resignation of his Fellowship, Trinity immediately offered him a lectureship in its place. The abolition of University Tests enabled him in 1883 to be elected Knightbridge Professor of Moral Philosophy, which chair he held until his death in 1900. Throughout this time he worked for the reform of university teaching in general. He was concerned to enhance the importance of lectures, which included improving their quality. He was also eager to encourage colleges to take back into their own hands and to take much more seriously the provision of supervisions, small-group, sometimes one-to-one, teaching. Hitherto this was something undergraduates had gone out – or not – and found for themselves, relying on the market and their imperfect knowledge of it. In Trinity, the largest, richest and – with St John's – the trend-setting college, Sidgwick and his close ally, Henry Jackson, Regius Professor of Greek, succeeded in changing the pattern; and gradually other colleges followed suit. Obviously the new women's colleges could not and did not wish to allow their students to shop for supervisors on the open market and from the beginning, their tight and careful control of supervision conformed to the Sidgwick/Jackson model.

Sidgwick was also much concerned with the content of the curriculum. A campaign which triumphed only after his death was that against compulsory Greek. Again, this was a requirement which bore particularly heavily upon the women students, since the slowly emerging girls' secondary schools found it even harder to muster decent teaching of Greek than of Latin. More generally, there were many aspects of the male curriculum Sidgwick thought outmoded and he was not prepared to allow, let alone require, the women students to go through the same hoops as the men, simply for the sake of it.

A number of his male allies shared this view, some of whom undoubtedly saw the cause of women as a lever for other changes. J. R. Seeley, Regius Professor of History, fell out with Miss Davies over her insistence on existing Tripos courses or nothing, and withdrew his teaching, complaining about 'stationary' education:

> I cannot take any pleasure in attending to the details of a College where the old and to me obsolete routine goes on. I do not cease to wish it success . . . I hope for times when you may feel able to be bolder and more progressive.[11]

Gradually the differences between the styles and populations of the two institutions abated. As systematic provision for the secondary schooling of girls spread across the country, more students came up better prepared to cope with Cambridge courses. Both colleges did all they could to raise funds for scholarships and bursaries to help with fees for the less affluent. The campaigns of Sidgwick, Jackson, Seeley and others to modify and, as they saw it, modernise, traditional Cambridge courses for all students gradually bore fruit.

And although, with regard to curricula, they were prepared to construe equality differently, the early supporters of Newnham and Girton were at one in having no truck at all with another version of the 'women-can-be-equal-but-different' argument, the case for a separate women's university. Emily Davies had set her face against this in making the move from Hitchin to Cambridge. Sidgwick had become involved with the schemes for a house for women students in Cambridge because he thought they had a right to access to the best teaching currently available. Yet the idea had a long history and proved surprisingly resilient.

It had first surfaced in Tennyson's poem, *The Princess*, in 1849; and it was one of the possibilities considered by the patent medicine manufacturer, Thomas Holloway, when he left his huge fortune to found a college for women at Egham, in Surrey.[12] In December 1897 the Governors of Royal Holloway College organised a great conference on the issue, at the Society of Arts in London, attended by representatives of all the institutions of higher education for women in the country, of the leading girls' schools and of the Universities of London, Oxford and Cambridge. Emily Davies, Henry Sidgwick and Eleanor Sidgwick, who had succeeded Anne Jemima Clough as Principal of Newnham, were among them.[13]

The women themselves were virtually unanimous: their principal spokeswoman was Sophie Bryant, the first woman D.Sc. of the University of London and then Headmistress of the North London Collegiate School. Her argument can be summed up very simply: 'we want what other people understand by higher education'.

The point was underlined by Arthur Sidgwick, Henry's brother, who was among the representatives of the University of Oxford:

> How is the present education unsuited to women, I should like to know? Our experience at Oxford is rather curious in this respect: we ourselves began with the notion (being inexperienced and not having worked it out) of 'education adapted to women'; and the whole progress of our work has been towards realizing that the one thing wanted was systematic study and systematic study as it had been laid down by long experience for men.

But there was one dissenting voice among the women, Mrs A. H. Johnson of the Oxford Society of Home Students, and among her grounds was the following:

> University men are not willing that women should share fully in the life of the Universities. I don't mean to say they are not willing that women should go in for their examinations or have the advantage of the same education, because we know that they are, and since we began our work in Oxford we have all along been met with the greatest possible sympathy. But they are not willing that women shall share in the life of the University, or form part of its governing body, or be associated with men in all the higher work of the University. There-fore women will never be, so far as we can see, in the same position as the men who are managing the colleges for men. It may be right or it may be wrong, but the fact remains that we are no more liked now than when we began.

Mrs Johnson's warning was a real one, in Cambridge at least as much as in Oxford. For the education in which the women were asking to share was much more than attending lectures and sitting examinations: it was for the students a whole process of socialisation and shared experiences and for their teachers and elders a fiercely democratic intellectual commonwealth.

When in 1852 John Henry Newman articulated for his generation and its successors, *The Idea of a University*, he laid as much stress on process as on content, and admitted that if forced to choose between them, he would choose process: young men – and older men – learned far more from associating with each other than from any formal curriculum, however admirable its content.[14] The twentieth century would label these processes of association and exchange the 'hidden curriculum'.

The women and their supporters shared these ideals. In 1896 Eleanor Sidgwick addressed students at Liverpool on the university education of women and spoke of 'two gifts, one moral and one intellectual, which it . . . is the special privilege of the University to bestow'. The moral gift she saw as 'the sense of membership of a worthy community, with a high and noble function in which every member can take part, and at the same time not so vast in extent as to reduce the individual to insignificance'. The intellectual gift was 'the habit of reasonable self-dependence', which she saw as shaped in particular by three experiences: first, 'the kind of labour and care and precision of thought that is required to arrive at sound conclusions in any department'; second, 'living and learning among students who are studying other subjects [and thus imbibing] an adequate sense of the limits of their own knowledge and its relation to other parts of the vast system of modern science and learning'; and finally, encounters with teachers 'who are thinking for themselves and advancing as well as imparting knowledge'. She concluded:

> To know where one is intellectually, what one can do and what one cannot do, – this knowledge is of inestimable value for life. No institution can be relied upon to impart it; but I know of no institution that can do so much to aid men and women to learn it as a University that is doing its duty.[15]

For women to lay claim to a share in these processes of intellectual socialisation, intellectual encounter and ultimately academic self-government was a profoundly subversive act. It entailed asserting that these processes were not intrinsically and fundamentally determined by sex; that their present mode of conduct was a matter of gender, socially constructed. The women were doing so, however, in a society which felt that exchanges between the sexes should be strictly regulated, formalised and often limited, particularly within a given social class. One mid-Victorian observer, the barrister, A. J. Munby, maintained that friendship between a man and a woman was only possible across class boundaries. He had spent an evening alone in her room with a milliner named Louisa Baker, drinking tea and discussing her employment prospects and whether she should emigrate to Australia. Afterwards he reflected: 'with the men of her own class it would be indelicate to associate as friends; for modesty is an affair of *class* as well as sex, and with them such intercourse would certainly be misconstrued'.[16] The Cambridge into which the first two women's colleges ventured had hitherto set unfettered intellectual exchange, discourse, enquiry – and friendship – in an exclusively male context.[17]

The founders of Newnham and Girton were hardly unaware of this and its implications at all levels. Henry Sidgwick lamented the 'unfortunate personal appearance' of the first five students at Newnham; by which he meant 'they were all remarkably good-looking women'.[18] More happily, he referred to them on another occasion as 'my Garden of Flowers'; although this was rather coarsely translated by his friend and supporter, F. W. H. Myers, as Sidgwick's 'harem or collection of girls reading at Cambridge'.[19]

Both Miss Davies and Miss Clough were in a state of constant alert lest the behaviour of their students should even hint at impropriety. This had been one of the factors contributing to the start at Hitchin; and even there the first five students were castigated for engaging in private amateur theatricals. Dress, behaviour, conduct and company were scrutinised minutely. 'There was, we were told', wrote Shena Potter, later Lady Simon of Wythenshawe, 'a group of Cambridge ladies – wives of Professors – who kept an eagle eye on our behaviour and every lapse would be immediately reported to the University and would delay the granting of equal rights.' Mary Ann Hingston, who came up to Newnham in 1899, remarked: 'I don't think I spoke to a man my first year. I had cousins at various colleges but we never met. It wasn't done.'[20] Chaperonage survived to the beginning of the 1920s.

The College authorities were impaled on the horns of a dilemma. Unconventional behaviour might give the opposition an additional weapon; yet conformity with the existing social mores hardly equipped or enabled their students to take part in unfettered intellectual discourse and exchange. Such scrupulous conformity laid the women and their male supporters wide open to a resurgence of arguments for a separate, women's university, at the beginning of the 1920s.

In the course of that discussion, a flysheet issued by two very distinguished Fellows of Trinity, E. D. Adrian, a future Master of the College and Chancellor of the University, and H. A. Hollond, shortly to be elected Downing Professor of the Laws of England, argued that what made Cambridge so precious was the college system, which 'offers the free intercourse of men of congenial minds with a clash of diverse intellectual opinion and some association with older men who have intellectual ideals if not achievement to their credit'. The addition of women would, 'by altering the habits of undergraduate life, impair the heritage of the men'. Intercourse between the sexes was likely to be of a trivial nature and would 'diminish the time spent by students either in work or in more valuable intercourse with others of the same sex'.[21] In the intensity of their anxiety, the hard-pressed women's college authorities had largely restricted 'intercourse between the sexes' to trivialities.

Yet it is impossible not to sympathise with their predicament. For they knew only too well that the opposition, however measured the tones in which it was expressed in the flysheets of University debate, had powerful emotional dimensions and deep, hardly rational, almost visceral roots. To provoke this too far might not only jeopardise the concessions so far won but risk extrusion altogether.

The year 1897, the very year of the great London debate about a separate women's university, had produced some terrifying scenes in Cambridge, when the admission of women to degrees had been rejected by 1,713 votes to 662. On the day of the vote a crude effigy of a woman student in blue bloomers, mounted on a bicycle, had been suspended outside what is now the Cambridge University Press bookshop, opposite the Senate House. The surrounding streets were thronged and MAs going to vote were pelted with flour and fireworks by the undergraduates of Gonville and Caius. Once the result of the ballot was announced, triumphant undergraduates marched to Newnham, there to be faced down by the grim-faced women dons, assembled behind barred gates. They turned back to the construction of a huge celebratory bonfire in the Market Square, doing hundreds of pounds worth of damage.

The next time the issue came to a vote, in 1921, both Henry Sidgwick and Emily Davies were dead, and Eleanor Sidgwick was living in retirement. But their successors had to face another defeat at the ballot box and stand by while demonstrating undergraduates smashed the lower half of the handsome bronze gates at Newnham, erected as a memorial to Miss Clough in 1894.

These were ugly scenes. They serve to remind us that changing a culture takes very much more than changing formal rules and regulations. Such changes require some fundamental shifts in attitudes and expectations. In 1866 Emily Davies wrote, 'a great part of the difficulties which beset every question concerning women would be at once removed by a frank recognition of the fact, that there is between the sexes a deep and broad basis of likeness'.[22] We are still contending for and trying to act out that 'frank recognition'.

NOTES

1 The principal study of Cambridge remains Rita McWilliams-Tullberg, *Women at Cambridge: A Men's University – though of a Mixed Type*, London 1975, now sadly out of print; see also Christopher N. L. Brooke, *A History of the University of Cambridge vol. IV, 1870–1990*, Cambridge 1992, chs. 9, 17 and 18. For Oxford, see Vera Brittain, *The Women at Oxford*, London 1960 and the chapters by Janet Howarth forthcoming in the nineteenth- and twentieth-century volumes of the *History of the University of Oxford*. For London, see Negley Harte, *The University of London 1836–1986. An Illustrated History*, London 1986 and Gillian Sutherland, '"The plainest principles of justice": the University of London and the higher education of women' in *The University of London and the World of Learning 1836–1986*, ed. F. M. L. Thompson, London 1990.

2 For Cambridge student numbers, see *Cambridge University Reporter*. Special No. 18, 19 August 1992; for numbers nationally, see *Universities' Statistical Record, University Statistics 1990–91*, published on behalf of the Universities' Funding Council, Cheltenham 1992, vol. 1, *Students and Staff*; also *Forty Years On . . . : The CUWAG Report on the Numbers and Status of Academic Women in the University of Cambridge*, Survey Committee of the Cambridge University Women's Action Group, Cambridge

1988; and John Carswell, *Government and the Universities in Britain. Programme and Performance 1960–1980*, Cambridge 1985, p. 45 and Appendix I, Tables 3 and 4.

3 For a fuller discussion, see Gillian Sutherland, 'The movement for the higher education of women: its social and intellectual context in England *c.* 1840–1880' in *Political and Social Change in Modern Britain: Essays presented to A. F. Thompson*, ed. P. J. Waller, Hassocks 1987.

4 For an excellent short account of Emily Davies, see Janet Howarth's introductory essay to her edition of Emily Davies's, *The Higher Education of Women (1866)*, London 1988. Barbara Stephen's *Emily Davies and Girton College*, London 1927, still remains indispensable, although Daphne Bennett's *Emily Davies and the Liberation of Women 1830–1921*, London 1990, offers a vivid, if partisan, introduction.

5 Quoted Stephen, *Emily Davies*, p. 29.

6 For the importance of this, see Sheila Fletcher, *Feminists and Bureaucrats. A Study in the Development of Girls' Education in the Nineteenth Century*, Cambridge 1980.

7 See n. 4 above.

8 Mrs Humphry Ward, *A Writer's Recollections*, London 1918, pp. 96–7.

9 For an analysis of the student population to 1880, see Sutherland, 'Movement for higher education of women', pp. 100–4.

10 The basic biographical source on Sidgwick remains *Henry Sidgwick: A Memoir*, by A[rthur] S[idgwick] and E[leanor] M S[idgwick], London, 1906. See also Sheldon Rothblatt, *The Revolution of the Dons: Cambridge and Society in Victorian England*, London 1967; McWilliams-Tullberg, *Women at Cambridge*; and the admirable study by Christopher Harvie, *The Lights of Liberalism: University Liberals and the Challenge of Democracy 1860–86*, London 1976.

11 Quoted McWilliams-Tullberg, *Women at Cambridge*, p. 65.

12 See Sutherland, '"The plainest principles of justice"' for a fuller discussion.

13 *University Degrees for Women: Report of a Conference Convened by the Governors of the Royal Holloway College, 4 December 1897*, London 1898; the direct quotations that follow in the text are taken from pp. 47, 52–3.

14 See in particular Discourse VI, 'Knowledge viewed in relation to Learning', s. 9.

15 Mrs Henry Sidgwick [*sic*], *University Education of Women: A Lecture Delivered at University College, Liverpool, in May, 1896*, Cambridge 1896. The only biographical study remains Ethel Sidgwick, *Mrs Henry Sidgwick: A Memoir*, London 1938. It is plain not only from this but also from the Newnham archives that her administrative and financial talents, her good sense and dispassionate judgement made a huge contribution to the affairs of the college over the whole period 1876–1921.

16 Derek Hudson, *Munby, Man of Two Worlds*, London 1972, p. 20.

17 Gender and segregation in Victorian society in general and Cambridge in particular are huge topics; some sense of both can be gained from David Newsome's study of Henry Sidgwick's nephew, A. C. Benson, Master of Magdalene College, Cambridge, 1915–25, *On the Edge of Paradise*, London 1980.

18 Ann Phillips (ed.), *A Newnham Anthology*, Cambridge 1979, p. 1.

19 Quoted McWilliams-Tullberg, *Women at Cambridge*, p. 59.

20 Phillips, *Anthology*, pp. 59 and 46.

21 Quoted McWilliams-Tullberg, *Women at Cambridge*, p. 166.

22 *The Higher Education of Women*, 1988 reprint, pp. 163–4.

CHAPTER 4

Radioastronomy in Cambridge

ANTONY HEWISH

One of the most exciting aspects of modern science has been our growing understanding of the structure of the Universe and how it has evolved since the beginning of time. Scientific books do not usually rank amongst the best-sellers, but the outstanding success of Stephen Hawking's famous book *A Brief History of Time* shows how this subject has captured the popular imagination. To a large extent our present picture has come about through discoveries in radioastronomy in which Cambridge has played a leading role. In this chapter I shall sketch a few highlights of the Cambridge work.

The beginnings of radioastronomy in England were stimulated by the wartime discovery of radio waves emitted by the Sun. In the dark days of February 1942, shortly after the German warships *Scharnhorst* and *Gueisenan* had made their dash to base through the English Channel, anti-aircraft radar stations experienced severe jamming signals. At first assumed to be enemy activity, it was later found by J. S. Hey, engaged in operational research, that the signals came from the Sun's direction and were associated with an active sunspot, also seen by optical astronomers at the Royal Observatory, Greenwich. Systematic investigation of this unexpected type of solar radiation was an obvious choice for a university research group in radiophysics starting up again after the war. In Cambridge, Martin Ryle, who had wartime experience as a scientist in radar research, used surplus military equipment to construct sensitive receivers and succeeded in detecting radio emission from the Sun at all times, not just outbursts connected in some way with sunspots. He also found other objects in the sky to be emitters of natural radio waves.

At first it was thought that the radio emission was coming from other stars, perhaps similar to the Sun, but obviously much more distant and more powerful in the radio waveband. So the emitters were called 'radio stars'. It was clear, however, that they had nothing in common with the well-known bright stars – there was no positional agreement with the important members of well-known constellations. A serious problem was the relative inaccuracy of the early charts of the radio sky due to the primitive nature of the first radio telescopes. Locating a radio star within an area of sky comparable to that covered by the full Moon, corresponding roughly to the accuracy attainable then, meant that there were several hundred visible stars as possible candidates.

New techniques were needed and Ryle was a pioneer in the development of radio interferometers, in which two receiving aerials spaced at a considerable distance were connected to the same receiver. Waves from a given source in the sky reach the two aerials at slightly different times, depending on the direction in relation to the baseline separating the aerials. Wavecrests can arrive at the receiver in step, or out of step, thus adding or subtracting in a manner that depends precisely upon the source direction. This principle allows positions to be measured more accurately than by the use of a single aerial, and was exploited by Graham Smith, who joined Ryle as a research student in 1947. Using a pair of parabolic reflectors, similar to those employed in satellite communications today but recovered from German radar installations, Graham Smith obtained a highly accurate position for one of the most prominent radio stars called Cygnus A.

A long exposure photograph was subsequently taken by American astronomers at the 200-inch optical telescope on Mount Palomar and this revealed a striking image of a type of galaxy never seen before. Two features were of outstanding interest. First, the galaxy was located at a vast distance, more than 100 times further away than our near neighbour, the spiral galaxy Andromeda. This was deduced from the redshift of the light and implied that the radio-emitting galaxy was at the outermost limits of the known Universe at that time. Secondly, the quality of the light – its spectrum – was unlike that of any other galaxies. Galaxies are huge collections of stars similar to the

Sun but of many different sizes ranging from white dwarfs to red giants. A typical galaxy contains around 100 billion stars, something like the number of peas required to fill King's College Chapel, so its light has the quality of average starlight. By contrast, most of the light from the galaxy identified with Cygnus A was coming from disrupted atoms, indicating an extremely hot gas. It was thought that we might be witnessing a collision between two galaxies.

Whatever radio-emitting galaxies might be – and that mystery took many years to solve – it was immediately evident that radio galaxies provided new and important information about the past history of the Universe. This was because of the time taken for the radiation to travel across space before reaching the Earth. A useful measure of the vast distances involved in astronomy is the light-travel time. It takes about 8 minutes for light to reach us from the Sun, and several years from the nearest stars. In terms of light-years our Milky Way galaxy has a diameter of about 100,000 light-years. Andromeda is around 2 million light-years distant and Cygnus A is close to 1 billion light-years away. Hence the image of Cygnus A tells us how this object looked 1 billion years ago. We are looking back in time as though we were time-travellers, and the fact that many fainter radio galaxies could be detected strongly suggested that these were even further away in space, and therefore seen earlier in time. It should be noted that measurements of redshifts, and hence of distances, depends on recognising the characteristic wavelengths of light emitted by atoms such as hydrogen and oxygen. At radio wavelengths the radiation is emitted by free charged particles and has no characteristic wavelength, so redshifts cannot be observed with radio telescopes.

In the early 1950s there were two main theories about the origin and evolution of the Universe. It was generally agreed that the Universe was expanding in the sense that galaxies were moving apart. That was the only straightforward explanation of Hubble's observation that the more distant galaxies had larger redshifts. One reason for the expansion is the supposition that the Universe erupted from a highly condensed state long ago. Using Einstein's theory of general relativity to calculate how gravitational forces slow down the expansion, it follows that the Universe originated in some kind of 'Big Bang' about 15 billion years ago. The other cosmological theory avoided the problem of a singular origin by assuming that matter is being created steadily all the time. The theory of 'Continuous Creation' involves the formation of new galaxies to replace older ones as they are carried away by the overall expansion. The creation of one atom every hundred years or so in each volume of space comparable to a lecture hall would be sufficient to maintain the whole population of galaxies. This process of constant regeneration, analogous to water boiling away in a kettle and being replenished from a dripping tap so that the level remains the same, leads to a 'Steady State' Universe which, on average, does not change with time. The Steady State theory avoids the problem of a singular origin by spreading the creation process over the whole of time.

In principle, these two theories could be distinguished by observing how the Universe is changing with time. On the 'Big Bang' theory the galaxies are formed by some process in the expanding sea of primordial matter which fills space, and they subsequently evolve as the stars burn up their nuclear fuel. One can envisage an early time before the galaxies were born. The Steady State theory, on the other hand, specifies a Universe which always remains roughly the same. Before the advent of radioastronomy it seemed unlikely that telescopes could detect galaxies at the very large distances needed to look far enough back in time to reveal temporal evolution. But a radio galaxy at, say, ten times the distance of Cygnus A would be seen 10 billion years ago, which is more than half the age of the Universe on the Big Bang theory, so evolutionary effects should be pronounced.

The possibility of testing cosmological theories by observations of radio galaxies was appreciated soon after the optical identification of Cygnus A, but more advanced radio telescopes were needed to detect radio galaxies in sufficient numbers. Radio telescopes demand large structures, both to collect enough radiation for detectable signals and to achieve a high angular resolution for distinguishing between different sources in the sky. Conventional parabolic reflectors are not suitable because the necessary size involves structures too large to be built. In the late 1950s Martin Ryle saw how computers could be used for a novel process, called aperture synthesis, which enabled powerful radio telescopes to be achieved without enormous structures. The essential idea was to store the radio signals obtained from a two-element interferometer, while moving one component from place to place so that, ultimately, it gave the same results as if all the components were in place at once. The effective size of such a radio telescope is then given by the maximum spacing of the elements, and giant radio telescopes can be effectively synthesised from relatively small and easily constructed parts.

The most advanced development of the synthesis technique makes use of the Earth's rotation to move the components. How this works is readily seen by imagining one element sited at the North Pole, so that in one day the other element, as seen from a fixed direction in outer space, moves around it in a circle of radius D, where D is the separation of the elements. Thus one element sweeps out an annular ring, which may be regarded as a section of a large circular area. By increasing D successively from day to day virtually any size of radio telescope can be synthesised, provided that the necessary computations can be carried out. The relative moment of the elements is the same when one element is not at the Pole, and a detailed analysis of the process shows that no information is lost if observations are made for only twelve hours each day. Since Ryle's first demonstration of the power of the synthesis method, it has been widely applied at many radio observatories around the world, and the sensitivity of radio telescopes has increased in step with the advance of computer technology.

The first evidence supporting the Big Bang origin of the Universe came from sky surveys of radio galaxies made by Ryle and his team in the early 1960s. The observations showed that radio galaxies were much more numerous in earlier phases of the Universe than they are today. It seems as if there was a preferred epoch for the birth of radio galaxies such that they blazed forth more dominantly then. This type of evolution on a cosmic timescale has no place in the Steady State theory, but would be a natural feature of a Universe emerging from a singular origin. Further evidence for the Big Bang was the discovery in 1965, by Penzias and Wilson in the USA, of the cosmic background radiation. This chance discovery was made during tests of antenna systems for satellite communication when it was found that very weak heat radiation was coming in from all directions in space. Presumably the Universe must be filled with this radiation, because there is nothing special about the location of our own galaxy, and the only satisfactory explanation for it is that it represents the final glimmer of the explosion which marked the birth of the Universe. In case it seems surprising that this radiation occurs as a radio signal, rather than a visible glow, it should be noted that the radiation corresponds to a temperature only just above absolute zero, equivalent to about 270 degrees below freezing-point. The radiation remains in space because there is not enough colder matter to absorb it. At times less than one second from the beginning, however, it must have been too hot for any of the known sub-atomic particles to exist.

Later surveys of radio galaxies at Cambridge, which probed the Universe at even greater distances, showed that we could look back to a time before these galaxies came into being. At those epochs, condensation of the primordial gas into galaxies had not progressed sufficiently far for the radio galaxies to have formed, and there was a dramatic reduction in their numbers. Comparing the statistics of the radio galaxy population with theoretical models of cosmological evolution is still an active field of research in radio astronomy, but another feature of early work in the mid-1960s which must be mentioned is the discovery of quasars.

In those days it was impossible to obtain good images of radio galaxies because they were so distant and therefore looked extremely small. Following on from Ryle's work in charting the positions of large numbers of radio galaxies, attempts were made to measure their angular sizes by using interferometers on longer and longer baselines. Henry Palmer, one of Bernard Lovell's team at Jodrell Bank, succeeded in estimating many angular sizes, but some radio galaxies seemed to fall into a special category and were far smaller. Then Cyril Hazard, who had left Jodrell Bank to work in Australia, used a new radio telescope recently constructed there to obtain a highly accurate position for one of these by noting the precise time when the Moon passed in front of it and obscured the radio signals. An astronomer at the 200-inch Palomar telescope subsequently found what seemed to be a star in this position, but the 'star' lay at a distance of more than 1 billion light-years. To be visible at this distance the light must have been 100 times more powerful than the total starlight emitted by normal galaxies. Hence the term 'quasi-stellar galaxy', or 'quasar', was coined for this and similar objects sometimes found to coincide with radio galaxy positions.

The inference that some galaxies could emit such powerful radiation caused a few astronomers to question the use of the redshift of light for estimating distances. Even today there is a small minority which does not accept the redshift evidence, but no other satisfactory explanation for the redshifts has been given. As telescopes became more sensitive, the quasars were studied more closely and it became clear that some galaxies contain centres of activity which can generate tremendous power. When detailed pictures of radio galaxies were finally achieved they revealed further remarkable properties of these active galactic nuclei.

The last radio telescope to be built by Martin Ryle, completed in 1972, used eight parabolic reflectors spaced out along a line of nearly 3 miles. The aperture synthesis method gave computer-generated images sharper than can be obtained with any optical telescope, except the Hubble Space Telescope, launched only a few years ago. These radio images began to provide the detail needed to understand the physical processes at work in radio galaxies. Earlier studies had shown that the radio emission was generated in large clouds which typically lay on either side of a central galaxy like a giant dumb-bell. The clouds contained electrically charged particles, most probably electrons and positrons, moving at high speed along randomly curved paths in weak magnetic fields which fill the whole volume. What Ryle showed was that the particles were continuously supplied from an active central nucleus and travelled out in two narrow beams on either side. Precisely how these beams are accelerated and directed is still unknown, but they are probably ejected along the rotation axis of a spinning central condensation of matter which could be a black hole formed by the gravitational attraction of several million stars. For these advances in radioastronomy Martin Ryle shared the Nobel Prize for Physics in 1974.

While radio galaxies are the most common celestial objects revealed by radio telescopes, this account of Cambridge work would be incomplete without some mention of radio emitters in our own galaxy, such as the remnants of supernova explosions and neutron stars. In fact one of Ryle's first discoveries in 1948 was the supernova remnant known as Cassiopeia A. When stars several times more massive than the Sun have exhausted their supply of nuclear fuel, they eventually shrink, because the internal pressure can no longer resist the large compressive force resulting from gravitational attraction towards the centre. Matter near the core of the star is then crushed into a new form with properties quite different from those of normal matter found on Earth. In effect, the positive and negative charged particles which constitute normal matter are squeezed together and converted into new uncharged particles called neutrons. It has been known since the 1930s that some neutrons exist in atomic nuclei, but outside the nucleus they are unstable and convert spontaneously into electrons and protons. This process is reversed at the extremely high pressure which exists inside massive stars that have been compressed by gravity. Matter composed mainly of neutrons has unimaginably high density and a teaspoonful would contain 100 million tonnes. In this state a star as massive as the Sun would have a diameter of only just over 10 miles.

From the behaviour of compressed matter, it can be deduced that the inward collapse of massive stars that have run short of fuel is a short-lived and violent event. Ultimately the matter is attracted towards the centre at a speed exceeding 200,000 miles per second, and the resultant collision blows most of the star apart, leaving a residue of neutrons in the middle. This is believed to be the cause of stellar explosions, or supernovae, which occur about once per century in a typical galaxy like ours. The explosions are usually seen as a short-lived brightening of the stars which lasts for several days before fading away, but radio emissions from the expanding cloud of debris generally lasts for over a thousand years. The radio image of Cassiopeia A clearly shows the expanding cloud which, as viewed in the sky, must have exploded about 250 years ago.

The probable existence of stellar bodies formed inside supernovae and consisting almost entirely of neutrons had been conjectured since the 1930s, but it was thought that they would be very difficult to observe because of their tiny size. Fortunately, this is not so and it was a lucky chance that my own research led to their discovery in 1967. I had designed an unusual type of radio telescope for a new search for quasars, exploiting a previous discovery that quasars 'twinkled' far more strongly than other radio galaxies. The twinkling is a flickering of intensity caused by hot gas from the Sun which blows past the Earth as a solar wind and disturbs radio waves entering the solar system from outside. The effect is most pronounced at the longest radio wavelengths and occurs when the distant radio emitters have, like quasars, a very small angular extent. During analysis of all the twinkling sources Jocelyn Bell-Burnell, who worked in my team as a graduate student, pointed out one which seemed, occasionally, to be showing too much flickering. I decided we should make special observations to clarify the mystery and, with improved recording apparatus, it turned out that the signals were not random twinkling, but a highly regular sequence of radio pulses. When I began to time the pulses I found that the pulse rate was accurate to one-millionth of a second per day and the signal looked so artificial that I contemplated the possibility that it might have been caused by extraterrestrial beings. I checked this by looking for orbital motion of the source, since extraterrestrial intelligence is most likely to evolve on a planet, but found no evidence for planetary motion. Knowing that the pulses, because of their short duration, must have been emitted from a source no larger than the Earth, I finally concluded that they could have been generated by the vibrating surface of a neutron star.

My theory was nearly, but not quite, correct. One year later, after a number of similar pulsing emitters, which we called 'pulsars', had been located, a rapid pulsar was discovered near the centre of a well-known supernova remnant – the Crab Nebula. Not only was this the expected site for a neutron star, but other characteristics, such as a steady slowing down of the pulses, confirmed an alternative theory that neutron stars were spinning rapidly and sending beamed radiation like a lighthouse. So it was rotation, not vibration, which caused the clock-like regularity of the signals, and only neutron stars could spin just enough without fragmenting.

The unexpected discovery of neutron stars opened a new field of research in physics and astronomy and also caused many scientists to regard the theoretical possibility of black holes in space far more seriously. After all, the fact that general relativity predicts that a high enough concentration of matter can actually trap light and form a closed region of spacetime does not mean that such situations actually occur. However, the mere existence of neutron stars suggests that the formation of black holes is quite probable. Neutron stars themselves are surrounded by such intense gravitational fields that they are already on the brink of further gravitational collapse and calculations indicate that a neutron star twice as massive as that in the Crab Nebula would rapidly become a black hole.

The early decades of radioastronomy, in which Cambridge featured so prominently and which was recognised by the award of the Nobel Prize to Ryle and myself, can be seen in retrospect as a 'golden age', but what are the prospects for the future? One of the outstanding questions in astronomy today concerns the origin of galaxies. What caused these structures to condense out of the expanding primordial gas? Several theories have been suggested for the initial blueprint which set the pattern for the galaxies that we now observe, but to check whether any of them is correct it is vital to look far enough into the past by probing to still greater distances. It is hoped that clues will be found by careful imaging of the microwave background radiation which presents a picture related to the distribution of matter less than 1 million years from the beginning, long before the galaxies emerged. This demands a new kind of radio telescope because the radiation is so feeble, and the patterns imposed upon it are so very faint. Cambridge radioastronomers are actively engaged with this challenging problem and the next few years should see the beginnings of an answer to the question of galaxy formation.

CHAPTER 5

Three Cambridge prehistorians

COLIN RENFREW

My theme is the development of prehistory as a coherent discipline:
a discipline in whose development Cambridge has played a significant role. Prehistory is generally defined as the study of the human
past before the existence of written historical records (which first
emerged in the Near East around 3000 BC). Such study relies almost
exclusively upon the techniques of archaeology – the study of the
human past using the material remains of human activity. Much of
the story of the development and growth of prehistory as a discipline
is thus bound up with the invention and application of new archaeological techniques, as well as new frameworks of interpretation. Only
through such advances has the vast panorama of the human past been
made available to us, and our own understanding of our place in the
world and in the scheme of things been clearly established.

The Chair of Archaeology established in Cambridge by John
Disney in 1851 was the first in Britain. It was instituted eight years
before that other Cambridge graduate, Charles Darwin, with the
publication of his *On the Origin of Species*, defined the context in
which prehistoric archaeology would become established. It was not
until 1927, however, that the Disney Chair became a full-time,
teaching position: its sixth incumbent, Sir Ellis Minns, was a man of
quiet erudition, whose *Scythians and Greeks* remains a standard work.

Already, with the first lectures in prehistoric archaeology,
delivered in 1916 by Miles Burkitt, the subject had been systematically taught in Cambridge. But three major figures who were to
succeed Minns in the Disney Chair – Dorothy Garrod, Grahame

Clark and Glyn Daniel – established a distinguished tradition of scholarship which has governed the future growth of the subject in Cambridge and indeed beyond. During their time also a whole series of energetic scholars worked to enlarge the scope of the discipline. To three more of these – Charles McBurney, Eric Higgs and David Clarke – I shall also draw attention.

Several other figures of distinction have worked in the formation of Cambridge archaeology. But in this retrospective review I have chosen not to refer in detail to younger scholars, but rather to deal with those no longer with us, or in the case of Grahame Clark, with one who is still active and highly productive but who retired already from the Disney Chair in 1974. His *Prehistory at Cambridge and Beyond* refers in detail to the scholars mentioned here.

PREHISTORY IN CAMBRIDGE

Prehistory has to be a mixture of theory and of practice. Without theory the subject scarcely exists. It was not until the middle of the nineteenth century that the pioneering work was undertaken to establish that the antiquity of humankind extends back well before the traditional date for the Creation, calculated from biblical genealogies to the year 4004 BC. The much vaster perspective inferred from the French quarry and cave sites discovered and investigated during the nineteenth century allowed the study of human biological and cultural evolution to flourish systematically for the first time. But if the earlier theoretical contributions of the mid-nineteenth century were indispensable to the growth of the discipline, so too were the important discoveries made in many parts of the world from that time onward.

Various approaches to archaeology may be discerned. John Lubbock in 1865 was one of the first to claim that prehistory could be regarded as a science. But alongside and sometimes counter to this view has been the notion of archaeology as a humane, historical discipline. Each generation sees its own tensions between these tendencies, as the following diagram indicates.

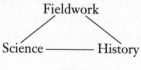

Of my three scholars, each reflecting aspects of all three directions, each most clearly exemplified one of these approaches.

DOROTHY GARROD

Dorothy Garrod, an outstanding field archaeologist, was one of those pioneering women in whom the discipline of archaeology has been so very fortunate. Among her redoubtable contemporaries, for instance, was Gertrude Caton-Thompson, who contributed so significantly to the understanding of the earlier prehistory of Egypt, and Kathleen Kenyon, based in London and then in Oxford, who undertook pioneering excavations at Jericho and Jerusalem. But to Dorothy Garrod came the additional distinction of being the first woman to hold a chair in any subject in the University of Cambridge.

Born in 1892, Dorothy Garrod was one of the first British scholars to contribute, by fieldwork and excavation as well as by works of synthesis, to the understanding of the earlier episodes in the human story in the Old Stone Age or palaeolithic period. Like Miles Burkitt before her, she was a pupil of the great French prehistorian, the Abbé Breuil. During the years 1922–4 she studied at the Institut de Paléontologie Humaine in Paris. It was at Breuil's suggestion that she set out to review the evidence for the occupation of Britain in the late palaeolithic period. Her *The Upper Palaeolithic Age in Britain*, published in 1926, may be regarded as the first work of modern synthesis in British palaeolithic archaeology.

Dorothy Garrod was personally quiet of manner and relatively slight in physique. She was, however, intrepid in her approach to archaeology, both intellectually and physically. She was a pioneer, and it was her great contribution to develop the study of the early human story well beyond the homeland of palaeolithic research in France itself, where, since the nineteenth century, and notably in the Dordogne, it had become so well established.

Her first excavation, undertaken at the suggestion of the Abbé Breuil, was in Gibraltar. There she had the great good fortune to discover evidence of Mousterian occupation, including some fragments of the skull cap of a Neanderthal child. Already it was well established that the Neanderthal hominids, and their associated Mousterian industry of flint tools, were the immediate predecessors in France of modern or 'Cro-Magnon' man – i.e. of our own species,

Homo sapiens sapiens. As Gertrude Caton-Thompson later wrote: 'Her report appeared in 1928. Few documents of comparable importance have been more tersely and coolly written by a beginner, who has just added a chapter to history.'

In 1928 there began her association with the Near East in which her most important contributions were to be made. She undertook first an exploratory visit to Kurdistan, at the invitation of the Iraq Department of Antiquities. Excavations were undertaken at two main sites, Hazer Merd and Zarzi: both required the presence of an armed guard, in view of local lawlessness. Hazer Merd produced the first good evidence of Mousterian occupation in this region, then little explored archaeologically. As we shall see, the Near Eastern Mousterian poses problems for human biological and cultural evolution which are still unresolved. At Zarzi she found ample remains of upper palaeolithic occupation. When R. S. Solecki excavated at Shanidar in the same area, after the Second World War, he was able to obtain radiocarbon determinations of *c.* 12,000 years ago for the Zarzi-type upper palaeolithic, and *c.* 50,000 for the Shanidar Mousterian.

In 1928 she also began work for the first time in Palestine, in the cave of Shukbah, in the Syrian desert. Deep deposits were found, rich in microliths, those small stone tools which in northern Europe are characteristic of the mesolithic period. She confidently diagnosed these also as belonging to the period following the local upper palaeolithic, and termed the industry 'Natufian', after the Natuf valley below the cave.

The great significance of these finds emerged only twenty years later when the origins of farming and the neolithic way of life were energetically being sought. Robert Braidwood's excavations at Jarmo in Iraqi Kurdistan focused renewed attention on the preceding Zarzian upper palaeolithic of several millennia earlier. And Kathleen Kenyon's work at Jericho clearly showed that the earliest farming levels there and elsewhere in the Levant were preceded by the remains of hunter-gatherer villages of essentially Natufian type. Dorothy Garrod's 1957 paper on the Natufian is a landmark study for the transition from hunter-gatherer to farming economy.

Between 1929 and 1934 she undertook seven excavation seasons at Mount Carmel in Palestine, in caves which, as Gertrude Caton-Thompson put it:

supplied in her memorable words 'the key to a large section of the prehistory of this part of the Near East' in as much as they provided between the three of them, a still unique and nearly but not quite unbroken series of deposits with a combined total of 24 metres, representing the main industrial levels with subdivisions covering in time something in the order of 80,000 to 100,000 years.

A notable feature of the work was the collaboration with scientific specialists, notably the zoologist Dorothea Bate and the geomor-phologist E. W. Gardener (as well as the anatomist Sir Arthur Keith). The faunal and climatic evidence were brought together with the archaeology in the pioneering interdisciplinary publication *The Stone Age of Mount Carmel* in 1937.

Her assistant T. D. McCown discovered a Mousterian cemetery of twelve individuals in one of the caves. This part of the Levant (today Israel and Jordan) remains of crucial importance for the under-standing of the emergence of our own species *Homo sapiens sapiens* and its relationship with *Homo sapiens neanderthalensis*.

Between 1934 and 1937 Dorothy Garrod was based mainly in Cambridge, teaching and writing, and in 1938 she undertook a reconnaissance in Anatolia. Sadly, the work there was held up by bureaucratic delays, and Anatolian palaeolithic studies did not benefit from her excavation skills and her careful analysis as the Levant had done and as Bulgaria was to do. For she and her colleagues (James Gaul and Bruce Howe) turned next to Bulgaria and excavated the Bacho Kiro cave, once again adding to knowledge of the Mousterian, of the upper palaeolithic and of the later phases prior to the onset of farming.

As Glyn Daniel records in his autobiography, her appointment to the Disney Chair of Archaeology was announced in 1937, on her birthday. Her tenure of the Chair was interrupted by the war, when she worked in the Intelligence Unit at Medmenham. As Glyn Daniel later wrote: 'The creation of a Part II archaeology which started in 1949 was one of the reasons for the growth in importance of the Cambridge school in the post-war years – that and Dorothy's uncompromising view that students should be taught archaeological facts, get acquainted with artefacts and site reports, and travel.'

She retired early, in 1952, and built herself a house in France, continuing to collaborate with Suzanne de Saint-Mathurin, another former pupil of the Abbé Breuil, in her excavations at the rock shelter of Angles-sur-l'Anglin.

I had the privilege of meeting Dorothy Garrod only once, in 1965, accompanied by my wife Jane, on our honeymoon in Paris. Glyn Daniel, knowing that we were to be in Paris, where she was then living, wrote to suggest a meeting. Suzanne de Saint-Mathurin was also present at lunch. The quiet clarity of mind of Dorothy Garrod is the clearest impression which I retain of that meeting.

Dorothy Garrod became a Fellow of the British Academy in 1952, was the recipient of several honorary degrees and received the Gold Medal of the Society of Antiquaries of London in 1968, the year of her death. She was one of those scientists whose fieldwork is driven by a sense of problem which transcends local concerns. She was first and foremost a field archaeologist, the first in a notable series in Cambridge archaeology.

It is appropriate perhaps to compare with her another great field-worker, Charles McBurney, whose greatest contributions were also made in exploring the palaeolithic period in lands beyond Europe. Charles McBurney worked principally in North Africa. Born in 1914 and educated in Cambridge before the war, he worked in Cyrenaica and in 1948 discovered the Hauah Fteah cave. The publication of the excavations at this site in 1967, and McBurney's work of synthesis, *The Stone Age of Northern Africa*, were contributions which may be compared with those of Garrod. His later work in Iran, and then at the Cotte de St Brelade in Jersey, contributed to the same tradition of well-directed pioneering fieldwork. Charles McBurney, by then the holder of a personal chair, died in 1979.

It is not possible to leave the palaeolithic period and the contributions of Dorothy Garrod and Charles McBurney, without mentioning also three more Cambridge scholars who went out to work in Africa, where such great strides have been made in palaeolithic studies. Louis Leakey, Desmond Clark and Glyn Isaac are among those who have established that the earliest steps in the human story took place in Africa, with the emergence of *Australopithecus*, *Homo habilis* and *Homo erectus*, and then the emergence of our own species *Homo sapiens*. But these were scholars who started in Cambridge and then went on elsewhere. Instead I turn to Grahame Clark, currently the doyen of British prehistorians, now in his 86th year.

GRAHAME CLARK

If Dorothy Garrod was the first scholar to establish in Cambridge a fine tradition in systematic archaeological excavation and a well-focused interest in early humankind, Grahame Clark was the first to develop a whole new approach to the subject. His *Prehistoric Europe – the Economic Basis* developed in an impressively sustained way the ecological approach to the subject – an approach which harmonises in many ways with the growth of archaeological science. Grahame Clark brought to archaeology in mid-century the rigour of the sciences.

Grahame Clark was born in 1907 and came up to Cambridge in 1928, turning to archaeology in 1930. His doctoral dissertation, *The Mesolithic Age in Britain*, was published in 1932. As he himself put it: 'The basis from which I began my research on the Mesolithic phase in British prehistory was the ten-page treatment of what Dorothy Garrod termed "epi-palaeolithic" cultures in her book *The Upper Palaeolithic Age in Britain*.'

His approach, however, was a different one. In the first place he looked closely at the links across the North Sea with the contemporary cultures of Germany and Scandinavia. And he saw clearly the possibility of following the interdisciplinary methods being developed by German and Scandinavian archaeologists in collaborating with geologists and palaeontologists in the field of Quaternary Research. Dr (later Professor Sir) Harry Godwin had learnt the techniques of pollen analysis from the Swedish scholar Lennart van Post and went on to trace the history of British vegetation since the last Ice Age. Clark and Godwin collaborated in work at various Fenland sites, notably Peacock's Farm at Shippea Hill, Cambridgeshire.

Through Godwin's work, the pollen and climatic sequence was established as securely for Britain as it had been for Scandinavia, taking definitive form in Godwin's *The History of the British Flora*. And on this experience Clark's ecological approach was ultimately based. This keen ecological awareness may have underlain the thematic approach adopted in one of Grahame Clark's most original works, *Archaeology and Society*, published in 1939. Most introductions to archaeology up to that time had taken a chronological, period-by-period approach. Here instead there was a broader view, less concerned with narrative than with the broad and perennial themes of environment, technology and social structure.

The war brought an inevitable interruption: Clark, like many archaeologists in the war, was involved in military intelligence and in particular with air-photographic interpretation – he had already been a pioneer in the archaeological use of aerial photography.

After the war, in 1949, Clark set out to excavate a mesolithic site at Star Carr near Scarborough in Yorkshire. What might have been a small excavation of a waterlogged site, and mainly of British interest, was transformed into a significant episode in the development of archaeological method through the fine preservation of organic remains at the site and the manner of their recovery and interpretation. Animal bones, plant remains and pollen were very systematically recovered (along with the usual stone and bone tools). This was of necessity interdisciplinary work. But Grahame Clark made it into something more than this with his view of human settlement and human activity as components of the complete ecosystem.

Clark's view of prehistoric life as a series of varying productive activities was developed in a whole series of articles in the 1940s, and these formed the basis for what must be regarded as his most influential work, published in 1952, *Prehistoric Europe – the Economic Basis*. With its ambition to transcend the limitations of preservation imposed by the archaeological record, and to consider the full range of human endeavour, this was, I believe, one of the works which helped to shape the 'New Archaeology' of the late 1960s. It influenced the 'functional-processual' thought of such scholars as Lewis Binford and David Clarke, and the systems approach of Kent Flannery and others.

Clark's thinking harmonised well with the multi-disciplinary fieldwork initiated by the American scholar Robert Braidwood in Iraqi Kurdistan in 1948, with its reliance on faunal specialists and on the recovery of carbonised plant remains, pioneered by his colleague, the Danish palaeobotanist Hans Helbaek. This work indeed built on the foundations laid by Dorothy Garrod in the same area twenty years earlier: significantly, perhaps, Braidwood's environmentalist collaborator Bruce Howe had worked with Garrod in Bulgaria in 1938.

Here again the interaction between well-designed fieldwork and the developing conceptual approach is very clear. The research questions, properly formulated, govern the nature of the fieldwork to be undertaken. But, as at Star Carr, it is the specific opportunities offered by the fieldwork which lead to the further developments in the conceptual basis. The theory and the finds are mutually beneficial: in the jargon of the systems approach, there is 'positive feedback'.

Grahame Clark's interdisciplinary interests led him to keep fully abreast of the developments of archaeological science. When the technique of radiocarbon dating was developed by Willard Libby in Chicago, Clark encouraged the institution of a radiocarbon facility in Cambridge, and a project was implemented to date the mesolithic and neolithic culture sequence established in the Fens twenty years earlier. He was one of the first to use radiocarbon dates coherently, on a continental scale, with his study published in 1965 entitled: 'Radiocarbon dating and the spread of farming economy'. This same approach was employed in 1961, this time on a global scale, with the publication of *World Prehistory*, and, especially in the second edition in 1969 when more dates were available, the culture sequence fully established on the basis of radiocarbon determinations, for each continent in turn.

Grahame Clark presided over the Department of Archaeology in Cambridge during a period (1952–74) when universities were expanding and archaeology as a subject was becoming more popular. He himself took great pride in the diaspora of Cambridge pre-historians to different parts of the world, where they undertook a wide range of significant work. Research in Africa had been pioneered already by Louis Leakey and Desmond Clark – contemporaries rather than students of Grahame Clark. But in other areas – most notably in Australia and the Pacific – prominent senior figures, such as Jack Golson and John Mulvaney, had studied in Cambridge during Clark's time as lecturer or as Disney Professor. And, as he recounts with evident pride in his *Prehistory at Cambridge and Beyond*, many notable figures in a younger generation such as Isabel McBryde, Charles Higham, Wilfred Shawcross, Rhys Jones and Peter Belwood took first degrees or higher qualifications in Cambridge.

Grahame Clark, perhaps more than any other single prehistorian, worked to establish rigorously scientific standards both in his own research and in his publications. In the domain of excavation method

Sir Mortimer Wheeler was the leading pioneer, while the great master of synthesis in the prehistory of Europe was Gordon Childe, who came from Australia and was successively Professor of Archaeology in Edinburgh and then, following Wheeler, Director of the Institute of Archaeology in London. But Clark made a further contribution to the publication of prehistoric research at a level of high professional competence. For many years he was editor of the *Proceedings of the Prehistoric Society*, the organisation which he and others had transformed in 1935 from the Prehistoric Society of East Anglia, giving it a national and ultimately global scope by dropping the regional restriction.

As first Chairman of the Science-Based Archaeology Committee of the Science Research Council, he presided over the systematic development of archaeological science in this country, building upon the pioneering work of the Research Laboratory for Archaeology at Oxford.

Grahame Clark was knighted for services to archaeology in 1992 – placing him in the very select company of archaeological knights, among them Sir John Evans, Sir Arthur Evans (who inherited his father's title), Sir Flinders Petrie, Sir Leonard Woolley, Sir Max Mallowan and Sir Mortimer Wheeler, to whom must certainly be added their female counterparts Dame Kathleen Kenyon and Dame Joan Evans. Many of these were known principally as field archaeologists. Grahame Clark will be remembered above all as an interdisciplinary pioneer and as a scientist. His most recent work, published in 1992, *Space, Time and Man*, gives a prehistorian's view of the world in which we live, comprehensive in its scope.

In discussing Grahame Clark it is relevant to mention another worker who further developed the ecological approach which Clark had himself pioneered: Eric Higgs. Coming late to archaeology, Higgs took the Diploma in Prehistoric Archaeology in 1953, and worked with Charles McBurney in North Africa. He studied the animal bones from the important early neolithic site at Nea Nikomedeia in northern Greece and then went on to do pioneering work in the palaeolithic of Epirus in northern Greece, following here the direction indicated by Dorothy Garrod in the Levant and Bulgaria, and by McBurney in North Africa. Higgs was also Director of the Early History of Agriculture Project in Cambridge from 1966 until his death in 1976. Here he inspired a series of students to work on animal and plant remains, very much in the ecological tradition pioneered by Grahame Clark.

For Glyn Daniel, ideas were associated with people. His own personal warmth carried with it an ability to catch the imagination. Humour, and an eye for the foibles and idiosyncrasies of personal life were never far from the surface. In this and in other ways he was pre-eminently a humanist. These qualities underlay his two most notable contributions to archaeology. He was the first historian of archaeology. And he was one of the great popularisers of archaeology, on radio and television, as well as through the written word.

His childhood is recaptured in vivid detail in his autobiography, *Some Small Harvest*. Coming up to Cambridge in 1932 to read geography, he found the lectures unexciting and (although obtaining first-class honours in the qualifying exams) decided to read archaeology in his second year. It was at this time that the megalithic monuments of Britain and then of Brittany first seized his imagination, and in his autobiography he describes his first visit to the Morbihan area of Brittany, famous for the great sites of Carnac and Locqmariaquer, as well as for its oysters: 'I lived in a heaven of megalithic sunshine and good food . . . I went back to south Wales in a haze. I knew that I was going to study megalithic monuments for as long as I could, that I was fascinated by France and its archaeology.'

The quality of personal experience and personal contact underlay much of Glyn Daniel's archaeological contribution. It was what made him an outstanding communicator, and such a well-known figure nationally from the mid 1950s.

Glyn Daniel's doctoral dissertation was completed in 1938 and later published as *The Prehistoric Chamber Tombs of England and Wales*, and it earned him a Research Fellowship at St John's College. His academic career was interrupted by the war, where he served in India as Commanding Officer of the Central Photographic Interpretation Unit. His work on the British megaliths was the first of a number of studies on these enigmatic monuments, and I recall with great pleasure his lectures on Stonehenge and on the Maltese temples, which I attended as an undergraduate. Frequently he would report new and unpublished radiocarbon dates which, as editor of *Antiquity*, he received: there was an acute and stimulating sense of changing perspectives as the dates consistently came out earlier than predicted.

Glyn Daniel's first book *The Three Ages: an Essay on Archaeological Method*, was written in 1940, and from it developed an enduring interest in the history of archaeology and the history of ideas. His *A Hundred Years of Archaeology* was the first systematic history of archaeology written in English, and it was followed in 1962 by *The Idea of Prehistory*. In these works the shifting perceptions of the human past over the centuries and the development of prehistory as a study and archaeology as a discipline are chronicled with considerable insight. Glyn Daniel made a good historian of archaeology because he was interested in the people who undertook the research and could situate them and their thought very skilfully in the context of their time. In some respects his work created a part of the self-awareness, the self-consciousness of the thinking archaeologist about the nature of our discipline which set the scene for the 'New Archaeology' of the late 1960s. His clear image of an archaeology of developing and shifting perceptions is one which could be regarded as heralding also the 'post-modern' or 'post-processual' approach advocated by many writers today who no longer aspire to the ideal of archaeology as a scientific discipline.

Glyn Daniel was not a man for elaborate theories or models of the past. He judged archaeological research through the quality and nature of the individual research worker. That was a natural consequence of his personal humanism. So he was unimpressed by the 'New Archaeology' or 'processual archaeology' of David Clarke or Lewis Binford, just as he would, I fear, have been unimpressed by the 'post-processual' archaeology which became fashionable during his tenure as Disney Professor (from 1974 to 1981). I believe, however, that the clear image conveyed in *The Idea of Prehistory*, of changing archaeologies and prehistories, of differing perspectives and different prejudices, is one which is very much in keeping with the relativism of much current thought. Glyn Daniel, however, did not relish long passages of theoretical writing. He related ideas directly to people.

This quality was central also to his success as the first and perhaps the most influential exponent of a new genre of communicator – the television don. In 1952 came the first broadcast of the television quiz game *Animal, Vegetable, Mineral?*, of which he was question-master and, with Sir Mortimer Wheeler, one of the stars (Wheeler was

Television Personality of the Year in 1954, and Daniel in 1955). It was an instant success – this was in those far-off days when nearly all programmes were live and there was only one television channel. *AVM?* was produced by Paul Johnstone, who followed it with *Buried Treasure*, and then the series *Chronicle*. As a broadcaster, Glyn Daniel was the leading member of a group of communicators, including Wheeler and Jacquetta Hawkes, who generally had something of interest to say, and for whom the medium was not entirely the message.

The same zest for the whole scope of archaeology and for wide friendship and acquaintance made him a very suitable editor of Ancient People and Places, a remarkable series of books published by Thomas and Hudson, which produced more than a hundred volumes. And when the founder and editor of *Antiquity*, O. G. S. Crawford, died in 1957, he was the natural successor to take on the responsibility for what was and remained a periodical which achieved that difficult mission of being at once popular and scholarly.

This was the time when archaeology really became established in public awareness in Britain, where it had long been an interest of the informed amateur. It now became more than this; it achieved popularity at a mass level. It was the time also that the number of students reading archaeology in universities increased substantially. The increase in numbers is related, of course, to the growth in university education as a whole. Yet through a combination of factors archaeology has entered the public awareness as a discipline, part humanity, part science, which is relevant to all times and all places. That it has done so is due in large measure to the process of *haute vulgarisation* in which Glyn Daniel was the leading academic figure.

There are, of course, many other strands in the public growth of archaeology, not least the development of rescue archaeology and of the general awareness that the proper conservation of the heritage is a matter of appropriate national concern. But these ideas are related to that humane interest in the past which Glyn Daniel experienced so fully and communicated so warmly.

Mention earlier of the name of David Clarke allows me to refer briefly to one other notable Cambridge mind. Born in 1938, he sadly died in 1976 at the early age of 38. David Clarke was indeed a theoretician: his *Analytical Archaeology*, published in 1968, is the most ambitious work of archaeological theory ever written – and in my own view in many ways the best. His article 'Archaeology, the loss of innocence', published in *Antiquity*, remains the most clear statement of the intellectual scene in the mid-1970s, when it was written. He had a vision of archaeology as an ambitious discipline, scientific in the best sense, and he evoked this even more clearly than the other principal exponent of the 'New Archaeology', Lewis Binford. In choosing to discuss three major figures of a more senior generation I have been unable to do justice to Charles McBurney, Eric Higgs or David Clarke or indeed to other figures such as Geoffrey Bushnell, a champion of Americanist archaeology, John Alexander, a great supporter of the cause of African archaeology, and a number of other active figures.

But the three principals in my story – Dorothy Garrod, the field-worker; Grahame Clark, the scientist and exponent of economic prehistory; and Glyn Daniel, the humanist and champion of archaeology in the common understanding – effectively expounded and exemplified three of the fundamental approaches upon which the disciplines of archaeology and prehistory are founded.

CHAPTER 6

John Maynard Keynes

GEOFFREY HARCOURT

I

The obituarist of *The Times* of London wrote on 22 April 1946:

> Lord Keynes, the great economist, died at Tilton, Firle, Sussex, yesterday from a heart attack.
>
> By his death, the country has lost a very great Englishman.

This is a faultless judgement: Keynes was a 'great economist', arguably the greatest of the twentieth century, and he was, indisputably, 'a very great Englishman'. In order to have a proper perspective on his life, his economics and his contributions generally, these attributes have always to be remembered. Keynes was a proper patriot. He was as aware of the faults of his fellow citizens as he was of their virtues; but he always attempted to devise policies and to design institutions which would enable them, if they so wished, to be able to live better, while at the same time fitting his and their society into an international order in which there could be desirable outcomes for all. Even more important, we should remember that Keynes's own life was an example of a person who was wrestling unceasingly but increasingly optimistically with the Moorean problem: Is it possible both to *be* good and to *do* good?

In the end Keynes literally killed himself for his country and for the wider international community. His heroic efforts and his death are the ingredients of a Greek tragedy, not least because it was the Americans and not Keynes and the British who triumphed at Bretton Woods concerning the details, and especially the orders of

72

magnitude established for the new international institutions. The new international order thus set up contained within it the seeds of its own destruction.

In this chapter, though, I concentrate on the developments which led to Keynes's greatest intellectual achievement, the writing of *The General Theory of Employment, Interest, and Money* (1936).

II

To understand Keynes's economics, it is vital to remember that, though he read mathematics as an undergraduate at King's, he seems to have spent as much time on philosophy. He was in fact an outstanding and original philosopher in his own right. (Keynes himself always regarded economics as a branch of moral philosophy – and, as Andrea Maneschi has reminded me, Adam Smith was Professor of *Moral Philosophy* in Glasgow and always viewed political economy as a branch of philosophy.)

His philosophical understanding brought to his economics at least three vital characteristics, the neglect of which literally makes it impossible correctly to interpret his books or articles and especially the arguments of his *magnum opus*. Economists who have neglected this aspect of Keynes's thought have been pushed, still puzzling, into acknowledging it when they themselves have worked on the issues and problems which Keynes addressed. A candid admission of this was made by Frank Hahn in 1982 when, in his admirable crusade against the disastrous effects on theory and policy of the new classical macroeconomics, he said that he found himself at times able only to provide 'arguments that are merely plausible rather than clinching'.[1]

Keynes's first major research project, as we would say now, was on philosophical issues; published in 1921 as *A Treatise on Probability*, it was originally written as his Fellowship dissertation for King's in the first decade of the century. Though he was to respond to criticisms of it, especially by Frank Ramsey, it nevertheless continued to provide the base for all his subsequent intellectual work.

How did it affect his economics? First, there is the argument that, in a discipline such as economics, there is a whole spectrum of languages, moving continuously from intuition and poetry to mathematics and formal logic, taking in lawyer-like arguments on the way. *All* these languages *may* be relevant at appropriate steps in arguments and for particular issues, or aspects of issues, in economics. *The General Theory* has puzzled many modern economists just because they are unaware of, or unwilling to accept that, economic *theory* may be done in this manner. Even as shrewd and as deep a thinker as Keynes's colleague and friend in King's, Gerald Shove, fell into this trap. When he first read *The General Theory*, he wrote to Keynes that he had been trying to bring expectations, and the influence of current and immediate past experience on them, into the analysis of the industry and firm, but that he could not make the analysis 'precise'. Keynes in effect told him that he need not do so. 'As soon as one is dealing with the influence of expectations and of transitory experience, one is, in the nature of things, outside the realm of the formally exact'.[2] As I said above, on the path between intuition and formal logic, we come to lawyer-like arguments, the sorts of balances of probabilities and the use of evidence which Keynes himself captured in the term 'weight' and which is the essence of those plausible but non-clinching arguments experienced by Hahn. As Richard Kahn has told us, Keynes became increasingly more comfortable (indeed, was probably always so) with this part of the languages spectrum. He much preferred to write for a wider public audience (even if his essays were often 'the croakings of a Cassandra', ahead of his time and taken notice of too late, as has happened again to another Cassandra of the Fens, Wynne Godley), than to write formal economic theory, especially of the kind which now dominates the economic journals.

Secondly, there is Keynes's realisation that, again in a discipline such as economics, the whole *may* be more than the sum of the parts, a realisation which he came to long before he wrote *The General Theory* but in which it played a crucial role. My favourite quote which illustrates this point comes from his biographical essay on Edgeworth. Keynes is discussing 'The application of mathematical method to the measurement of economic value': 'We are faced at every turn with the problems of organic unity, of discreteness, of discontinuity – the whole is not equal to the sum of the parts, comparisons of quantity fail us, small changes produce large effects, the assumptions of a uniform and homogeneous continuum are not satisfied.'[3]

Thirdly, Keynes thought of probability as a form of objective belief and of uncertainty as an absence of probabilistic knowledge – 'We simply do not know'.[4] This distinction and understanding permeated the whole of his economic reasoning, especially in relation to the formation of expectations, decisions concerning investment expenditure and the formation of portfolios, including the holding of money. In this Keynes was both drawing on and deepening greatly the tradition in which he was brought up and which he himself taught, Cambridge economics as dominated by Alfred Marshall. Marshall had a wide and detailed knowledge of 'mankind in the ordinary business of life' and he framed his own principles of economics so as to illuminate the behaviour of sensible people doing the best they could – as business people, as consumers, as workers – in environments characterised by uncertainty. This led Shove to apply to Marshall, Wildon Carr's dictum that 'it is better to be vaguely right than precisely wrong'[5] – a dictum which is even more applicable to Keynes.

Next, to stress the obvious, Keynes, as well as being an intellectual, was a deeply practical person, well versed in the ways of the world, wanting his philosophy and his economics to be applicable to practical issues of explanation and policy, and right behaviour. Robert Skidelsky has charted this development in his first two volumes of biography, showing how Keynes's friendships and experiences in the First World War brought this particular member of the Bloomsbury set from being a superbly clever (but perhaps too flippant, too brilliant) all-rounder to becoming a deeply serious and committed political economist. Keynes was outraged by the behaviour of the politicians at Versailles and determined to speak up for decent, humane values, not only because to do so was morally correct but also because it was intelligent *Realpolitik* as well.

Keynes's system of thought started from observations on, and intuitions and conjectures concerning, reality as such. The *Treatise on Probability* abounds in homely examples which are then generalised in propositions which are vital links in his arguments. Though he was not a great mathematician in any formal sense, he did have that characteristic of the greatest mathematicians of intuitively knowing the answer, stating a conclusion, long before the steps in the argument needed to reach them were stated, a priceless gift for someone as interested in policy as in theory and explanation. Because of these traits, it was no accident therefore that he soon became and remained primarily a monetary economist. He was fascinated by the properties of money: what caused it to arise and then become a vital institution of what he was eventually to call a monetary production economy, how it operated in society and how dispassionate intelligent people, by taking thought, could tame it so as to make it a good servant instead of a bad master. (He did *not* have in mind independent central bankers.) It is true that the first serious work in economics that he read was by Jevons and that Marshall, as his teacher, encouraged him to read all of Volume 1 of the *Principles*. But his interest in value (and distribution) theory was only a means to the end of constructing an appropriate structure of thought through which to understand the monetary aspects of the system. Real long-period theory, 'the real business of the *Principles*', Kahn called it,[6] left Keynes cold, a subject suitable only for undergraduates – or the dead. Keynes especially loved making up policies for the short term, though he tried always to be conscious of the ensuing implications of them for the medium to the longer term. From the *Tract on Monetary Reform* (1923) on, he directed his theoretical apparatus towards making understanding of the short period, and policies appropriate to it, central objects of study in their own right.

Let me enter a further slight caveat at this point. Both in *The Economic Consequences of the Peace* (1919) and right at the end of his life in his speech to the House of Lords, he did emphasise the longer term. Having in mind those longer-term persistent and dominant forces at work in healthy, competitive societies, Keynes said: 'Here is an attempt to use what we have learnt from modern experience and modern analysis, not to defeat, but to implement the wisdom of Adam Smith'.[7] But explicitly, in both sources, there is a presumption that the *appropriate* short-term policies have been designed and implemented.

In his first example there is his justly famous description[8] of how the European economy functioned before the First World War. Here, the importance of institutions and of tacit understandings between classes, combined with mutual knowledge of the rules of the game, are brilliantly evoked. Keynes also admits that there may be forced acceptance of all this by one class and he gives a dire warning concerning the 'unstable psychological' base on which the whole edifice is placed. In the second example, with his appeal to Smith, our founder, Keynes keenly appreciated the stress by Smith on inter-relationships between regions and nations, on cumulative processes which, if benign, could bring harmony and well-being, but also discord and increasing misery if inappropriate institutions and behaviour were allowed to dominate.

III

At first Keynes was inhibited in his endeavour to make the short period and accompanying appropriate policies centre stage because of the structure of the ideal *Principles* which Marshall had imposed on the profession as Keynes understood it. Volume I was to be on real things, relative quantities and relative prices, primarily long period and normal, Volume II on money and the absolute or general price level, and never the twain should meet. True, in the *Tract*, while Keynes pays lip service to this, he nevertheless concentrates on the short-period consequences of changes in the velocity of circulation for the twin but opposite processes of inflation and deflation, such as had plagued the economies of Europe after the war. He was cheeking his old teacher in the passage in which his best known quote, '*In the long run* we are all dead', appears. For he adds: 'Economists set themselves too easy, too useless a task if in tempestuous seasons they can only tell us that when the storm is long past the ocean is flat again',[9] a reference to the analogy of storm and sea beloved by Marshall himself.

Nevertheless, the *analysis* was still strictly Marshallian. Moreover, Marshall's shadow was to continue to lie over *A Treatise on Money* (1930), the publication of which Keynes hoped would establish him as *the* outstanding monetary economist. That it might not do so Keynes himself realised, so that he wrote to his mother when the book was finished, that 'Artistically it is a failure'.[10]

It is important to understand the nature of this 'failure' and the details of how Keynes liberated himself from the hold which Marshall had on his thinking. In the process we should note, as well as Keynes's own critical and creative genius, the crucial role played by his favourite and most devoted disciple, Richard Kahn, and the group of brilliant young people who were Keynes's colleagues and/or pupils – and friends. In Cambridge itself there was the 'circus' in which, in addition to Kahn, there were Piero Sraffa, Austin and Joan Robinson – Austin has just been taken from us in his 96th year – and James Meade, still happily with us in his 87th year and then 'learning his

77

trade' by having a year in Cambridge before starting teaching at Hertford in Oxford. (An index of how fast economics was advancing is that ten years or so earlier Roy Harrod only needed six months!) Then we must mention Keynes's *alter ego* of many years, Dennis Robertson, and Roy Harrod, Ralph Hawtrey and Gerald Shove.

The hold which Marshall had can be reduced to two interrelated propositions – Say's Law and its corollary, the Quantity Theory of Money (of which Kahn in particular had always been sceptical as a *causal* explanation of the general price level). I mention this not only because of its biographical and historical interest but also because of the grip which this former approach has taken again on modern theory and policy-making. From this development stems in considerable part the misery of those who had been condemned to poverty, unemployment and insecurity because of the often man-made malfunctioning of our economies over the past two decades.

Marshall used partial equilibrium analysis in Volume I to examine the workings of individual industries in the short period in order to build up to the long period and show how in competitive conditions there was a tendency for markets to clear, for prices to settle at levels where voluntary demands and supplies matched. This model was as applicable to the market for labour as it was for the market for peanuts. Nevertheless, he had a general equilibrium model – a model of all markets of the system taken together – hidden (as ever) in an appendix where, he argued (as Walras had before him), the same result went through for the system as a whole. It follows that the question 'What determines employment and output as a whole?', while clearly of practical significance, for Marshall knew much about the trade cycle, was neither an interesting nor a necessary *theoretical* question. Hence Say's Law that, as a tendency, total supplies create total demands so that undesired unemployment and a general glut of commodities were not a long-term possibility was established as a deduction in Volume I without the need, *analytically*, to mention the role of money or financial institutions at all.

Moreover, when accumulation was discussed, it was in terms of the market for saving and investment which was equilibrated by its own particular price, the natural rate of interest, a *real* not a monetary phenomenon. Its role was to equilibrate the desire to spread consumption out of income over the lifetimes of the individuals in society with the incentive of business people now to use postponed consumption and available resources in productive investment in the best known techniques of production, in order to convert them into streams of consumption in the future, in the process deciding the *composition* but not the sizes of the Say's Law levels of overall employment and output.

In the ideal Volume II this Say's Law level was carried over in order to determine, with the help of V, the velocity of circulation (which was historically and institutionally given), and M, the quantity of money (which was the provenance of the monetary authority), the overall level of prices, P – in the (in-)famous Quantity Theory of Money which in fact is a theory of the general price level. This provided the long-period background for a discussion of why economies might fluctuate around such positions – the trade cycle and all that – and how institutions could be designed to allow economies to recover as quickly as possible from shocks and return to these positions, or move as smoothly as possible to new positions if the fundamental determinants of the Say's Law positions – tastes, techniques, resources – had changed.

IV

When Keynes was writing *A Treatise on Money*, even though he was getting more and more interested in cycles and prolonged lapses from full employment, he nevertheless told us that he felt constrained from following out too far the intricate theory of short-period production because it was not an acceptable way to proceed in a treatise on money. He still thought he was providing a more usable version of the Quantity Theory of Money and that his 'fundamental equations', which 'explained' the price levels of available (consumption) goods and unavailable (investment) goods, as well as the overall price level, were just another way of writing down the Quantity Theory. Indeed they were, especially in the long-period position, but they also drew attention to another theory of price formation in which wage costs were a key element, an innovation which was to have lasting consequences.

In the *Treatise on Money* it was still true that real things ruled and monetary things have to adjust to them. For example, if the economy was malfunctioning, this meant that the banking system had set money rates of interest which were inconsistent with the underlying natural rate and that the malfunctioning would continue until the banking system came to its senses.

However, Keynes was too impatient to be completely true to himself – after all, unemployment in the United Kingdom in the 1920s had never been less than 1 million people. He therefore analysed short-period production and employment problems in, for example, his famous banana plantation parable. In the parable there is no endogenous process which can stop a cumulative process once it has started. Keynes tells the story of a thrift gospeller who comes to 'help' the people of this economy where investment is setting up plantations and consumption is harvesting bananas. The thrift campaigner tells the inhabitants to save more. As a result, on the *Treatise on Money* equations, there is a cumulative downturn in prices, employment and production until the inhabitants either starve to death or decide to change their investment behaviour or scrap their new-found habits with regard to thrift.

Peter Clarke has told us the fascinating story of the inter-relationship between Keynes's evidence and arguments before the Macmillan Committee and the writing and rewriting of the proofs of his book as he responded to the debate. We need also to note the important intervention by Keynes and Hubert Henderson in the election at the end of the 1920s when they wrote *Can Lloyd George Do It?*, a reference not to the obvious answer which history was to provide but to the case for using expenditure on public works to lower unemployment. In both places Keynes was taking on the so-called 'Treasury View' (which still more than lingers on today) that public works could not cure unemployment because there is only so much saving around for society's investment, so that what goes into the public sector must be at the expense of the private sector.

Keynes used the apparatus of his book in these debates. Wherever there was a difference between saving and investment (on the definitions of the *Treatise on Money*) cumulative processes occurred, principally with respect to movements of prices but also, as we have seen, with regard to output and employment as well. But he did not have a convincing answer as to where the saving would come from or a coherent answer as to how the process would stop, until Richard Kahn, using Keynes's theoretical apparatus and aided by 'Mr Meade's relation', provided them in his famous 1931 *Economic Journal* article on the multiplier. Kahn and Meade provided the endogenous process whereby activity and employment would change, following a change in investment expenditure, until voluntary saving was again equal to the new level of investment, even on the *Treatise on Money* definitions. Investment led and saving followed, a tremendously liberating move which allowed Keynes to go from his 1930 book to *The General Theory*. For Kahn's article and Meade's demonstration that, as income changed, so, too, did saving until it too had reached the new level of investment, gave an explicit answer to the Treasury View that there was only a certain amount of saving to go round.

Actually Keynes rather blew it as a debater because he revealed prematurely his answer in the exchanges at the Macmillan Committee. The Treasury witnesses were therefore able to counter by saying that this was not their argument after all. Rather, they were arguing that the public sector is so inefficient that it should not be allowed to invest because private people would do so much more efficiently and profitably. (This has a certain modern ring to it.)

Keynes now began to realise that Say's Law did not hold and therefore that the Quantity Theory was not an explanation of prices. He started to rebuild his system of thought, with money there right from the start. He argued that the Marshallian dichotomy between the real and the monetary was wrong, that we had to have a theory of a monetary production economy in which money had several roles to play – as a medium of exchange, as a unit of account, and as a store of value, *all at the start of the story*.

What other changes occurred? Keynes liked to make things stark so that the fundamental strands of the argument could be seen in very simple outlines before he put in the modifications. As we have seen, in the earlier book the natural rate of interest equilibrated real saving and investment and the money rate of interest had to be consistent with this. By the time Keynes came to *The General Theory* he had turned all this around by 180°. He argued that the money rate of interest, determined by the demand for money including liquidity preference (which reflected its store of value role) and the supply of money, ruled the roost. His version of the natural rate of interest, which had now become the expected rates of profit on potential investments (he called them marginal efficiencies of capital), had to measure up to the money rate of interest. This is the subject principally of chapters 11 to 17 of *The General Theory*, and of the papers Keynes published in 1937 in reply to his critics.

Another major change was to build up the theory of consumption and saving for the economy as a whole – the propensity to consume and to save schedules – and the theory of investment, on which we have already touched. Together they constituted the theory of aggregate demand in the form of an aggregate demand function, a concept which goes back at least to Malthus – the first Cambridge economist, Keynes called him – but which Keynes considered had been lost to sight following Ricardo's (alleged) trouncing of Malthus in the debate on general gluts after the Napoleonic Wars. Finally, there was chapter 21 on the general theory of prices, in which he said we should bring again to the fore those 'homely but intelligible' concepts of short-period elasticities of supply and marginal costs. Here, Keynes was Marshallian, adapting Marshall's great gift to the profession (and parrots) of supply and demand curves, to obtain an *overall* short-period Marshallian supply curve as the basis of the aggregate supply function. The point of intersection of the aggregate demand and aggregate supply functions was christened by Keynes the *point of effective demand*. He argued that it could be associated with considerably high and sustained levels of unemployment, involuntary unemployment in the sense that wage-earners wished to work but that it was not profitable for them to be employed. Moreover, there were no actions that they could take, either individually or collectively, which would make it profitable for them to be employed.

The base on which total demand was built was the desire to accumulate by business people – 'Accumulate, accumulate, that is Moses and the prophets' – was a theme common to both Marx and Keynes. The desire itself depended primarily on their expectations of *future* sales and profits in relation to the cost and availability of finance, and the prices of capital goods. Moreover, there was nothing in the signals of the system which would ensure that the combined outcome of these interacting forces would be such as to ensure, *even on average*, that investment would be at the level which could absorb the saving that the community would make if the work force and the capacity of existing capital goods both were fully employed. And for all the sophisticated advances in theory that have been made since then, this basic insight still holds concerning the operation of industrialised economies, the activities of which are predominantly determined by the decisions of private business people.

v

When *The General Theory* was published in early 1936, Keynes only
had ten years more to live, two of which were (relatively) washed out
by his severe heart attack in 1937. Yet in those years he was to leave
us more major contributions. First, in replying to his critics he
showed that, while investment was not constrained by saving (unless
the economy were to be fully employed), it could be constrained by
lack of finance, primarily from the banking system and ultimately
from the stock exchange and the other financial institutions which are
designed to gather up and allocate or reallocate new and past savings,
both domestic and from abroad.

Secondly, while naturally the policy emphasis and analysis initially
concerned unemployment and recession, when war came in 1939, he
showed how his system could equally well tackle the problems of
shortages and inflationary pressures. He identified an inflationary
gap – demands in real terms which outstrip even the full employment
supplies of the system, such as happens (alas, usually only) when there
is full mobilisation for a war effort. This aggregate excess demand
would show its effects in tendencies for prices to rise and/or for
queues to form and it would be a *cumulative* inflationary process *unless*
steps were taken to reduce demands in real terms in order to match
them with available supplies. Here again the significance of his use of
the word 'general' in the title of the book and his warning that we
should be on our guard against the fallacy of composition – what may
be true for an individual taken in isolation may not be so for all
individuals taken together – come to the fore. Moreover, had
Keynes's aggregate supply and demand analysis gone into the text-
books, understanding and analysing the post-war stagflation episodes
would have been so much easier and better informed.

And, finally, there were his valiant efforts to help design
institutions and new rules of the game for the post-war world so that
unemployment would never again be a scourge and the benefits
of the international division of labour through free trade and flow of
capital funds could do their thing in raising world living standards.
This is what Bretton Woods tried to establish through the creation
of the IMF and the World Bank. Keynes himself returned to his
long-sustained interest in the functioning of the international order,
something which he had temporarily suppressed in order to set out

the crucial new ingredients of how the economic system worked. Donald Moggridge, in his official biography of Keynes, has given us in his superb historical chapters on the two world wars, the details of Keynes's contributions. Here I wish only to emphasise that Keynes's sense of the need to have or to design appropriate institutions for the implementation of effective policy was never more in evidence. His last major act was to try to persuade his compatriots and their government to accept the harsh conditions of the American loan. There, all his greatest qualities came together – his high intelligence, his persuasive eloquence, his proper patriotism, his fine sense of orders of magnitude and interrelated processes of nevertheless different time spans, his realisation of what was possible as opposed to what may have been ideal. Exhausted by his efforts, Keynes died on Easter morning 1946.

VI

Let me close by quoting Austin Robinson's reflections on the death of Keynes.

> His death left a gap everywhere [in the Treasury, the world of academic economics, his college and university, the world of ballet and the arts]. Not least, in his own family. But perhaps some day we may learn to say that it was right that he, like others whom the gods love, should die young. At sixty-two he was in the plenitude of his powers. That brilliant mind was still at its best – rapier sharp, leaping always with intuitive rapidity far ahead of the rest of us. The memory that will remain is of that mind at its perfection.[11]

In this chapter I have concentrated on Keynes's greatest intellectual achievement. But it is only the tip of an iceberg in the story of a man who not only did good but who was also, despite many unattractive features (which his biographers report, it must be said, with some glee), truly good himself.

NOTES

I want to record here my indebtedness to Rod O'Donnell's seminal work on the relationship between Keynes's philosophy and his economics, *Keynes:*

Philosophy, Economics and Politics, Basingstoke: Macmillan 1989, and to John Coates's Ph.D. dissertation, 'Ordinary language economics. Keynes and the Cambridge philosophers', Cambridge 1990. My thanks also to Andrea Maneschi for his comments on a draft of the chapter.

1 F. H. Hahn, *Money and Inflation*, Oxford: Blackwell 1982, p. xi.

2 J. M. Keynes, *The General Theory and After: Part II, Defence and Development (Collected Writings* vol. xiv, 1973, p. 2).

3 J. M. Keynes, *Essays in Biography (CW* vol. x, 1972, p. 262), London: Macmillan 1933.

4 Keynes, *CW* vol. xiv, p. 114.

5 G. F. Shove, 'The place of Marshall's *Principles* in the development of economic theory', *Economic Journal* 52 (1942), 294–329, p. 323.

6 R. F. Kahn, *The Economics of the Short Period*, London: Macmillan 1989, p. xxiii.

7 J. M. Keynes, *Activities 1940–1946. Shaping the Post-war World: Employment and Commodities (CW* vol. xxvii, 1980, p. 445).

8 J. M. Keynes, *The Economic Consequences of the Peace (CW* vol. ii, 1971, pp. 11–13), London: Macmillan, 1919.

9 J. M. Keynes, *A Tract on Monetary Reform (CW* vol. iv, 1971, p. 65), London: Macmillan 1923.

10 J. M. Keynes, *The General Theory and After: Part I, Preparation (CW* vol. xiii, 1973, p. 176).

11 Austin Robinson, 'John Maynard Keynes 1883–1946', *Economic Journal* 57 (1947), 1–68, p. 66.

CHAPTER 7

Mathematics in Cambridge
and beyond

JEREMY GRAY

Arthur Cayley's appointment to the Sadleirian Professorship in 1863 may be taken to mark the start of a new, recognisably modern period in the study of mathematics at Cambridge. The appointment is significant not just because Cayley was the first mathematician with a truly international reputation to work at Cambridge since the days of Newton; the Sadleirian Chair was itself a new position, created to replace nine University lectureships in mathematics that had become moribund. In his inaugural lecture Cayley defined his task in these terms: he was to explain and teach the principles of pure mathematics and to apply himself to the advancement of that science.

Cambridge could hardly have found a better person for the job. Cayley, then 42, was a dazzling mathematician: energetic, prolific, eager to promote the subject, congenial to talk to, knowledgeable in nearly all branches of the subject and original in many. He also belonged to the first generation of English mathematicians for over 100 years who were not insular in their outlook. It was only within Cayley's day that British mathematics connected to European mainstream developments, whatever may have been its earlier claims to innovation. Cayley in particular wrote extensive survey articles, describing the state of the art in various branches of the subject. This is an invaluable service for any nation that is cut off from the research tradition. In every respect, Cayley was the man for the job. And yet he did not create a school of mathematics.

The reasons for this lie in the nature of the University. Mathematics in Cambridge when Cayley first studied there was influenced by the attempts of Herschel, Peacock and Babbage at reform in around 1820. These reforms, started when they were still under-graduates, are well known. The crucial point for many years was that the Cambridge degree was still a degree in mathematics, so the subject was adapted to its role as a general training of the mind. Although it was not intended to be a step on the road to research, only after 1851 was it permissible to study mathematics for one year before switching to either moral or natural sciences. This change allowed for research to enter the life of a Cambridge mathematician, because it no longer could be argued that advanced topics were inappropriate to the education of a gentleman.

Nevertheless, a degree in mathematics retained its high status throughout most of the rest of the nineteenth century. Cambridge degrees were publicly ranked, and those obtaining what today would be called first-class honours were called Wranglers. The list of Wranglers was published in order of merit, so each year it was known who had come first (the Senior Wrangler), second, and so on. Success in this manner led on almost inevitably to success in later life; not just because it was evidence of an agile mind, but because it opened doors. Distinguished British judges and bishops were testimony to the merits of the Cambridge Senior Wrangler. This being so, there grew up a system of coaches, of whom Routh was the most famous. Of the situation in the 1870s Forsyth, Cayley's successor, wrote that '[The Professors] did not teach us. We did not read their work'.[1] College lecturers did not always exert themselves, and promising students would be sent out to coaches for training in how to pass the Tripos. The Tripos itself grew to become several days of examinations in detailed and difficult mathematics, all to be carried out at high speed, and coaches trained candidates in this arcane skill. The would-be Wranglers solved artificial problems right and left, and graduated to spend the rest of their lives in the law, the City, or the church.

Some who watched from afar found this very strange. Here is Max Born's parody from his Göttingen days, around 1904: 'On an elastic bridge stands an elephant of negligible mass; on his trunk sits a mosquito of mass *m*. Calculate the vibrations of the bridge when the elephant moves the mosquito by rotating his trunk.'[2] He recalls it when describing lecturing as a professor in Edinburgh in the 1930s, so it was not only Cambridge that took mathematics this way. Of the Tripos when he sat it, A. R. Forsyth said that one was expected to know any lemma in Newton's *Principia* by its number alone, as if it were one of the commandments or the 100th Psalm. This was not an ethos that encouraged a conceptual, let alone critical, approach to mathematics. Alongside Cayley, whom even Forsyth found incomprehensible when he was an undergraduate, there were college lecturers who openly boasted of their inability even to pronounce the names of Euler and Cauchy correctly.

Cayley's own temperament was gentle. In her obituary of Cayley, C. A. Scott painted an attractive picture of him. Speaking of the 'childlike purity and simplicity of his nature', she wrote:

> He was ever ready to say what he was working at, to indicate the lines of thought, to state what difficulties he was encountering. It is not every mathematician that will lecture to a class of specialists on the incomplete investigation of the night before, and end up with the remark, obviously genuine, 'Perhaps some of you may find this out before I do'.[3]

On the other hand, there is no one who can be said to be a pupil of Cayley's. Cayley did not gather students about him, not even Forsyth.

Who else was at Cambridge in, say, 1890? J. W. L. Glaisher, the Second Wrangler in 1871, after which he became a Fellow of Trinity, was a staunch advocate of pure mathematics. In 1890, he became the President of the British Association for the Advancement of Science. In his Presidential address he spoke of recent changes in mathematics in England, but confessed that at Cambridge there were still more generals than soldiers (meaning that there was no organised school for the study and advancement of mathematics by research). He was the author of more than 400 papers, none of which, it is probably fair to say, are remembered today. But that would be to misunderstand his importance. His interest in differential equations and elliptic functions was passionate, and it is due to him that they made their way onto the Cambridge syllabus. His lectures never mentioned the Tripos but developed the subject systematically from the beginning, albeit in a narrowly algebraic style that avoided all mention of complex function theory.

H. F. Baker, the joint Senior Wrangler of 1887, and a Fellow of St John's from 1888, had studied informally under Klein at Göttingen. The result was Baker's book *Abelian Functions* of 1897, which rightly established his reputation. The subject was a central part of contemporary mathematics. Baker presented it in as rigorous a manner as possible from a Riemannian standpoint, although he avoided the contentious way in which Riemann had sought to establish the existence everywhere of holomorphic integrands on a Riemann surface. Klein was the largest single influence, but Baker was well-read, aware of the rather different theories of Kronecker, Dedekind and Weber, and of Noether.

Baker particularly respected his colleague, the Irishman Joseph Larmor, another Fellow of St John's, and Senior Wrangler in 1880. He is remembered today for his version of the Lorentz transformation in what was to become the special theory of relativity, and published in his book *Aether and Matter* of 1900. The book, dubbed by Lamb 'Aether and no matter' because of its emphasis, undoubtedly helped Larmor become the Lucasian Professor in 1903.

Soon to be at Cambridge was E. T. Whittaker, who graduated as Second Wrangler in 1895, and became a Fellow of Trinity College. His first work was on a new branch of complex function theory called automorphic functions, and some still bear his name. He had a lively interest in celestial mechanics, and he reported on the state of play in the three body problem to the British Association for the Advancement of Science in 1899 and again in his masterly *Analytical Dynamics*, 1904. On the strength of that he was asked by Klein to write about it for the *Encyclopädie der Mathematischen Wissenschaften* (in 1912, by which time he was at Dublin, and about to go to Edinburgh). In 1902 he published the first edition of Whittaker and Watson (the one without Watson) which became the standard English language introduction to complex analysis and elliptic function theory. Quite indefatigable, he lectured every term for fifty years.

But W. H. Young, who graduated in 1886, spent fifteen years of drudgery as a tutor, before he emigrated with his wife Grace Chisholm, not to return to England until 1916, and then to Liverpool. Hardy called him 'one of the most profound and original of the English mathematicians of the last fifty years'. Others have considered Grace Chisholm the better mathematician of the two, and, needless to say, she did not get a job in Cambridge either. One of Young's achievements while at Cambridge was to coach Miss Fawcett, the woman who was ranked above the Senior Wrangler in 1890. Philippa Fawcett went on to have a distinguished career in education, and a college is named after her in South London. Shockingly, she is not even mentioned in the *Dictionary of National Biography*, even in its recent volume, *Missing Persons*.

Reasonably enough, Cayley's successor, Forsyth, had the greatest impact. The Senior Wrangler in 1881, he was also able at once to commence research, and wrote a well-received doctoral thesis on a topic in the theory of Abelian functions, specifically the theta functions of several variables. In 1886 he became an FRS, and when Cayley died in 1895 there was no surprise when Forsyth, then 37, became the next Sadleirian Professor. Forsyth continued Cayley's tradition of trying to bridge the gap between English and Continental mathematics. Curiously, and sadly, this was to be his undoing. The book that did the damage was his second one, a two-volume *Theory of Functions of a Complex Variable*, 1893. The topic was one that was widely agreed to be of central importance in contemporary mathematics. The difficulty can be measured by Forsyth's observation that the Cambridge of 1880 was a place where $\sqrt{-1}$ was suspect even in trigonometric formulae, 140 years after Euler had introduced it there. Indeed, Forsyth credited Lamb's *Treatise on the Motion of Fluids*, 1879, with being the first book to reveal the use of the complex variable in mathematical physics. That it was put to good use in Maxwell's *Treatise on Electricity and Magnetism* of 1873, as Klein knew very well, just shows that the book was way beyond the comprehension of any Cambridge student at the time.

Forsyth set himself the task of writing a book that brought together the best features of the three traditions then in vogue: the complex analysis of Cauchy, Riemann and Weierstrass. To oversimplify a little, the first emphasises the concepts of contour integral and residue; the second global, topological considerations; and the third rigorous power series methods. There was in fact no book in any language that had attempted such an ambitious feat (Harkness and Morley's book came out in America in the same year). German authors were to comment favourably on the attempt and lament the polarisation of books in their own language. Moreover, complex analysis was then unknown in Cambridge. Forsyth, with his broad knowledge and his zeal for exposition, was exactly the right man for the job.

For his local audience, the book was a complete success. Neville said that it 'burst in 1893 with the splendour of a revelation',[4] and

Whittaker that the book 'had a greater influence on British mathematics than any work since Newton's *Principia*'.[5] This is indeed the book that brought modern analysis to England. It alerted all who read it to the existence of rich fields of rigorous analysis, and made it plain how far the British lagged behind. Initially, Forsyth's reputation soared. But on the Continent and in America the reception the book earned was only lukewarm, for in truth it was not rigorous, nor did it truly bring together the three strands its author had hoped to interweave. Osgood, for example, was a Professor at Harvard who had studied under Klein at Göttingen and had a sharp eye for rigour. In a detailed summary of several pages published in the first edition of the Bulletin of the American Mathematical Society in 1895, Osgood found much to criticise and something to praise. He wrote: 'But we cannot stop without pointing to the loose form in which theorems are often stated and proofs given; it only too often happens that the ideas on which the proofs rest are lacking in rigour, or that important matters are overlooked.'[6]

No matter: bad reviews are the author's lot. Forsyth was also good at bringing Europeans to Cambridge (Klein was reputedly scandalised by the high living and low intellectual standards of Trinity on one of his visits). They too alerted Cambridge mathematicians to the existence of rigorous mathematics. Forsyth sparked the taste for the real thing, but could not gratify it. Like Moses, he was to be left behind, as a generation of mathematicians searched the living Continental tradition for its vision of modern mathematics. He was in fact doubly unlucky, for his penchant was handling invariants in the manner of one of the inventors of the theory of them, Arthur Cayley. But David Hilbert had just transformed the subject utterly, and little interest attached to the huge formulae that Forsyth could manipulate with such skill. While still a comparatively young man, Forsyth found himself reduced to the role of one who encourages but cannot keep up.

Yet for a time he was the conspicuously successful head of the Cambridge school of mathematics, and active in University politics. In 1897 he opposed the admission of women to Cambridge degrees, arguing instead for the creation of a separate women's university. There was a forceful lobby among those who favoured the feminist cause for keeping out of Cambridge and setting up a women's university on its own, not least because in mathematics the Tripos system was so unacceptable. So Forsyth may have been progressive on the issue. On the other hand, women were already established at Cambridge, so perhaps his position had become a more reactionary one. Girton College had been founded in 1869 and housed safely away from the male colleges. Sympathetic men, of whom Cayley was one, helped with the teaching.

Indeed, the Tripos of the year before Forsyth's success had been most newsworthy. On the appointed day, 31 January 1880, the customary excited audience gathered at the Senate House to hear the Chairman of the Examiners of the Mathematical Tripos at Cambridge read out the list of that year's students found worthy of the honours degree. The list of Wranglers was read out from the bottom (the weakest candidate) to the top, the man who thereupon became the Senior Wrangler. And he would be a man – women were allowed to sit the exam, but not to claim a degree. This year there had been a leak. As the chairman reached number 8, a boisterous and jovial crowd of undergraduates (all of them men, of course) in the gallery cried out 'Scott of Girton, Scott of Girton!' and threw their hats in the air. Thus entered the public arena the first distinguished woman mathematician from Cambridge: Charlotte Angas Scott. The public excitement that attended a woman's doing so well at mathematics was intense. *The Times* took it up, and Cambridge began to change its ways. By a vote of 398 to 32, from 1881 women were to be ranked with the men in the Tripos – but still they could not claim a degree; that had to wait until 1948.

Jobs were likewise hard to come by. In 1885 Scott successfully completed her doctorate (a London D.Sc., since Cambridge awarded no higher degrees to women) and for a time she taught at Cambridge. But prospects for pay were poor and for promotion almost negligible. No opportunity came up in London either. But at that time the women's college of Bryn Mawr, Pennsylvania, was founded and Scott was offered a position as associate professor. She accepted, and went to Bryn Mawr in September 1885, the only woman among the five associate professors.

The natural sciences (applied mathematics and physics) at Cambridge seem to have been more successful. Klein, in his *Entwicklung*, stressed the contributions of Stokes, Thomson and Maxwell. The School of Natural Sciences at Cambridge got off to a slow start, but under J. J. Thomson's leadership it began to grow in the 1880s and 1890s. Matters came to a head in 1906 when yet another reform of the Mathematical Tripos was proposed. The suggestion was to produce a syllabus more in line with the needs of the students, as they themselves seemed to perceive them, and of the nation, as mathematicians at Cambridge conceived of that: less mathematics of an artificial kind, more that would help the scientist, a move that J. J. Thomson supported. Leading the debate in the absence of Forsyth, who was ill, was E. W. Hobson.

Hobson not only deplored the 'unsatisfactory influence [of the Tripos] on the course of studies' of the average student, but also on the best. He noted that the ideas of many Continental mathematicians 'had never permeated the teaching of Cambridge to a sufficient degree to form a real school of mathematics'. Whittaker agreed, arguing that 'A man who takes a good degree and goes on to India, say, was quite unable to keep in touch with mathematical opinion in later life because . . . he was not sufficiently advanced to understand what was being done in mathematics'. Hobson also argued that the new syllabus should be accompanied by changes in the system accompanying the Tripos. No longer would students be ranked, no longer would there be a Senior Wrangler. His colleagues supported him, and he was opposed by the elderly Routh, putting up a lone rearguard action for the coaches. The debate could not be resolved when it was first begun, in May, and at a second debate in December 1906 one finds the melancholy spectacle of Forsyth himself rebutting the revered old man's arguments. The proposals were accepted, and old Cambridge modernised.

What undoubtedly helped carry the day, beyond the genuine dislike the mathematicians felt for the old Tripos system in which they had grown up and which they had helped maintain, was the impact of Thomson's school of natural sciences. The Natural Sciences Tripos had begun to erode interest in the Mathematics Tripos. Hobson quoted persuasive figures to support his claim that the danger of a collapse in mathematics was all too obvious. From an average of 105 students who completed the Tripos in the years 1881–1885, the numbers had declined to 56 in 1905. The syllabus was reformed, and with it the ethos of studying mathematics. In line with wider University reforms, the distinction between the University and the colleges at Cambridge, a source of confusion to every visitor, was also confronted, and the syllabus was brought much more tightly under University control.

These changes were underlined by another, that in 1907 would have seemed unthinkable. During a visit of the British Association to Canada in 1909 Forsyth fell in love. On his return he resigned his Professorship and left Cambridge. All for love? Perhaps not all, but true and doomed love it was. The story is not quite as his obituarists told it. The correspondence between G. H. Darwin and Klein shows that in 1909 Darwin wrote to Klein to say that Forsyth had suddenly left Cambridge, in circumstances that Darwin could not properly relate. Could Klein suggest who might succeed him? Klein must have replied as anyone interested in people would, and so Darwin wrote to tell him what had happened. Everyone agreed, he said, that C. V. Boys badly mistreated his wife. But now she had not only left him, she had moved in with Forsyth. 'You will understand', wrote Darwin, 'that every door in Cambridge is henceforth closed to him.' This in the Edwardian era, that epitome of hypocritical hedonism.

Forsyth resigned his Professorship, which was only to be expected, but also his Trinity Fellowship, which was by then his for life, however he behaved. He settled in London, and became a Professor at Imperial College. He married the former Mrs Boys, but it was not to last. In 1920 she died of cancer, after a painful illness. He continued to write, but all his energy, his reading, his fluency in writing, his desire to inform were never again to find a suitable theme. Forsyth was succeeded as Sadleirian Professor at Cambridge by Hobson, almost his exact antithesis, in a move that upset Baker, who felt passed over. Although he had been Senior Wrangler in 1878, Hobson had long seemed a dull fellow. But rigorous real analysis was his transformation. His *Theory of Functions of a Real Variable* had appeared in 1907. It has been described (by Hardy) as the first rigorous textbook in English on mathematical analysis. Hobson became a man with a mission, and the embodiment of the new Cambridge. His rise, and Forsyth's fall, capture the decisive shift that Forsyth had begun but had been unable to follow. With the arrival of Hardy, and Littlewood in 1912, the reform of Cambridge was secure. To them came the remarkable Indian mathematician Ramanujan – but that is another story, remembered even in dance.[7]

In 1911, Baker's interests turned to geometry and he rapidly went on to become the leader of a prominent school of English geometers.

Then in 1914, at the insistence of Lord Rayleigh, Baker was appointed Lowndean Professor of Astronomy and Geometry. The move angered some astronomers, although it was true that astronomy was still well represented by two other professors at Cambridge, and Baker set to make amends by lecturing on Poincaré's work on celestial mechanics. After the war he returned to geometry, publishing the first of his six-volume *Principles of Geometry* in 1922. He organised a regular Saturday afternoon tea for many years which functioned as an informal seminar that did much to contribute a sense of élan to the place, thus moving Cambridge a little further from the days of Cayley and Glaisher. Real and complex analysis and geometry define Cambridge mathematics in the inter-war years. With them in place we may turn aside.

Did it have to happen the way it did? Why was it those subjects and not some others? The comparison with Harvard, another old institution, suggests that a similar process was at work, except – and this was to be greatly to the advantage of the American Cambridge – foreign influences were much more welcome. It is interesting to see that Klein figures prominently in the British, as in the American, story: visiting Forsyth, redirecting Baker's career, advancing Whittaker's, supervising Grace Chisholm and welcoming her husband. Klein is one source of the Cambridge interest in geometry and a decisive influence on its approach to complex analysis. The international consensus that complex analysis was a central branch of mathematics surely made its arrival at Cambridge inevitable. Real analysis likewise requires no explanation, except for the delay. On the other hand, one might argue that these topics are unadventurous: no axiomatisers in the style of Hilbert, such as Veblen was in America; no group theorists, although Burnside, a Cambridge man, might have accepted a call to return from Greenwich, where he had gone as a professor in 1885; unlike the Americans, no foreigners; reform would be conducted firmly from within. Logic was represented by Whitehead and Russell, even though one notes that Russell was often lecturing to three students, four with the arrival of Wittgenstein.

The teaching of women at Cambridge was achieved in the face of adversity, if not actual hostility. By contrast, Scott's contributions to Bryn Mawr, and to the cause of women in mathematics, were remarkable. She was the dissertation adviser to seven students, putting Bryn

Mawr third behind Chicago and Cornell, at a time when women were winning three times the percentage of Ph.D.s that they were to win in the 1950s. Her colleague Harkness and their mutual friend Morley (of Haverford) wrote the first textbook on complex analysis to meet with general acceptance. Cambridge mathematics may have changed during the years under discussion, but in deeper ways Cambridge did not.

One way to account for the pre-eminence of Cambridge once it woke up to mathematics is to observe that other places in England were still deeply asleep. Oxford had produced H. J. S. Smith, but after his death in 1883 the place slipped back. In 1892 it appointed E. B. Elliott to a new chair, the Waynflete Professorship. His book on Cayley's theory of invariants *The Algebra of Quantics*, which was based on his college lectures, was published in 1895. But he was a modest, hesitant, if helpful man, and the University did not prosper. It did produce J. E. Campbell, whose book *Lie's Theory of Finite Continuous Transformation Groups* came out in 1903; his name survives, rather generously, in the Campbell–Baker–Hausdorff formula relating a Lie algebra to its Lie group. But the death of his son in the First World War dimmed his enthusiasm for mathematics for quite some time, and that of the second Waynflete Professor, A. L. Dixon, appointed in 1922, had ebbed away by 1910. This was not the appointment of a university on the move. Perhaps its most successful appointment was that of A. E. H. Love, an expert on applied mathematics, notably the theory of elasticity (there was an old joke which ran: which famous mathematician's work suggests a tragedy? Love's *Elasticity*). Love died in 1940 as the Sedlein Professor of Natural Philosophy at Oxford, having been appointed for life in 1898. These life appointments at Oxford and Cambridge were another obstacle to reform, even though Love's tenure was energetic to the end. But even in Love's day there was no system of research students in the modern sense.

London University was from the first divided into competing colleges. The result was a lack of identity for the University as a whole. The colleges were not fortunate in their appointments, either. Clifford died young. T. A. Hirst, although energetic and well aware of Continental mathematics, was not first-rate, and O. Henrici, who emigrated to Britain to find work in 1865 and became Professor at Bedford College, is best remembered as a teacher. The military academies were a great deal more important than they are now. Greenhill taught at Woolwich from 1876 to 1908. He was the first to introduce Weierstrass's theory of elliptic functions to an English audience, and regarded Halphen's *Traité des fonctions elliptiques* as his bible. Firmly committed to the utility of mathematics, he was averse to Weierstrassian rigour, and called Hobson's pure mathematics a monstrosity. Burnside taught naval officers happily at Greenwich from 1885 while his own research took him from using complex function theory in the study of hydrodynamics in the style of Lamb to elliptic functions to automorphic functions to the theory of groups. He apparently felt that Greenwich gave him enough time to conduct his own research, and saw no reason to move. And of course in an imperial nation the military connection conferred status: W. D. Niven, an undistinguished professor at Greenwich, was eventually knighted, as was Greenhill when he retired. Greenhill probably enjoyed his social role, being described by one who knew him as a sociable recluse. A final example, Major P. A. MacMahon, who was educated at Woolwich, taught at a variety of military academies while doing important work on combinatorics. The combined talent in London, put in one place and working as a team, could surely have accomplished much more than it in fact did.

The provincial university situation is confused. The best was Manchester, where Lamb had gone on his return from ten years as a professor at the newly established University of Adelaide, Australia. During his stay in Manchester from 1885, or rather 1887 when he became Professor of Pure and Applied Mathematics, to 1920 the University flourished, not least because he was a born teacher and a prolific author. He brought Sidney Chapman, the distinguished geophysicist, there from 1919 to 1924, and the number theorist L. J. Mordell from 1923 to 1945. But the pre-war situation was rather different: when Wittgenstein registered there as a research student in engineering there were very few research students (two in mathematics), no formal course of study, and no supervisors were provided. Wittgenstein was not expected to work for a degree, but he was allowed to work in the laboratory and to consult professors if he felt the need. He did in fact consult Lamb, and also J. E. Littlewood, who was there from 1907 to 1910 and labouring under a teaching load that he later regarded as excessive. Through Littlewood he became interested in pure mathematics, then in its foundations, and was soon on the road to Cambridge, Russell, and the destiny he so eagerly and painfully sought.

Lamb's appointment is typical of another aspect of Cambridge's importance: it exported mathematicians who went on to argue for and exemplify the Cambridge style, to keep in touch with developments there, and often to return there at the end of their careers. Love, like Whittaker, chose to end up elsewhere; others, like Lamb (on his retirement at 71), Mordell and Hardy himself (who went for a time to Oxford) came back. The influence of these people was often considerable: Edinburgh continues to think highly of Whittaker, and one reason there is an internationally famous Institute for Advanced Study in Dublin with a strong focus on mathematics is because Eamon de Valera, the first President of independent Ireland, founded it, and he had been taught mathematics by Whittaker.

Pure mathematics came to Cambridge because it thrived so strongly in Germany, France and Italy that it would have been remarkable if it had not. It survived and flourished because Cambridge wanted it to, and provided an environment where research could be done, although not because it was conspicuously well planned. It took the threat from a growing school of natural sciences to carry out the necessary reforms, and its slow growth was never challenged from elsewhere in the country. It was lucky in its leaders, and finally rewarded by two mathematicians of genius (Hardy and Littlewood). By the 1920s the transition from a community of gentlemen (almost exclusively) and scholars (in some cases) to the modern organised system for producing researchers had begun at Cambridge, and the hopes of Forsyth, Hobson and others could increasingly be realised.

NOTES

1 A. R. Forsyth, 'Old Tripos days in Cambridge', *Mathematics Gazette* 19 (1935), 162–79.
2 M. Born, *My Life: Recollections of a Nobel Laureate*, London: Taylor and Francis 1978, p. 282.
3 C. A. Scott, 'Arthur Cayley', *Bulletin of the American Mathematical Society* 1 (1895), 133–41, p. 139.

4 E. H. Neville, 'Andrew Russell Forsyth', *Journal of the London Mathematical Society* 17 (1942), 237–56, p. 245.
5 E. T. Whittaker, *Obituary Notices of Fellows of the Royal Society* 4 (1942–4), 208–27, p. 218.
6 W. F. Osgood, 'The theory of functions', *Bulletin of the American Mathematical Society* 1 (1895), 142–54, p. 143.
7 R. Kanigel, *The Man Who Knew Infinity: A Life of the Genius Ramanujan*, New York: Charles Scribner's Sons 1991.

CHAPTER 8

James Stuart: engineering, philanthropy and radical politics

PAUL MCHUGH

Professor James Stuart is possibly the least remembered of this collection of 'Cambridge minds'. What, then, are his claims for inclusion in the company of say, the Darwins, Keynes or Wittgenstein? My subtitle offers a clue. His was an unusually wide range of interests, and in Stuart we see the academic venturing into the public sphere, ultimately at the cost of his reputation in Cambridge.

Stuart played a significant part in the movement for university reform in the mid-nineteenth century. He was anxious to extend the work of the University beyond Cambridge – to today's adult education, to provide opportunities for women's higher education, and to develop engineering as a proper subject for undergraduate study. But for Stuart reform went beyond the confines of the University. He was involved in one of the great moral reform movements of the period, the campaign to repeal the Contagious Diseases Act, Britain's only foray into the controversial area of regulated prostitution. He was later a Liberal MP on the radical wing of the party, he ran a major London newspaper, was a devoted member of the London County Council, and ended his career as an industrialist, managing the country's most celebrated mustard works.

Even this summary glosses over aspects of a career which reveals a spread of commitment far wider than would be found today. He was a robust and energetic individual who thought nothing of having to preside over a temperance meeting (addressed by Cardinal Manning) which was broken up by what he termed the 'publican faction' with the room wrecked and not a word heard. He had a passion for reform and a determination to battle to secure it whatever the cost to his reputation. There are grounds here for an examination, though perhaps it will have to be more an exhumation, of this Cambridge mind.

James Stuart was born on 2 January 1843 at Balgonie in Fife where his father was a flax mill-owner. His was a markedly radical background; his mother's family had been intimates of William Godwin and Mary Wollstonecraft, his father was an active Congregationalist and a keen public speaker on topics such as 'Democracy'. One of the young Stuart's earliest memories was hearing his father deliver a speech of welcome to Kossuth when the great Hungarian patriot visited Fife.

Stuart's education was acquired from a combination of tutors, a spell at an eccentric school, Madras College, in St Andrews and, most prized by himself, the 'irregular apprenticeship' of being allowed to work in the counting-house and mechanics' shop in his father's mill. He was an undergraduate at St Andrews University from 1858 to 1862 during a period in which it was still emerging from the decay into which it had fallen. He was its first honours graduate for many years and, thus equipped, he won a minor scholarship to Trinity College, Cambridge, graduating in 1866.

As a Junior Fellow of Trinity from 1866, he was a member of the group of reformers involved in the modernisation of Cambridge University; the Grote Club, of which he was for a time Secretary, was their focus. Stuart set himself two tasks: 'first, to make the University lectures generally open to all the Colleges, and of a more interesting type, and, second, to establish a sort of peripatetic university the professors of which would circulate among the big towns, and thus give a wider opportunity for receiving such teaching'.[1] He lost no time in achieving the first of these. Appointed an assistant tutor by Trinity in 1868, he immediately opened his lectures on physical astronomy to undergraduates of other colleges. Others followed and thus an important principle was established.

The 'peripatetic university' was the larger task but the opportunity to set about it came sooner. In the summer of 1867 the North of England Council for Promoting the Higher Education of Women, through its Secretary Miss Anne Jemima Clough, was seeking a lecturer to inaugurate a series of lectures on education. Stuart was invited to lecture on this general theme, but asked to be allowed to offer a practical series on the history of astronomy instead. His proposal was accepted, and in this way the first steps towards University Extension were taken. Stuart's lectures in Liverpool, Manchester, Sheffield and Leeds, for which he was paid a handsome fee of £200, were a great success and led to a series of further invitations: from the Crewe Mechanics' Institute, the Rochdale Equitable Pioneers Society, the North of England Council again in 1869, and a series of public lectures in Leeds. For four years Stuart carried on alone what he termed 'missionary work', but his intention was always to have this activity taken up officially. Involving Cambridge, and Oxford eventually, in responding to the demand for extra-mural education seemed natural to him since they were best placed to supply it, and, in doing so, the country as a whole would be associated with 'the immense educational traditions of the two Universities'. But, shrewdly, there was another motive also: 'I felt equally strongly that the Universities would have before long to face a fire of criticism, and that their position would be greatly strengthened if they ministered to the needs of a wider area than they did.'[2]

In the autumn of 1871 Stuart organised memorials to the University of Cambridge from the bodies to which he had lectured. All asked the University to take the extension lectures over and put them on a regular footing. He circulated a letter of his own, describing his experience and urging the appointment of a special syndicate to consider the issue. The University cautiously took two years to test demand for this work, but eventually set up the syndicate for which he had lobbied, and with himself as its Secretary and reformers such as Henry Sidgwick and the two Professors of Divinity, Westcott and Lightfoot, as members, the outcome was in little doubt. A two-year experiment was sanctioned from October 1873, and Stuart now became the Secretary of what was to be termed the Local Lectures Syndicate.

Stuart now threw himself into creating a network of extension classes with particular strengths in the East Midlands, in Yorkshire, on Merseyside and in the Potteries. He managed the entire operation, subsidising it to some extent from his own pocket and travelling constantly to set up new centres and supervise existing ones. In this second phase he delegated the lecturing to a group of younger Fellows, mainly of Trinity, but was always in overall control. In addition he continued with his tutorial duties in Trinity and, as we shall see, had substantial demands on his time from outside the University. Within two years he had put University Extension on a sound footing and with his election to a chair in November 1875 he felt that it was now time to step down. Extension work had been recognised as a permanent feature and it could now be entrusted to other hands. In 1876 he resigned as Secretary although he remained a Syndic until he left Cambridge in 1889.

Stuart retained his commitment to adult education and regularly addressed the large Summer Meetings of extension students. That he had an ambitious understanding of its purpose is made clear in a lecture to the 1892 Summer Meeting in which he explicitly associated this work with the creation of a democratic society:

> . . . it has been a great gain to the Universities. They have taken part in the forging out of a true democratic university system which could never have existed if they had not lent their aid. That system they have worked out by experience, by the people and for the people. And they have obtained as a rich reward the people's confidence. Said a pitman to me once: 'I cannot tell how much I owe to these University lectures. They have worked a revolution in my life.'[3]

As the extension work became established, his attentions shifted in another direction – towards the effective establishment of under-graduate studies in engineering. He had been elected to a newly-created Chair in Mechanism and Applied Mechanics and he found almost nothing to work with. In the early days he had to be and was a vigorous innovator, rationalising the provision of lectures between himself and Clerk Maxwell, the Cavendish Professor, and, from 1878, equipping an increasingly sophisticated workshop at his own expense. By the 1880s the Engineering Workshop was able to attract students – there were seventy working in it by 1884 – was producing equipment for other departments within the University and impressing a stream of distinguished visitors. Stuart was by then a figure of some influence within the University, being a member of the Council of the Senate and of the General Board: 'The reputation of the department stood high, both inside the University and in the industrial areas where Stuart had most of his contacts with the Engineering profession. All this was the creation of one man, and nothing like it had ever been seen in Cambridge before.'[4]

Unfortunately, Stuart's position within the University began to decline from the high point achieved in the mid-1880s. His attention was probably diverted by his growing interests outside Cambridge, and these, in turn, increasingly set him apart from mainstream opinion within the University. A symptom of his gradual disengagement was his wish to persuade the University to take over responsibility for what was still his workshop. This was accepted as perfectly reasonable but an unseemly dispute about the valuation of the 'fixtures and fittings' led to accusations that he had 'made a good thing out of the workshop' which thoroughly disheartened him in view of his considerable personal outlays in setting it up.

Moreover, this controversy came to damage the cause of engineering within the University. In 1887, proposals for an Engineering Tripos were unexpectedly turned down; more because of Stuart's association with them than for any inherent reason. Eventually a fresh attack on the running of the workshop, by now no longer his operational concern though still his responsibility, proved too much for him and he resigned his chair in December 1889. This ended his connection with Cambridge and, sadly, it was on an unfortunate note. For while there were those who disagreed with his concept of engineering education, it is likely that political animus better explained his troubles in the late 1880s.

For by then, James Stuart was established as a radical of the most ardent Gladstonian stripe. How had this come about? To explain the transition from University reformer to political activist, we must now turn to what was probably his major distraction from University affairs between 1870 and 1886, and certainly his most controversial. This was his position as one of the leaders of the campaign to abolish the Contagious Diseases Acts.

The Acts were a tentative venture into the sort of police-controlled regulated prostitution then widely employed throughout continental Europe. Passed in 1864, 1866 and 1868, they were to be suspended in 1883 and repealed in 1886:

> The object had ostensibly been to protect members of the armed forces from the consequences of venereal disease, and the government from the resulting financial penalties and loss of manpower. The method employed was to identify prostitutes and submit them to examination by designated official doctors; if they were found to be diseased they were detained in hospitals for specified periods. To

implement the Acts a specialised police force and purpose-built Lock Wards were provided.[5]

Stuart was in at the very start of what he always referred to as 'Mrs Butler's agitation', referring to its most charismatic leader, Josephine Butler. What was it which so outraged him about the Acts that he was willing to divide his attentions between his work for University reform and this campaign? He was certainly enthralled by Mrs Butler and was often by her side at the most difficult times – at dangerously rowdy by-elections, for instance, at Colchester in 1870 and Pontefract in 1872. His devotion even caused him to debate giving up education work, though he sensibly persuaded himself that 'my connection with Education is of more value to my work for our cause ... than the time devoted to Education is a loss to that work'.[6] He drove himself so hard that his health collapsed in the spring of 1875, but this prompted him to withdraw from organising extension work rather than ceasing to campaign against the Acts. This was a vital commitment.

Stuart was important to the repeal campaign in three ways: first, he shouldered much of the burden of spreading opposition to regulation internationally; he was Treasurer of the grandly named British, Continental and General Federation for the Abolition of State-Regulated Prostitution from its inception in 1875, and he and Mrs Butler effectively carried the international work between them, involving a vast correspondence and much travelling. Secondly, his Cambridge Professorship brought valuable academic status to the movement; he was treated as a senior figure (more than his years justified), above the splits and divisions to which it was prone, and was turned to as a conciliator – for which he seems to have had some aptitude. Thirdly, he was one of a group of influential radicals who steered the campaign towards an ultimately successful collaborationist strategy with the Liberal Party in the early 1880s.

Indeed, Stuart was particularly active in this last regard; dining Liberal frontbenchers such as Joseph Chamberlain and Sir Charles Dilke in Trinity to persuade them to get the government to back repeal; acting as correspondent with the National Liberal Federation; mobilising the sort of support which it was difficult for Gladstone and the Liberals to ignore. Stuart and his allies calculated that if they could show that their agitation would not be abandoned, however distasteful it might seem to 'respectable' opinion, they could eventually persuade a Liberal government that the Acts were not worth saving. This strategy worked and it fell to Stuart himself, by then an MP, to see repeal through the House of Commons in 1886.

It was surely his involvement in what was essentially a Liberal-based campaign which impelled him towards the next phase of his career. By the early 1880s he was well known as a devoted Gladstonian, even to the extent of being willing to run as a candidate for one of the University seats at a by-election in November 1882 (he was soundly defeated and said, privately, that he had not really wanted to win).

But within two years his attitude had changed. In November 1884, he entered the House of Commons as Member for Hackney, coincidentally succeeding another Cambridge Professor, Henry Fawcett. Hackney was a radical artisanal seat, previously unknown to Stuart, but he fitted the bill well, as Gladstone's Private Secretary Eddie Hamilton noted: 'Stuart, wholly unknown to the constituency, obtained a thumping majority, notwithstanding the attractive and treacherous cry of "Fair Trade". Stuart ought to do well in Parliament, but he has some nasty crotchets.'[7] This last patrician phrase refers to his radical enthusiasms including, of course, final repeal of the CD Acts. His successor in charge of Local Lectures, the Revd G. F. Browne, an ardent Tory, put it even more fiercely when he said that Stuart 'goes to Hackney and pours forth a flood of ultra-radicalism, of crazy fads, of coarse misrepresentation and vulgar abuse, which must make his Cambridge friends shudder'.[8] Here is evidence of his gradual estrangement from the mainstream of University opinion. His radical activism was now increasingly evident, setting him apart even from those less extreme than Browne.

Stuart insisted that he did not play an active part in parliament until 1886, but with the decimation of the parliamentary Liberal Party after the Home Rule election, it was more difficult to stand back. Moreover, radicalism was now in the ascendant within the depleted party. He became an assiduous backbencher, noted for two particular interests.

He now became the leader of the small group of London Liberal MPs, and from 1887 to 1898 was also the Secretary of the London Liberal and Radical Union. Although himself an individualist radical, he was regarded as sympathetic to those constituency activists preaching a new style of progressive and collectivist politics within metropolitan Liberalism.[9]

Even so, Sidney Webb thought Stuart was the principal opponent of permeation, the notion that Liberalism ought gradually to be infiltrated by working-class candidates, and was therefore delighted when Stuart failed to get round to drafting an official Liberal programme for London, enabling Webb to put forward his radical *London Programme* in 1891.[10] Stuart could be out-manoeuvred on what was for him unfamiliar ground, for his strength lay in effective parliamentary scrutiny on London's behalf of the local government measures of the late 1880s and 1890s. His commitment to municipal reform is also evident in his willingness to serve on the new LCC, initially as an Alderman, and from 1898 as an elected Councillor.

Stuart's other great enthusiasm was appropriately Gladstonian. After 1886 he became a passionate Home Ruler. He was Chairman of the Home Rule Union and visited Ireland in the late 1880s to observe British frightfulness at close quarters, urging the Irish tenantry to resist their landlords' exactions, and briefing Gladstone in a quite inflammatory manner on what was happening in Ireland.[11]

Support for the Irish cause must have made him even more of a marked man within the University, most of whose senior members were marching in the opposite direction. This was so even in his own College, as Henry Sidgwick noted in July 1886 during the Home Rule crisis: 'Unionists gaining slowly but steadily. Dined in Hall, and was surprised to find the great preponderance of Unionist sentiment among the Trinity Fellows, a body always, since I have known Trinity, predominantly Liberal.'[12]

Understandably, then, after resigning his Chair he gave up his rooms in Trinity and moved to London. He also married, in July 1890, Laura Colman, the daughter of a fellow radical MP, J. J. Colman, the mustard manufacturer. Besides his parliamentary activities, marriage now drew him forward a further career. He was no stranger to business since he had always played some part in the management of the family mill in Fife until its disposal in 1884; now he was invited to become Chairman of the *Star* newspaper, in which his father-in-law was a major shareholder.[13] This fitted in well with his other London interests, and during the 1890s, Stuart as Chairman and chief leader-writer of the *Star*, LCC Alderman and the most prominent London Liberal MP was a figure of reasonable note in Westminster politics.

However, when J. J. Colman died unexpectedly in 1898, Stuart was asked to move to Norwich and take an active part in the management of the Colman business. Thus this last phase of his varied career saw him as a benevolently paternalistic manager of the Carrow mustard works, while accumulating the customary honours which accrue to someone in public life towards the end of his career: Lord Rector of St Andrews in 1899, Chairman of the Governors of Norwich's King Edward VI Grammar School in 1903 and, finally, a Privy Councillorship in 1907.

Stuart's parliamentary career ended in 1910. In his final years he dictated his *Reminiscences*, which are disorganised and self-indulgent, probably not a worthy record of his solidly useful public life. Nobody thought to write anything more substantial about him. When he died in October 1913 his Gladstonian Liberalism had long been marginalised by the collectivist thrust of the New Liberalism, and the *Dictionary of National Biography*'s failure to commemorate him may be indicative of how low his stock had fallen (amends have recently been made in the *Missing Persons* supplement).

Stuart's work for adult education put Cambridge in the forefront of this development, and he was effectively the founder of the modern Engineering Department. While some of his judgements can be questioned, it was more likely his unusually profound radical commitment which set University opinion against him, and which has served to obscure his achievements, thus removing him from the ranks of the great reformers.

Similarly, his political career never quite took off. Nobody seems to have regarded him as front-bench material, and most of his years as an MP were spent in opposition. He was swept away in the Khaki election of 1900, and when he returned to the Commons in the landslide of 1906, Liberalism had moved on, leaving the individualist radicals of Stuart's generation stranded.

James Stuart did not achieve eminence in either of his two main areas of activity, but his reminiscences do not reveal any of the usual bitterness of frustrated ambition. He should be acknowledged as a radical figure of his times – in education, moral reform, local government and national politics; a useful man of affairs, industrious, creative and generally, if not spectacularly, successful. Not a bad record – and one which certainly deserves to be rescued.

NOTES

Stuart's *Reminiscences*, London 1912, provide the essential starting point. For his work as a pioneer of adult education see J. F. C. Harrison, *Learning and Living, 1790–1960*, London 1961, and Edwin Welch, *The Peripatetic University: Cambridge Local Lectures, 1874–1973*, Cambridge 1973. For engineering see T. J. N. Hilken, *Engineering at Cambridge University, 1783–1965*, Cambridge 1967. For the C.D. Acts campaign see my *Prostitution and Victorian Social Reform*, London 1980.

1 Stuart, *Reminiscences*, p. 152.
2 Ibid., p. 165.
3 James Stuart, *An Inaugural Address delivered at the opening of the Third Series of Vacation Courses of Study at Cambridge*, Cambridge 1892, p. 14.
4 Hilken, *Engineering*, p. 74.
5 McHugh, *Prostitution*, p. 16.
6 Fawcett Library (H. J. Wilson MSS), James Stuart to H. J. Wilson, 7 May 1873.
7 D. W. R. Bahlman (ed.), *The Diary of Sir Edward Walter Hamilton*, Oxford 1972, p. 737 (20 November 1884).
8 Cited Hilken, *Engineering*, p. 75.
9 John David, *Reforming London: The London Government Problem, 1855–1900*, Oxford 1988, p. 119.
10 Paul Thompson, *Socialists, Liberals and Labour: The Struggle for London, 1885–1914*, London 1967, pp. 99, 145; Michael Barker, *Gladstone and Radicalism: The Reconstruction of Liberal Policy in Britain, 1885–1894*, Hassocks 1975, p. 179.
11 Barker, *Gladstone*, pp. 82–3; T. W. Heyck, *The Dimensions of British Radicalism: The Case of Ireland, 1874–1895*, Urbana 1974, pp. 183, 189–95.
12 Cited Christopher Harvie, *The Lights of Liberalism: University Liberals and the Challenge of Democracy, 1860–1886*, London 1976, p. 219.
13 Stephen Koss, *The Rise and Fall of the Political Press in Britain. vol. I: The Nineteenth Century*, London 1981, pp. 310, 312.

CHAPTER 9

The Darwins in Cambridge

RICHARD KEYNES

The earliest member of the Darwin family to enter the University is recorded by Freeman as William Darwin of Lincoln (1620–75), who matriculated in 1640 from Magdalene College. He did not take a degree, presumably because he left in 1642 to serve the King as Captain Lieutenant in Sir William Pelham's troop of horse, as a result of which his lands were forfeited during the Commonwealth. He went to Lincoln's Inn in 1645, where he qualified, and after the Restoration he became Recorder of the City of Lincoln. His son, another William (1655–82), and his grandson Robert (1680–1754) did not come up to Cambridge, but Robert was a barrister described by a contemporary as 'a person of curiousity' from whom all the later Darwins with academic pretensions were descended.

Robert Waring Darwin (1724–1816), head of the family in the ninth generation listed by the genealogists, matriculated from St John's in 1743, but apparently did not take a degree. He qualified as a barrister, though he never practised, nor did he marry. Unlike his younger brother Erasmus he had strong taste for poetry, and setting a pattern for what was to come, was the first of the Darwins to write a book, *Principia Botanica, or a Concise and Easy Introduction to the Sexual System of Linnaeus*, which ran to three editions. One of his brothers, William Alvey Darwin, had a grandson, the Revd William Darwin Fox, who, as will be recounted, was a contemporary at Christ's, and thereafter a lifelong friend, of his cousin Charles Darwin. Another brother, John, took his M.A. from St John's in

1757, and was the first of three Darwins to join the Anglican priesthood.

The fourth and youngest brother of this ninth generation was Erasmus Darwin (1731–1802), who also went to St John's, and took his Cambridge M.B. in 1755 after completing his medical training at Edinburgh. He set up his practice first for some years in Lichfield, and later in Derby, and his fame as a physician became prodigious, matching his energy and, it would seem, his appetite. He had five children by his first wife, followed by two illegitimate daughters after she died. At the age of 50, a corpulent, stammering widower, he fell in love with one of his patients, a rich and witty young widow, Elizabeth Pole. Against strong competition, he carried off the prize, and the marriage was a happy one with seven further children.

His intellectual interests were all-embracing, and in 1766 he and the leading scientists and technologists of the area – Matthew Boulton, Josiah Wedgwood, James Watt, John Baskerville and Joseph Priestley among them – founded the Lunar Society, which met monthly for discussions, and rivalled the Royal Society in its distinction and vigour. He was a prolific and technically competent poet, and in his lifetime was best known to the general public as the author of *The Botanic Garden*, two long poems entitled *The Loves of the Plants* (1789) and *The Economy of Vegetation* (1792), though the overpraise that greeted their initial appearance was succeeded by a period of ridicule. His aim was both to amuse and to impart serious instruction, and *The Botanic Garden* deserves respect as the first and probably the last attempt to popularise science in verse.

Here is an example from his last poem, 'The Temple of Nature', in which he sums up the process of evolution in four prophetic couplets:

> Organic Life beneath the shoreless waves
> Was born and nurs'd in Ocean's pearly caves;
> First forms minute, unseen by spheric glass,
> Move on the mud, or pierce the watery mass;
> These, as successive generations bloom,
> New powers acquire, and larger limbs assume;
> Whence countless groups of vegetation spring,
> And breathing realms of fin, and feet, and wing.

Erasmus Darwin is best remembered nowadays for the two huge volumes that he published in 1794 and 1796 entitled *Zoönomia, or the Laws of Organic Life*, which was in effect a medical treatise, based on forty years of practical experience, that covered not only medicine and psychology, but much of animal biology, with physics, philosophy and religion thrown in as well. In section 39 of *Zoönomia* he put forward the first comprehensive theory of evolution, preceding that of Lamarck by some years. His grandson Charles wrote in his *Autobiography*, referring to talks with Robert Grant in 1826:

> I had previously read the *Zoönomia* of my grandfather, in which similar views [to those of Lamarck] are maintained, but without producing any effect on me. Nevertheless it is probable that the hearing rather early in life such views maintained and praised may have favoured my upholding them under a different form in my *Origin of Species*. At this time I admired greatly the *Zoönomia*; but on reading it a second time after an interval of ten or fifteen years, I was much disappointed, the proportion of speculation being so large to the facts given.[1]

Charles was uncharacteristically less than generous to his grandfather in writing thus, for Erasmus had not had the advantage of the rich harvest of facts that became available to his grandson while travelling in South America. There are many arguments in *The Origin of Species* that closely parallel those in *Zoönomia*. Erasmus was in the end less Lamarckian in his views than Charles, and as has been argued by King-Hele, deserves priority as originator of the first well-rounded account of evolution, though of course without the theory of natural selection in explanation, and with insufficient evidence for final proof. I have to confess that I have never properly read the *Zoönomia*, but my respect for my great-great-great-grandfather rose still further when I realised only recently that he was also a pioneer in my own field of research, having been one of the earliest to recognise the electrical nature of nerve impulses.

It may, I am afraid, be questioned whether Erasmus Darwin was strictly a 'Cambridge mind', because his period was one when studies in the natural sciences were not very flourishing in the University, and it is doubtful whether the education that he received in Cambridge deserves much of the credit for his subsequent achievements. All the same he was undoubtedly one of the most distinguished alumni of the eighteenth century, and earns an honoured place in my catalogue.

Erasmus Darwin had two sons by his first marriage who followed him into the medical profession, Charles (1758–78), after whom his famous nephew was named, and who died tragically young of a dissecting wound, and Robert Waring (1766–1848), but both received their training in Edinburgh. Robert Waring Darwin became a greatly respected and successful medical practitioner in Shrewsbury. In 1796 he married Susannah, daughter of Josiah Wedgwood I, by whom he had four daughters and two sons. In due course he sent his eldest son Erasmus Alvey Darwin (1804–81) to Christ's College and then to Edinburgh, where he qualified M.B. in 1828. This Erasmus moved to London, but did not practise, and spent the rest of his life entertaining his Whig friends and sitting on educational committees.

Robert's second son, Charles Robert Darwin (1809–82), was originally intended to follow his brother into medicine, which he studied in Edinburgh University from 1825 to 1827. But he found the lectures that he attended intolerably dull, and concluded in his *Autobiography*[2] that 'to my mind there are no advantages and many disadvantages in lectures compared with reading', an observation of which later educationalists might like to take note. He regretted later that he had not been urged to practise dissection, for 'the practice would have been invaluable for all my future work', but it has to be said that from the very start of the voyage of the *Beagle* only a few years later he was in fact displaying considerable skill at both dissecting and drawing marine invertebrates, and among his unpublished zoology notes in Cambridge University Library are a number of sheets of admirably neat drawings that he made to illustrate what he saw under his microscope.

Charles also attended two surgical operations at Edinburgh, and found the experience so distasteful that he lost all desire to pursue medicine as a career, and spent the greater part of his second year collecting marine animals with Drs Coldstream and Grant in the tidal pools of the Firth of Forth, listening to Professor Jameson's lectures on geology, which were so bad that he vowed never to study the subject again, and in his vacations riding and shooting with his Wedgwood cousins at Maer. His father was vehement against his 'turning into an idle sporting man', and proposed that he should become a clergyman, with this in mind sending him to Cambridge to join his cousin William Darwin Fox (1805–80) at Christ's College. He took up residence early in 1828, after a few months of private tuition to brush up his Latin and Greek.

The move proved decisive for his future, though not quite in the direction intended by his father. His distaste for lectures persisted, but by answering well the examination questions on Paley's *Natural Theology* and *Evidences of Christianity*, whose logic he admired, 'by doing Euclid well, and by not failing miserably in Classics', he was tenth in the list of January 1831 for those not competing for honours. He recorded that he got into a sporting set, 'including some dissipated low-minded young men', and spent much of his time indulging his passion for shooting, riding across country, and hunting. However, the pursuit that gave him the greatest pleasure was the collecting of beetles, to which he was introduced by W. D. Fox, and became notorious among his friends. He wrote in his *Autobiography*:

> But no pursuit at Cambridge was followed with nearly so much eagerness or gave me so much pleasure as collecting beetles. It was the mere passion for collecting, for I did not dissect them and rarely compared their external characters with published descriptions, but got them named anyhow. I will give a proof of my zeal: one day, on tearing off some old bark, I saw two rare beetles and seized one in each hand; then I saw a third and new kind, which I could not bear to lose, so that I popped the one which I held in my right hand into my mouth. Alas it ejected some intensely acrid fluid, which burnt my tongue so that I was forced to spit the beetle out, which was lost, as well as the third one.
>
> I was very successful in collecting, and invented two new methods; I employed a labourer to scrape moss off old trees during the winter, and place [it] in a large bag; and likewise to collect the rubbish at the bottom of the barges in which reeds are brought from the fens. And thus I got some very rare species. No poet ever felt more delight at seeing his first poem published than I did at seeing in Stephen's *Illustrations of British Insects* the magic words, 'Captured by C. Darwin, Esq.'.[3]

Most significant of all was the close friendship that he established early in 1830 with the Revd John Stevens Henslow (1796–1861), Professor of Mineralogy and then of Botany in Cambridge, and one of the founders of the Cambridge Philosophical Society, whose weekly gatherings for students interested in natural history were an important feature of the University's scientific life. Soon he was botanising almost daily with the Professor, and was known by some of the dons as 'the man who walks with Henslow'. To Henslow he owed his selection to sail on the *Beagle* with Captain FitzRoy; and it was to Henslow that he wrote the letters reporting his first impressions of the geology and natural history of South America that were published in 1835 by the Cambridge Philosophical Society. The great indebtedness to Henslow that Darwin always felt did not, however, rest on his scientific distinction, for as Darwin wrote in his *Autobiography*: 'His knowledge was great in botany, entomology, chemistry, mineralogy, and geology. His strongest taste was to draw conclusions from long-continued minute observations. His judgement was excellent, and his whole mind well-balanced; but I do not suppose that anyone would say that he possessed much original genius.'[4] Although Henslow's deeply felt religious views prevented him from ever fully accepting the revolutionary theories of his pupil, he was a man of sterling character, and the example of his scientific approach was an extremely important one to his protégé.

The following year, Henslow persuaded Darwin to overcome the distaste for geology that he had acquired in Edinburgh, and to accept some instruction from the Revd Adam Sedgwick, Woodwardian Professor of Geology from 1818 to 1873. In August 1831, Darwin accompanied Sedgwick on a three-week geological tour to North Wales that constituted almost his entire field training in geology before he accepted FitzRoy's invitation to become the *Beagle*'s geologist and naturalist. Darwin wrote forty-five years later:

> On this tour I had a striking instance how easy it is to overlook phenomena, however conspicuous, before they have been observed by anyone. We spent many hours in Cwm Idwal, examining all the rocks with extreme care, as Sedgwick was anxious to find fossils in them: but neither of us saw a trace of the wonderful glacial phenomena all around us; we did not notice the plainly scored rocks, the perched boulders, the lateral and terminal moraines. Yet these phenomena are so conspicuous that, as I declared in a paper published many years afterwards in the 'Philosophical Magazine', a house burnt down by fire did not tell its story more plainly than did this valley. If it had still been filled by a glacier, the phenomena would have been less distinct than they are now.[5]

Through Sedgwick, Darwin was brought into contact with the controversies over the past history of the Earth that had convulsed geology for the previous half-century, and was given an invaluable training in the established routines of structural and stratigraphical geology. But Sedgwick was not the most flexible of men, and inclined towards the catastrophist view of geology rather than the uniformitarianism of Lyell. His eventual reaction to a copy of *The Origin of Species* sent him by Darwin in 1859 was to write:

> I have read your book with more pain than pleasure. Parts of it I admired greatly; parts I laughed at till my sides were almost sore; other parts I read with absolute sorrow; because I think them utterly false & grievously mischievous. You have *deserted* – after a start in that tramroad of all solid physical truth – the true method of induction, and started us in machinery as wild, I think, as Bishop Wilkin's locomotive that was to sail with us to the moon.[6]

On 29 August 1831, Charles Darwin returned to Shrewsbury from his trip with Sedgwick, and found awaiting him at home letters from George Peacock and Henslow suggesting that he should accompany Captain Robert FitzRoy on a surveying voyage of HMS *Beagle* to South America as the ship's geologist and naturalist. His immediate reaction was to accept the offer, but his father felt that it would be a 'useless occupation' most unsuitable to his chosen profession as a clergyman. However, Robert Darwin qualified his opposition by adding, 'If you can find any man of common sense, who advises you to do, I will give my consent.' The following day, Charles rode over to visit his Wedgwood cousins at Maer, and found a strong supporter in his uncle and future father-in-law Josiah Wedgwood II, who at once provided a detailed list of arguments setting Robert's misgivings at rest. Paternal opposition was gracefully withdrawn, and on 1 September Charles wrote to accept the offer of sailing on the *Beagle*.

The role of the voyage of the *Beagle* in the development of Darwin's thinking about evolution lies beyond my remit, but by this time the period of scientific renaissance in Cambridge had begun, and considerable credit is due to Henslow for the correctness of his judgement in putting Darwin's name forward in the first place, and for helping to indoctrinate him in Cambridge with the critical and analytical approach towards his observations in the field that served him so well. The sound training that he received from Sedgwick was also invaluable, for it is not always appreciated that the importance of Darwin's contributions as a geologist was second only to those in biology. Much has been written by historians and philosophers of science about the ultimate origins of Darwin's great theory, but to my mind the most important factor of all was his intensively analytical approach to every one of his observations, and his invariable habit of enquiring with critical ingenuity into the why and wherefore of all that he saw. Coupled with his exposure in South America to a much wider range of facts than had come to the attention of any previous naturalist or geologist, the *Origin of Species* was the inevitable outcome.

Let me quote just one example. Within two weeks of sailing from Plymouth on the *Beagle*, Darwin was displaying the hallmarks of a practised professional. In his diary for 10 January 1832, he noted:

> I proved to day the utility of a contrivance which will afford me many hours of amusement and work. – it is a bag four feet deep, made of bunting, & attached to [a] semicircular bow. This by lines is kept upright, & dragged behind the vessel. – this evening it brought up a mass of small animals, & tomorrow I look forward to a greater harvest. –

The next day he continued:

> I am quite tired having worked all day at the produce of my net. The number of animals that the net collects is very great & fully explains the manner so many of a large size live so far from land. – Many of these creatures, so low in the scale of nature, are most exquisite in their forms and rich colours. It creates a feeling of wonder that so much beauty should be apparently created for such little purpose.[7]

This was only the second recorded use of a plankton net, preceding by some years the invention often credited to Johannes Müller. The first was that of J. V. Thompson, of which Grant had probably told him, and he had modified the oyster-trawl recommended to him by John Coldstream[8] so as to catch from the surface of the water.

Darwin's comments on the harvest of plankton are typical in two respects of many later entries in his diary and zoology notes. Who else at that period, having discovered the relative abundance of these tiny organisms in the ocean, would have immediately appreciated its relevance to the rest of the food chain? The other characteristic feature is that he always retained a sense of wonder at the beauty of nature, alike from the functional orderliness that he perceived as a scientist, and from the purely aesthetic viewpoint.

After his return to England in October 1836, Darwin lived in

London for a while, and in 1839 he married his cousin Emma Wedgwood. In 1842 they moved to Down House at Downe in Kent, where the rest of his life was spent. His theory of evolution by natural selection was set out for the first time in his private diaries for 1837. In 1839 he published the *Journal of Researches into the Geology and Natural History of the Various Countries Visited by H.M.S. Beagle*, his famous account of his travels, and later the *Zoology of H.M.S. Beagle*. He then set out to amass more evidence in support of his theory by enquiries into the variability of pigeons and other domesticated species, and, hampered always by his chronic illness, devoted some years to his monograph on barnacles. However, he kept his true objectives very strictly to himself, revealing them even to his closest associates Charles Lyell and Joseph Hooker only in 1844. In 1858 he received Alfred Russel Wallace's manuscript 'On the Tendency of Varieties to Depart Indefinitely from the Original Type', and after their joint papers had been read by Lyell and Hooker at a meeting of the Linnean Society, he set to work on an abridgement of the big book on evolution that he had been incubating in secret for so long, and *On the Origin of Species* was at last released by the booksellers on 24 November 1859. In the years which followed, a stream of further books appeared.

He returned rather seldom to Cambridge, but his spirit lives on there, for its University Library houses the bulk of his extant manuscripts and other papers. There, a team of scholars is engaged on editing his entire *Correspondence*, of which eight volumes have so far been published for the years 1821–60, and many more are still in the pipeline. The drawing of him as a young man made by George Richmond in 1840 presides over their labours in the Manuscript Room.

After his death in 1882, Emma Darwin bought The Grove on the south side of Huntingdon Road, so that she might spend the winters in Cambridge close to her sons. She died in 1896. Like several more of the family houses in the west of Cambridge, The Grove has subsequently provided space for college use, and is now divided between Fitzwilliam College and New Hall.

Charles and Emma had ten children, of whom three died in childhood. Their eldest son, William Erasmus (1839–1914), took his B.A. from Christ's College in 1862, and is said to have been looked after by the gyp called Impey who had also served his father. He became a banker in Southampton, and was the least academic and the least hypochondriac of the brothers, the only one who published nothing, and the only one who never grew a beard. He was adored by his nephews and nieces, and was famous for his lack of self-consciousness. In *Period Piece*[9] Gwen Raverat tells the story of how at his father's funeral in Westminster Abbey, he was sitting in the front seat as chief mourner, and felt a draught on his bald head. So he put his black gloves to balance on the top of his skull, and sat like that through the whole of the service, oblivious of the eyes of the nation.

The second son, George Howard (1845–1912), was educated at Clapham Grammar School, and then went to Trinity College, first as a commoner, though he was later elected a scholar. He took the Mathematical Tripos, was Second Wrangler and Second Smith prizeman in 1868, and was elected to a Fellowship of Trinity that autumn. He originally intended to make the law his profession, underwent training as a barrister, and was called to the bar in 1874; but he was dogged by ill health, and returned to Cambridge in 1873 to take up his Fellowship at Trinity and to resume his mathematical studies. In 1877 he wrote a long paper entitled 'On the influence of geological changes on the earth's axis of rotation', which was duly refereed favourably by Sir William Thomson (later Lord Kelvin), and published in the *Philosophical Transactions of the Royal Society*. The following year his father wrote enthusiastically from Downe:

> All of us are delighted, for considering what a man Sir W.T. is it is really grand that you should have staggered him so quickly & that he shd speak of 'your discovery etc' about the moon's period. I also chuckled greatly about the internal Heat. How this will please the geologists and Evolutionists. That does sound awkward about the heat being bottled up in the middle of the earth . . . Hurrah for the bowels of the earth & their viscosity & for the moon & for all the Heavenly bodies & for my son George (F.R.S. very soon).[10]

The prediction was correct, and George was indeed elected to the Royal Society in 1879, and four years later became Plumian Professor of Astronomy and Experimental Philosophy in Cambridge.

Even the most meticulous of mathematicians is not infallible, and Professor Walter Munk of the University of California has related the story of the marathon of errors involved in the long and sometimes heated controversy on polar wandering that had been set off by George Darwin's first paper, neither its author nor its eminent referee having noticed that early in the calculation there was a simple algebraic error that had the effect of reversing one of the basic conclusions. Nevertheless, it was fifty years before this slip was spotted, and it is doubtful whether there were others in the seventy-one subsequent papers on cosmology that came from George Darwin's pen, or in the famous book on *The Tides* that he published in 1898.

In 1884 George was married to a young American, Maud Du Puy, from a Huguenot family in Philadelphia, and in the following year they moved to Newnham Grange on Silver Street, where their three children were born. One of them was the artist and wood engraver Gwen Raverat (1885–1957), who at the end of her life lived at The Old Granary in the grounds of Newnham Grange, where she wrote and illustrated a magical account of her childhood in Cambridge, *Period Piece*, which has become a classic that is essential reading for anyone who wants to know what some of the Darwins in Cambridge were really like.

George Darwin's eldest son was Charles Galton Darwin (1887–1962). He came up to Trinity College in 1906 as a Major Scholar, and was classed 1.2 in the Mathematical Tripos in 1910. He proceeded immediately to Manchester University to join Rutherford as Schuster Reader in Mathematical Physics, which was a post intended for postgraduate training in research. Here he came into contact with the Braggs and Moseley, who were engaged on the early studies of the diffraction of X-rays by crystals, and in 1914 worked out a fundamentally new diffraction theory based on the mosaic structure of most crystals. On the outbreak of war he was sent to France, and with W. L. Bragg was engaged in the Royal Engineers on the detection of enemy guns by sound-ranging, for which he was later awarded the Military Cross. In 1919 he returned to Cambridge for the first time as a Fellow of Christ's College, and for the next five years worked on mathematical statistics with R. H. Fowler.

The German and British schools still had conflicting ideas for the correct calculation of the intensities of beams of X-rays reflected by crystals, and in 1925 Charles was summoned by Bragg to a conference in Bavaria as the British champion best able to hold his own with the powerful German theoreticians. Unfortunately, Charles had been working in other fields for some while, and, not having done his homework, had quite forgotten the details of his theory of 1914. The result was a fiasco. Bragg was not amused, but was led to write a paper with him and James, which summarised the earlier work, and is considered today as a major landmark in the use of quantitative data in crystal analysis.

In 1924, Charles was appointed Tait Professor of Natural Philosophy in Edinburgh, where he made further important studies in mathematical physics, and in 1925 he was married to Katharine Pember, herself a mathematician. In 1936 he was elected Master of Christ's College, and returned to Cambridge once more. But he stayed at Christ's for only two years, and, foreseeing the approach of war, he then accepted the Directorship of the National Physical Laboratory at Teddington, where he remained until his retirement and final return to Cambridge and Newnham Grange in 1949.

Many men have strong desires for the social betterment of the world when they are young, but lose them later on. In Charles the process was reversed, and, true to his ancestry, he published in 1952 *The Next Million Years*, in which he considered the future of the human race in Malthusian terms. The honesty of his reasoning was always impeccable, and his somewhat gloomy predictions erred only in that they now seem likely to be fulfilled in a much shorter time span than he expected. He died at Newnham Grange on 31 December 1962.

As has been related by my mother in *A House by the River*, three of the older colleges in the University, Gonville and Caius, St John's and Trinity, announced in 1963 the founding of a new graduate college. Enquiries about the possibility of acquiring Newnham Grange and the Old Granary for the housing of this new Foundation revealed that Lady Darwin and her family were warmly receptive to the idea, and of the suggestion that it should be named Darwin College. With the addition of a modern section linking Newnham Grange to The Hermitage next door, and of a dining hall at the corner of Silver Street, a successful conversion of the premises for college use was achieved, and a computer centre is now in course of construction in what used to be the kitchen garden.

Charles Darwin's third son, Francis (1848–1925), was educated, like George, at Clapham Grammar School and then at Trinity College, where he graduated with 1st class honours in 1870. He then qualified in medicine at St George's Hospital, London, but never practised, and during the first of his three marriages acted as his father's assistant at Downe, particularly with his experiments on the power of movement in plants. In 1883 he moved to Cambridge as a Fellow of Christ's College and University Lecturer in Botany, being appointed Reader in Botany in 1888, and retiring in 1904. In addition to his distinguished contributions on plant physiology, he is best known for his excellent editing of the basic biographies of his father, the three volumes of *Life and Letters* that appeared in 1887, and (with A. C. Seward) of the two volumes of *More Letters of Charles Darwin* that appeared in 1903. The house, called Wichfield, off the Huntingdon Road which he built in 1883 close to his mother at The Grove, now belongs to Trinity Hall, whose undergraduates it accommodates.

One of the two of Charles Darwin's grandchildren to be born in his lifetime was Francis's son Bernard (1876–1961). He was at Trinity College in 1894–7, and deserves a special mention in my list of Darwins in Cambridge because he was the only member of the family to have distinguished himself as an athlete, having played golf for the University. He later became golf correspondent of *The Times*, and for many years wrote elegant and amusing fourth leaders for the paper. He also wrote the Introduction to the second edition of *The Oxford Dictionary of Quotations*, which he described as 'a humble tribute to Oxford from another establishment over the way'.

Francis's daughter Frances (1886–1960) by his second marriage lived in Cambridge all her life, and was a much esteemed poet of the Georgian school whose most often quoted lines are in the triolet addressed 'To a Fat Lady Seen from the Train':

> O why do you walk through the fields in gloves,
> Missing so much and so much?
> O fat white woman whom nobody loves,
> Why do you walk through the fields in gloves,
> When the grass is as soft as the breast of doves
> And shivering-sweet to the touch?
> O why do you walk through the fields in gloves,
> Missing so much and so much?

Her husband, Francis Macdonald Cornford (1874–1943), was a Fellow of Trinity and Professor of Ancient Philosophy in the University. He is remembered not only for his edition of Plato, but as author in 1908 of *Microcosmographia Academica, Being a Guide for the*

Young Academic Politician. The basic principles of Cambridge politics at that time, which he described with superb wit, are still in force today, and indeed are equally applicable to every other walk of life. Thus:

> Every public action which is not customary, either is wrong, or, if it is right, is a dangerous precedent. It follows that nothing should ever be done for the first time.

And

> The Principle of Unripe Time is that people should not do at the present moment what they think right at that moment, because the moment at which they think it right has not yet arrived. But the unripeness of the time will, in some cases, be found to lie in the Bugbear, 'What Dr. —— will say.' Time, by the way, is like the medlar: it has a trick of going rotten before it is ripe.[11]

I am afraid that the *Microcosmographia* is out of print at the present time, but I believe that plans are in hand for the publication of a new edition.[12]

Charles Darwin's fifth son was Horace (1851–1928). He was educated at Clapham Grammar School like three of his brothers, went up to Trinity College, and graduated in mathematics as a Senior Optime in 1874. Whilst still an undergraduate, he began to display an extraordinary talent for scientific instrumentation, building an 'auxanometer' used by his brother Francis to measure the rate of growth of small plants, and the micrometer system for measuring the rate of sinking of his father's 'worm stone' at Down House. After three years' apprenticeship in mechanical engineering, he returned to Cambridge and joined forced with his contemporary at Trinity, Albert Dew-Smith, who was helping to provide instruments for research at the newly established Physiological Laboratory. In 1881, what had originally been known as 'Horace's Shop' was established as the Cambridge Scientific Instrument Company. The enterprise flourished, and was quickly playing an important role not only in building equipment of various kinds for other departments of the University, but instruments for temperature measurement and industrial pyrometry, oscillographs and galvanometers, paper recorders, seismology and sound-ranging; and after the 1914–18 war the Cambridge electrocardiograph was produced. The Company's present successor in Cambridge, now part of the Leica group, has maintained the tradition for innovation by manufacturing the first scanning electron microscope.

As his business expanded, so, too did Horace Darwin's involvement in the affairs of the town. In those days, Town and Gown were inclined to view each other with a suspicion that Horace was at pains to reduce. When Alderman Spalding proposed his election as Mayor in 1896, he was able to comment: 'Not very long ago Mr Horace Darwin described himself in the Council Chamber as a Cambridge tradesman.'

In 1880 Horace was married to Emma Cecilia Farrer, always known as 'Ida', whose father later became the first Lord Farrer of Abinger. They built a house which they called The Orchard, on spare land close to Emma Darwin at The Grove, which in 1954 was made over by their daughters as a site for the third women's college, New Hall. Ida Darwin, strongly supported by her husband, had over the years taken a keen interest in mental welfare, and her daughter Ruth (1883–1973) assisted her mother in this field, later becoming a Senior Commissioner at the Board of Control in London. In 1966 a tribute was paid to their work when a new wing of the Fulbourn Hospital, near Cambridge, was opened with places for 350 patients, and named the Ida Darwin Hospital.

Their second daughter, Nora (1885–1989), spent most of her life away from Cambridge, but returned there after the death of her husband, Sir Alan Barlow, and died a few years ago at the age of 104, the last survivor of Charles Darwin's nine grandchildren. Nora Barlow was the true founder of what is sometimes known as 'The Darwin Industry', having in 1933 transcribed and edited the diary that he kept for the benefit of his family during the voyage of the *Beagle*, following it up with editions of his *Autobiography*, his letters to Henslow, and some other manuscripts.

The male members of the family have thus made their contribution to Cambridge mainly in the scientific field, not only in biology but also in physics, mathematics and instrument design, while the women have been writers and artists. The tradition has continued, for Charles Darwin had 28 great-grandchildren, and some 16 Darwins, Keyneses, Cornfords and Barlows have taken degrees in Cambridge, mostly at Trinity. Two of them, Professor Horace Barlow and myself, have worked at the Physiological Laboratory for most of our careers. After that, the arithmetic gets beyond me, but three of his great-great-grandchildren are currently Fellows of colleges and members of the University staff, and I am happy to say that the supply of Darwins in Cambridge shows no signs of drying up.

NOTES

1 Nora Barlow, *The Autobiography of Charles Darwin*, London: Collins 1958.
2 Ibid.
3 Ibid.
4 Ibid.
5 Ibid.
6 F. Burckhardt and S. Smith (eds.), *The Correspondence of Charles Darwin* vol. VII, Cambridge: Cambridge University Press 1985, p. 396.
7 R. D. Keynes (ed.), *Charles Darwin's Beagle Diary*, Cambridge: Cambridge University Press 1988.
8 Burckhardt and Smith, *Correspondence* vol. I, p. 151.
9 Gwen Raverat, *Period Piece: A Cambridge Childhood*, London: Faber and Faber 1952.
10 Private letter.
11 Francis M. Cornford, *Microcosmographia Academica, Being a Guide for the Young Academic Politician*, Cambridge: Bowes and Bowes 1908, pp. 15, 16.
12 It is being reissued in *University Politics: F. M. Cornford's Cambridge and his Advice to the Young Academic Politician*, edited by Gordon Johnson, Cambridge: Cambridge University Press, due for publication in July 1994.

CHAPTER 10

How the Burgess Shale came to Cambridge; and what happened

SIMON CONWAY MORRIS

Does any family not have its legends? One of my family's is of the Scots ancestor (surely a Stewart) who was blown up during the construction of the Canadian Pacific Railway (CPR), catapulted on to a frozen lake – and survived. I am pretty sure the incident was in British Columbia and I like to think that this small drama was enacted somewhere close to the rail-town of Field, because if so it provides a link to my own life and a subject I have pursued for more than twenty years, the Burgess Shale.

It was inevitable that the building of the CPR led to exploration of the hitherto inaccessible hinterland, mostly of course for minerals, preferably gold. So it was that the amazing fossil beds on the north shoulder of Mount Stephen must have been discovered, at a locality only a few hours hike from Field. Henry Woodward, writing in 1902, noted that the first fossils on Mount Stephen were discovered by 1884 by L. M. Lambe, then a surveyor on the CPR, who went on to become a vertebrate palaeontologist in the Geological Survey of Canada (GSC). In a more recent account Desmond Collins narrates how a carpenter working on the tourist hotel in Field had also found trilobites. This information was given to Otto Klotz, an astronomer and surveyor taking geodetic measurements along the new railroad. Klotz passed on the information to the GSC geologist R. G. McConnell, who was mapping the area. In mid-September 1886, McConnell climbed Mount Stephen to discover several acres of scree upon which were scattered millions of slabs of a yellow-weathering calcareous shale with profusely abundant trilobites. It was not long before specimens were being sent for scientific study and description, the first trilobites being described in 1887.

By this time the overall complexion of Cambrian life was becoming clear, but the Mount Stephen fossil beds, known as the *Ogygopsis* Shale on account of a particularly abundant trilobite, also yielded stranger fossils, harbingers of things to come. In 1892 the Canadian palaeontologist, J. F. Whiteaves, described what he thought was the abdomen of a primitive crustacean (today represented by such animals as lobsters and crabs), but denoted its strangeness by calling it *Anomalocaris*. As we will see, the scientific career of *Anomalocaris* has been somewhat chequered, and even now our understanding of it as a primitive arthropod, but not a crustacean, is still incomplete.

WALCOTT: DISCOVERER OF THE BURGESS SHALE

At this time the leading intellect and exponent of Cambrian stratigraphy and palaeontology was undoubtedly Charles Doolittle Walcott. His interests in the area had developed whilst he was employed by the United States Geological Survey, and continued to flourish when he was appointed to the Smithsonian Institution in Washington, DC, where ultimately (in 1907) he was to become Secretary. Walcott had conducted extensive fieldwork in the Cambrian of the American West and it was natural that he should extend his activities north along the Cordillera, into the southern Rockies of west Alberta and British Columbia. Walcott was well aware of the *Ogygopsis* Shale and had published descriptions of some of the fossils as early as 1888. Following fieldwork the previous July, in 1908 Walcott published a further description of the *Ogygopsis* Shale, noting again *Anomalocaris* and also describing a number of other lightly skeletonised fossils. The discovery of the Burgess Shale was now only a matter of time. Indeed, Woodward wrote, 'Mount Field, which faces Mount Stephen, remains still unexplored, but is a part of the same massif, and will no doubt yield the same Cambrian fossils' (*Geological Magazine*, 1902, p. 506).

How the Burgess Shale was found has become part of palaeontological folklore, but Walcott kept a diary and at least the outline of events is clear. The dislodged slab, rich in soft-bodied fossils, was presumably close to the trail that runs on the west side of the ridge that connects Mount Field and Wapta Mountain. It was noticed on 31 August 1909. Apparently Walcott spent about five days on the ridge, but it was only in the following year that he located the parent stratum and began serious excavations of the site, in what is now known as the Walcott Quarry. During five seasons of excavation Walcott amassed tens of thousands of specimens, which at the end of each season were dispatched to the Smithsonian by rail from Field.

Walcott described a large percentage of the fauna, at least in preliminary fashion, and clearly planned to extend his studies because undescribed material in the Smithsonian often has photographs associated with it. Tressilian C. Nicholas, a Fellow of Trinity College, who died in 1989 at the age of 101 years, described to me how he once travelled near to the Burgess Shale, and he also indicated that Walcott discouraged visitors. Nicholas was on one of the excursions (Transcontinental Excursion c1) in 1913 as part of the International Geological Congress. According to Desmond Collins, of the Royal Ontario Museum, Walcott came down to Field to give a talk to the excursion. Even after Walcott had completed his own excavations it appears that he gave the impression that work on the Burgess Shale was largely complete and discouraged further visits to the quarry when his time was being increasingly consumed by administration. Thereafter, geological summer field parties certainly continued to visit the Walcott Quarry and a dribble of specimens must have been removed. Most significant, however, was an excavation by Percy E. Raymond, who in 1930 secured a significant collection that now lies in the Museum of Comparative Zoology in Harvard University.

WHITTINGTON: THE BURGESS SHALE UNFOLDS

Over the years Canadian palaeontologists began to realise that the Burgess Shale was one of their prime localities. Obviously there was no hope of the Smithsonian relinquishing Walcott's huge collection, which I counted in 1979 as consisting of about 30,000 slabs and approximately 65,000 fossils. Moreover, the overall setting of Burgess Shale, its regional stratigraphy and sedimentology, were scarcely understood. The impetus for restudy came from the Geological Survey of Canada (GSC), who designated the Burgess Shale reappraisal as part of the Bow-Athabasca project. The director of the GSC Calgary Office was Digby McLaren, and it was he who invited Harry Whittington to lead the palaeobiological investigation. The choice, which turned out to be inspired, was logical. It was clear from Walcott's papers that the Burgess Shale fauna was dominated by arthropods, and Whittington was clearly the world's leading specialist on trilobites, not least because of his superb work on beautifully preserved silicified faunas from the Ordovician of the United States.

Although English, Whittington had been in the Museum of Comparative Zoology, Harvard, for many years. It was fortunate for Cambridge that he did not remain in the United States, because in 1966 he was elected to the prestigious Woodwardian Chair. Thus, Whittington arrived in Cambridge shortly after completing the first season of fieldwork with the GSC. Whittington's connections with the trilobites meant that the first research team to be assembled consisted of David Bruton, who had joined the second and last (1967) field party, and Chris Hughes, recently appointed to the post of Assistant Director in Research in Cambridge. Bruton took on *Sidneyia*, an arthropod named after one of Walcott's sons, and Hughes tackled another arthropod, the eponymous *Burgessia*. In the meantime, Whittington began work on the most abundant of the arthropods, *Marrella*, which was named in honour of John Marr, an earlier Woodwardian Professor. In August 1969 Whittington was able to present the first fruits of the Burgess Shale programme at the North American Paleontological Convention in Chicago. Both the paper and the symposium in which it was delivered are landmarks. Apart from setting out a brief review of former work, Whittington established three cardinal points, using *Marrella* as his example. First, the fossils show exquisite anatomical details and an essential adjunct in their interpretation is the preparation of camera lucida drawings. Although laborious to prepare (some of my drawings of *Wiwaxia* took several days to complete), the use of a camera lucida has two advantages. First, it forces the observer to interpret all aspects of the fossil, including faintly preserved structures that may only be visible at certain angles and intensities of light. Second, the fossils are buried at various angles, evidently as a result of turbulent transport in a muddy cloud of sediment. The angles at which the carcasses came to rest are not entirely random, and each species has a tendency to settle in a particular fashion, governed by the greatest stability. A number of specimens, however, are orientated at 'unusual' angles, say, on their sides or even end-up. Thus, even though the fossils are greatly flattened, accurate three-dimensional reconstructions are possible because of their varying orientations. A further observation is that the various parts of the body of *Marrella*, especially the appendages, are separated by thin layers of sediment. This has two important consequences. First, it means that by careful use of a micro-chisel parts of the fossil can be removed to reveal underlying parts of the specimen. Second, quite often the split through the rock that originally exposed the specimen runs at an angle, so that a section of the fossil is restricted to either the part or counterpart. In other words, for a complete understanding of a specimen ideally one needs both part and counterpart. Unfortunately, Walcott appears not to have realised this and made little attempt to keep parts and counterparts together. In some cases the counterpart was never collected, in others either it is in another part of the collection or had been sent to other museums and institutions for exchange. In my census of the Smithsonian collection I estimated that about 20 per cent of specimens were available as part and counterpart.

As far as I recall, my own interest in the Burgess Shale was ignited during a practical class in Bristol, where I was an undergraduate. The display of material was derived from a small collection in the Museum, and I recollect looking up some of Walcott's publications in the library. In due course I wrote to Whittington about research prospects in Cambridge, which was followed by an interview in his vast room at the far end of the Sedgwick Museum (since converted into a mineral display). Whittington explained that an undergraduate from Trinity College, Dublin, one Derek Briggs, had already been offered a studentship in Whittington's own college, Sidney Sussex, and so had first pick of possible projects. Briggs had elected to study the second most abundant arthropod, *Canadaspis*. Whittington was a little uncertain what might be suitable, but somewhat diffidently suggested the worms. That sounded fine, but it was only in August that I learnt I was definitely able to take on the project, when news of a special studentship came through from the Natural Environment Research Council (NERC).

No sooner had I arrived in Cambridge than I developed appendicitis, followed by a nasty bout of septicaemia. So it was early in November that I was well enough to start work, other than flicking through Walcott's monographs in the sick bay of Churchill College. The bulk of the collections made by the GSC were in Cambridge, but the sooner we could get to the Smithsonian the better. The huge collections were readily accessible and we were given a free hand by the Collections Manager, Fred Collier, to browse, borrow and prepare the fossils. The type specimens could not be loaned, so photographs and camera lucida drawings had to be prepared in the Smithsonian. For the most part this presented few problems because a substantial number of the taxa had been described by Walcott at an early stage of his quarrying while material was still being amassed. In other words the main collections housed as good, if not better, material.

SIGNIFICANCE OF THE BURGESS SHALE

To date well over a hundred technical papers, books and popular articles have been written on the Burgess Shale fauna by the team originally based in Cambridge. Amongst the thousands of pages and hundreds of thousands of words, what is the general significance of the Burgess Shale and why has it attracted so much attention? At the time of the main research effort, the production of monographs, it was certainly difficult to distinguish the wood from the trees. The intensive study of the specimens, sometimes themselves highly problematic, the exhaustive camera lucida drawings and the days spent in the eerie glow of the ultra-violet light used for photographing the specimens were not conducive to simple consideration of wider issues. The full significance of the Burgess Shale has taken time to emerge.

In the first place, it was only when a substantial part of the fauna had been adequately documented that an overall view of the ecology and community was possible. To achieve this I combined data from the Smithsonian and GSC collections, together with as many of the smaller collections scattered around the world as I could find out about. Two cardinal facts emerged. First, the proportion of animals with hard skeletons, that might be expected to fossilise readily, against those with either very delicate skeletons or soft bodies, was overwhelmingly small. The exact figure depends on various assumptions, especially how many of the shelly fossils were actually inhabited at the time of burial. A reasonable estimate is that about

75 per cent of taxa and perhaps 95 per cent of individuals would not fossilise outside the exceptional environment of the Burgess Shale. When one remembers that palaeontologists usually have available only remains of skeletons, these figures suggest that normal Cambrian faunas are very seriously impoverished samples of the original communities. The second observation was that the range of ecologies present in the Burgess Shale was much wider than would be inferred from earlier knowledge of the Cambrian. Burrowers, crawlers, swimmers and those stuck in the mud could all be identified, as could the styles of feeding ranging across all the main types of deposit, suspension and predatory. The abundance of the last category was a particular surprise because hitherto it was widely assumed that Cambrian ecology was unusually benign, with few or perhaps even no predators. The Burgess Shale revealed a very different story. Most unequivocal were prey in the intestines of worms and arthropods, in *Sidneyia*, for example, forming a crushed mass. Mouth parts are always more equivocal, but the armature on trilobites such as *Olenoides* and worms like *Ancalagon* are certainly suggestive. The net result of this ecological investigation was to reveal a complex world, rich in taxa, pursuing a wide variety of life styles that ranged from stout worms probing deep in the sediment to delicate organisms drifting through the seawater. The marine world has, of course, changed enormously in the half billion years that separate today from the Burgess Shale, and there is little doubt that not only have animals become more effective but that the intensity of predation and competition have also escalated. But nevertheless, the groundwork of the ecological systems had clearly been established by Burgess Shale times.

However, if the palaeontologist travels slightly further back in time, a feat easily achieved by walking across any outcrop of rock that straddles the Precambrian–Cambrian boundary, then a dramatic change is observed. Prior to about 650 million years there is no evidence of animals, at least in the fossil record. A substantial number of palaeontologists believe that animals had evolved by then, but were microscopic and so unpreservable. It might be objected that delicate algae are often preserved in Precambrian cherts, but these mostly formed in inhospitable tidal flats whose extreme saltiness would discourage animals. Recently, the very careful preparation of Precambrian shales has revealed not only superbly preserved algae, but organisms as small as bacteria. Perhaps animals will also be found in these shales.

Approximately 650 million years ago there was an ice age that seems to have been of unusual severity, with glaciers forming even in lowland areas of the tropics. Glaciers deposit particularly charac- teristic types of sediment (known as tillites) and shortly after the cessation of the ice age we find the first evidence of animal life. These are the Ediacaran faunas, named after the Ediacara Hills in South Australia, but known to have an effectively global distribution. To many palaeontologists the bulk of the Ediacaran fauna can be interpreted as a primitive assemblage of cnidarians (represented today by sea anemones, corals and jellyfish), segmented worms, arthropods and perhaps echinoderms. Most notable, however, is that none of these fossils have any hard parts. Why these Ediacaran fossils are so abundantly preserved – in some Australian localities it is possible to collect hundreds in a day – when they have no skeletons is still rather mysterious. There are other problems. The bulk of the Ediacaran fauna disappears before the Cambrian, and the exact relationships between these animals and those found in the Cambrian are not clear.

It is near the base of the Cambrian that the fossil record plainly reveals one of the most dramatic of evolutionary events, the so-called 'Cambrian explosion'. This has long been obvious from the abrupt appearance of hard parts, acquired by a wide range of animals. Less remarked upon is the parallel diversification in the burrows and trackways, collectively known as trace fossils. Many of them were made by soft-bodied animals, the sort that account for the bulk of the Burgess Shale fauna. Clearly the 'Cambrian explosion' involves much more than simply the acquisition of hard parts, but the drawback of trace fossils is that very seldom is the original animal associated with them. The bonus, however, is that trace fossils record an animal's behaviour and so in some sense its neurological complexity. Trace fossil diversification at the beginning of the Cambrian tells us unequivocally that something of major importance was happening, but not exactly what.

Re-enter the Burgess Shale fauna, now ready to be integrated with the 'Cambrian explosion'. It might be objected that its age in the Middle Cambrian makes it too young and too far removed from the main event, perhaps 20 million years earlier. There is some truth in this; many of the early species must have become extinct, to be replaced by modified descendants. Paradoxically, however, the Burgess Shale fauna seems to be rather conservative, as is evident when comparing it to the equivalent Chengjiang fauna from the Lower Cambrian of south China. The faunas are certainly not identical, but they show strong similarities. Why should the Burgess Shale show such sluggish evolution when the Cambrian is meant to demonstrate a spectacular adaptive radiation: The reason may be that the Burgess Shale fauna lived in deeper water, in a sort of refuge from the biotic hurly-burly of the shallower shelves. In modern marine communities a similar conservatism is observed: those in deeper water seem to house more archaic elements.

THE BURGESS SHALE AND THE ORIGIN OF PHYLA

In what way then does the Burgess Shale enhance our understanding of the 'Cambrian explosion'? I have mentioned its rich diversity and complex ecology. Without the Burgess Shale to hand to add to our knowledge of Cambrian life would be rather like depending on the history of the Second World War solely on the basis of Soviet records, interesting but biased. But the Burgess Shale has played a more crucial role than that. It has long been recognised that many and probably most of the major designs or body-plans of animals appeared in the Cambrian. In other words, phyla such as brachiopods, molluscs, echinoderms and arthropods are all readily identifiable in the Lower Cambrian. Many phyla, however, are entirely soft-bodied and their first appearances are more likely to have been controlled by chance occurrences of exceptional fossilisation. So it is that the Burgess Shale has the first record of the phylum to which we as vertebrates belong, the chordates represented by *Pikaia*.

Right at the beginning of the Cambridge investigations it was clear that a number of the fossils were deeply puzzling, with strange and unfamiliar anatomies that seemingly precluded easy comparison with known groups. The degree of apparent bizarreness varied. For example, *Marrella* was clearly an arthropod, but, despite being reminiscent of the trilobites and crustaceans, was not similar enough to pigeonhole in either of these groups. Other fossils seemed to be totally peculiar. The problems were exemplified by *Hallucigenia*, an extraordinary fossil that had been very briefly described by Walcott

as a polychaete (*Canadia*) in a posthumous paper. My first examination showed that this could not be correct, and I reconstructed the
animal as walking on a series of sharp spinose appendages, while on
the opposite side of the trunk a row of tentacle-like structures
projected upwards. Reasons to doubt this reconstruction only
emerged recently when a remarkable array of lobopod animals was
discovered in the Chengjiang fauna of China. These lobopods may be
related to the living velvet-worm (*Peripatus*), which is typically found
in leaf litter or within rotting logs in areas such as Australia and South
Africa. Unlike the living velvet-worms, some of the Cambrian
lobopods bore a 'shoulder pad', a discoidal structure sometimes with
a protruding spine above each leg. What bearing does this have on
Hallucigenia? Work by Lars Ramsköld and Hou Xianguang suggest
that this animal is also a lobopod, and if so then my initial reconstruction must be upside-down. The supposed walking spines are a
defensive array, and it now transpires that the tentacles are actually
a double row of walking legs, remarkably slender and ending in
sharp claws.

Another animal that has had a distinctly chequered career is
Anomalocaris. Recall that it was first described some time before the
Burgess Shale was discovered and interpreted as the abdomen of an
arthropod. Briggs recognised that the fossils were much more
credible as appendages, and proposed that *Anomalocaris* was rather
like a millipede. However, the limbs are large, up to 20.5 cm in
length, so the millipede analogy would lead to *Anomalocaris* being
reconstructed as at least a metre long. In the meantime I had been
restudying a curious specimen that Walcott had considered to be a
holothurian (sea cucumber). At one end of the animal was a discoidal
structure and this was clearly the same as a strange fossil known as
Peytoia, that Walcott had earlier described as a jellyfish. *Peytoia*
resembled a pineapple ring, consisting of a series of plates that
encircled a central space. I assumed that the association of *Peytoia*
with the supposed holothurian was one of chance. It was
Whittington who solved the enigma. While excavating a large
specimen collected by the GSC he recognised at its anterior a pair of
the *Anomalocaris* limbs, while on the ventral surface was the structure
known as *Peytoia*, but clearly part of the mouth.

What does all this have to do with the origin of phyla? With
the inestimable advantages of hindsight, our research strategy for the

Burgess Shale can be seen to have been flawed, although not fatally. A useful way to consider the problem might be as follows: Imagine that you are an extra-terrestrial visitor to the planet, a trained zoologist but unfortunately with very limited time and access to only three collecting sites (say Hyde Park, central Patagonia and some marine muds off Massachusetts). The extra-terrestrial might be able to collect several hundred species (including some highly vociferous bipeds). With such a limited sample, however, it would be extremely difficult to gain much of an idea of the evolutionary relationships of these animals and plants. In particular, where only a single representative of a major group had been collected then its evolutionary position would be obscure. Indeed, many taxa, including perhaps those chattering bipeds, would look decidedly bizarre.

This is effectively what we did in our Burgess Shale study in Cambridge. It was a first and very preliminary trawl through the riches of the Cambrian seas. Since those marvellous days much has changed. Obviously some of our interpretations have proved incorrect, as is always the case in science. More importantly, other Cambrian deposits with Burgess Shale-type fossils have been recognised. I mentioned the discoveries in Chengjiang, and there is little doubt that ultimately this deposit will rival that of the Burgess Shale.

In terms of Cambridge, however, the story has been extended to the far Arctic of Peary Land in north Greenland. In May 1986 I was at a meeting of Cambrian specialists in Uppsala. Among those attending was John Peel, at that time a palaeontologist working in Copenhagen and employed by the Geological Survey of Greenland. While working in Peary Land some of his colleagues had discovered a locality with Lower Cambrian fossils. Only a few slabs had been collected, but a number of Burgess Shale-type fossils could be readily identified. An expedition was clearly imperative and in 1989 a four-man team visited the locality, to be followed by a return visit in 1991. A rich haul of fossils resulted, including numerous arthropods as well as worms and sponges. The great surprise, however, was the discovery of a scaly worm, belonging to a group known as the halkieriids. The importance of this find was twofold. First and principally, the halkieriids previously had only been known from their isolated sclerites (tiny calcareous plates) and their overall configuration on the original animal was rather conjectural. Second, in the Burgess Shale itself a somewhat similar worm had been described by Walcott as *Wiwaxia*. He had thought it to be a polychaete annelid (that is related to the living ragworms and more distantly the earthworms) but Stefan Bengtson and I had concluded that *Wiwaxia* was related to the halkieriids and, as the former was known from articulated specimens, it could provide a template for sclerite reconstruction in halkieriids. The discovery of the Greenland specimens broadly confirmed our hypothesis.

Perhaps the major problem in zoology has been determining the true interrelationships of the phyla. Anatomical, embryological and biochemical data have all been employed, but overall with little success. For example, whether the annelids are more closely related to the arthropods or the molluscs remains deeply controversial. At first sight the fossil record from the Cambrian supports this view: phyla appear early and are readily recognisable. How then can we ever establish the interrelationships of the phyla? One answer is that we don't: if the phyla evolved independently from different unicellular ancestors then the question is almost meaningless. But this idea, once quite popular, is now considered unlikely. Another possibility is that the phyla have long cryptic histories, and we need to search more thoroughly in Precambrian sediments. It may well be that Ediacaran fossils hold more clues to the evolution of early animals than we presently realise, but the answer to the origin of phyla will probably be solved in the time between the Ediacaran and Middle Cambrian, rather than deep in the Precambrian.

The renewed impetus to crack this problem has come from molecular biology where comparisons of sequence data, especially nucleotides in ribosomal RNA, throw interesting new light on the interrelationships of phyla. These data are far from unambiguous, but they do support some widely accepted ideas and throw interesting new light on other relationships. But molecular methods are not of unlimited use. Even if relationships between phyla are established, this tells us nothing about what the common ancestor looked like, how it operated, how the evolutionary transitions were achieved and by what mechanisms. Outside the imagination of zoologists, such information is only available from the fossil record. This is the unique importance of the supposedly problematic taxa from the Burgess Shale and other Cambrian deposits. In a colloquial sense these fossils are now being recognised as the 'missing links' between phyla or other major taxonomic groups. More precisely they are taxa that retain primitive characters that are also possessed by the common ancestor of two or more phyla.

What about some specific examples? Among the arthropods there has been a concerted effort by Briggs and his colleague Richard Fortey to produce a coherent evolutionary scheme for the Burgess Shale arthropods, including not only the known groups (crustaceans, chelicerates, trilobites), but the plethora of other 'problematic' arthropods. In addition, it now seems likely that the earlier stages of arthropod evolution will become clearer by including *Anomalocaris* and the various lobopods in the consideration. Similarly, it is now apparent that the halkieriids are involved with the very early stages of the evolution of molluscs (and perhaps annelids also).

These are early days and many of our existing ideas will need modification or scrapping. The flood of molecular data will help to shape new hypotheses, while the deliberate search for key taxa in the Cambrian necessary to elucidate the earliest stages of animal history will help with the emergence of a coherent phylogeny. Burgess Shale-type faunas have to play a critical role in this search because only in such deposits are the special conditions conducive for exceptional fossilisation. Nevertheless, this information must be integrated with the more orthodox skeletal record and, so far as possible, the trace fossils.

CONTINGENCY IN EVOLUTION

In a review article published in 1987 in *Geology Today* I wrote:

> Whatever evolutionary mechanisms are invoked to explain these bizarre creatures from the Burgess Shale, it seems that all were geologically short-lived and probably became extinct during the early Palaeozoic. It is perhaps natural to dismiss forms such as *Hallucigenia* as 'mere experiments', doomed to speedy extinction by the onslaught of superior competitors. Such a proposition is difficult to test, especially if the longer-term history of a group is not known. There is, however, some reason to believe that chance factors played just as important a part, if not the predominant role, in the weeding out of the different groups that arose during the 'Cambrian explosion'. The reason for thinking this lies in the sheer diversity of forms now known to have populated the Cambrian seas. With the benefit of hindsight we can dismiss these apparent oddities as mere freaks, sideshows to the evolutionary pageant that was to unfold during the rest of the

Phanerozoic. But just imagine that a team of zoological systematists, say the entire staff of the Natural History Museum of South Kensington, were to travel in a time machine back to the Cambrian. How would they proceed to classify this pot-pourri of metazoan evolution that was still in the process of rampant diversification? What appear to our eyes, in the privilege of hindsight as 'extinct phyla', would be shown to be more or less closely related to other species which happened to be successful in ultimately giving rise to myriads of descendant species that together would define the phyla we recognize today. In other words, our hypothetical time travellers would have no means of predicting which groups would be destined to success, and which to failure by extinction. Therefore, out of the vast diversity of forms, each with its own peculiar body-plan, only a small proportion survived to populate ultimately the entire planet with their evolutionary progeny. If the 'Cambrian explosion' were to be re-run, I think it likely that about the same number of basic body-plans would emerge from this initial radiation. However, there seems little guarantee that the same phyla would emerge. In the Burgess Shale the phylum to which we belong, the chordates, is represented by some rather insignificant looking worms [*Pikaia*] that are not dissimilar to the modern amphioxus. Looking at these creatures, would our Cambrian time-travellers dare to speculate that their descendants would include the sharks, dinosaurs, ostriches, and the readers of this article?

This seems to be a hardly exceptional statement, at least at the level of precise predictability. At another level, however, it may be that given certain starting conditions, the directions of life's branching are by no means unconstrained. There are at least two ways to consider this problem. One is via the phenomenon of convergent evolution, which is agreed by biologists to be rampant. In effect, this says that the number of evolutionary options is not unlimited. For example, there are only a few ways of moving through water or air, obtaining oxygen in a terrestrial environment, or cementing oneself to a rock. The other way of consideration is similar, and looks at the number of ways a structure can be assembled. Roger Thomas and Wolf Reif (*Evolution* 47 (1993), 341–60) give a useful example using the many different types of skeleton in animals. They show that a relatively large number (*c.* 720) of categories are recognisable. Significantly more than 50 per cent are widely employed, over 66 per cent are quite common and very few categories have never been exploited. In both cases the evolutionary options appear to be far from unlimited.

So if the history of the 'Cambrian explosion' was re-run would things be so different? In one sense completely. I the writer and you the reader would almost certainly not be here. Equally, if our respective parents hadn't met at that respective party, again we would not be here, but presumably other humans would be. But how likely is the evolution of humans from the perspective of the Cambrian? presumably very small indeed. Is this, however, a very interesting question? Seemingly not. What matters first is the likelihood of intelligence evolving. Here at least the convergent development of sophisticated neural systems in vertebrates and molluscs suggests that we are not dealing with the wildly improbable.

Contingency in history is accepted by evolutionary biologists, historians (take Winston Churchill's essay on what might have happened if the American civil war had gone the other way), and theologians (see numerous references by St Thomas Aquinas). Our presence may have been via the most convoluted of mazes and via a hair thread of continuity, and for that we must be ever thankful. But it might be unwise to confuse our personal history from whatever common ancestor – ?Pliocene ape, ?Triassic mammal, ?Cambrian chordate, ?Precambrian eukaryote – with possible inevitabilities of evolution given initial conditions. Within the debris of the 'Cambrian explosion' were the seeds of the most remarkable of all evolutionary innovations, the ability of matter to understand itself.

ACKNOWLEDGEMENTS

I thank Professor H. B. Whittington and Dr D. Collins for reading an earlier draft, and Sandra Last for typing the manuscript. My work is supported by the NERC, the Royal Society, and St John's College. Earth Sciences Publication 3705.

FURTHER READING

Collins, D. 1986. The great *Anomalocaris* mystery. *Rotunda* 19 (3), 51–7.
Conway Morris, S. 1986. The community structure of the Middle Cambrian Phyllopod bed (Burgess Shale). *Palaeontology* 29, 423–67.

1990. Palaeontology's hidden agenda. *New Scientist* 1729 (11 August), 38–42.

1993. The fossil record and the early evolution of the Metazoa. *Nature* 361, 219–25.

Whittington, H. B. 1985. *The Burgess Shale*. New Haven: Yale University Press.

CHAPTER 11

Ludwig Wittgenstein

P. M. S. HACKER

Ludwig Wittgenstein (1889–1951) was the youngest son of a wealthy and cultured Viennese family. In accordance with his father's wishes, he had studied engineering in Germany. In 1908 he came to England to pursue research in aeronautical engineering at the University of Manchester. In the course of research into the design of a jet-reaction propeller he was led into problems about the foundations of mathematics. He apparently read Russell's *Principles of Mathematics* and it was probably the appendix to Russell's book which led Wittgenstein first to read the works of the German logician Gottlob Frege, and then to visit him in Jena. On Frege's advice, the young Wittgenstein approached Russell with a view to studying philosophy with him. He came to Cambridge in 1911, and remained there until 1913, working with Russell, first as pupil and within six months as equal, on fundamental problems in the philosophy of logic and metaphysics.

Frege and Russell were the moving spirits behind the philosophical revival of interest in formal logic that dominates twentieth-century philosophy. They were the inventors of modern mathematical logic. Both had been motivated by the desire to establish mathematics on logical foundations. Russell, whose interests were wider than Frege's, believed that the application of the new logical techniques to traditional philosophical problems would herald a transformation of philosophy. It would make possible the application of scientific methods to philosophy and set philosophy on the path to achieving a gradual accumulation of secure knowledge on the model of the growth of scientific knowledge. Both philosophers thought of their new logical notation as a *language* (admittedly a formal one), indeed as a *logically perfect language*, unlike the natural languages of mankind. The propositions of logic they conceived of as true descriptions, of relations between abstract entities (e.g. propositions) – as Frege thought, or of the most general features of the universe, as Russell argued. The nature of the adamantine necessity of logical truths was a question neither faced up to.

Russell rapidly recognised the young Wittgenstein's genius, and expected him to take up work on philosophy where he himself had left off. In 1913 Wittgenstein left Cambridge in order to live in solitude in Norway while working on the problems he had inherited from Russell. He was not to live in Cambridge again until 1929. With the outbreak of the First World War, he returned to Vienna and volunteered for military service. Despite the exigencies of war service, in which he was twice decorated for gallantry, Wittgenstein continued to work on what was to become one of the great classics of philosophy. In the summer of 1918, shortly before he was taken prisoner of war, he completed the only book he ever published, indeed the only book he ever definitively completed, the *Tractatus Logico-philosophicus* (published in 1921). It ranges from the deepest problems in metaphysics, the nature of logic, language and truth, to the essence of the self, of mathematics and scientific theory, of intrinsic value, and of the logical character of the philosophical enterprise itself.

The *Tractatus* is the culmination of a long tradition in analytical philosophy, bringing to their climax ideas that run through both the empiricist and the rationalist strands in European thought. Stimulated largely by the writings of Frege and Russell, Wittgenstein rejected their solutions, and indeed their very conception of philosophy. He widened the scope of his investigation, taking as his central task the elucidation of the general conditions of the possibility of representation. The clarification of the essence of the proposition, of its essential form and relation to the reality it depicts, must, he argued, also clarify the essential form of reality – the metaphysical nature of the world. The new logic, he claimed, is not a new, logically perfect language, but a symbolic notation that aims at (but does not wholly achieve) logical perspicuity. Natural languages are not, and cannot be, logically defective, for logic is a condition of sense. Every language is logically adequate – otherwise it would not be able to express a sense, and would not be a language. But the surface grammatical forms of natural languages conceal their underlying, essential, logical forms. The logical form of any possible language *must* reflect the logico-metaphysical form of reality, for only thus is representation by means of a symbolism possible. The propositions of logic, however, are not descriptions at all – neither of a super-sensory realm nor of the most general properties of the universe. They are such combinations of descriptive propositions by means of logical connectives as ensure that all descriptive content cancels out. The propositions of logic say nothing (one who knows that either it is raining or it is not raining knows nothing about the weather). They are vacuous tautologies (which correspond to rules of inference). Their adamantine necessity merely reflects the mode of combination of the constituent propositions, namely that they are so combined as to exclude nothing (and hence say nothing). Wittgenstein rejected the Fregean–Russellian foundationalist endeavour to derive arith-metic from set-theory. So, too, he repudiated Russell's conception of scientific method in philosophy. The task of philosophy is not the pursuit of knowledge at all. It is the pursuit of (strictly ineffable) insight into the essential forms and possibility of expression of knowledge – a task Wittgenstein thought he had definitively achieved, and the elucidation of philosophically problematic propositions by means of logical analysis – with a view to showing that what is problematic about them stems from an unwitting misuse of language.

Wittgenstein, convinced that he had fulfilled his vocation as philosopher, abandoned philosophy. Having given away his inherited fortune to his sisters, he became a primary school teacher, and taught at peasant village schools for the next five years in the mountains of Lower Austria. It was not a happy experience, and came to an end in 1926, when he returned to Vienna. After spending a summer working as a gardener, he designed and supervised the construction of a mansion for his sister Margarete. In the meantime, the *Tractatus* had come to the attention of the Vienna Circle, a group of scien-tifically minded philosophers led by Moritz Schlick, and was recognised by (some of) them as a turning-point in the history of philosophy. They admired its clarification of the nature of propositions of logic, which they harnessed to their anti-metaphysical crusade, applauding the thought that pure reason alone can achieve no knowledge and that there can be no synthetic *a priori* propositions. They welcomed the idea that the task of philosophy is the logical clarification of empirical propositions, an idea they harnessed to their admiration for science as the only route to knowledge and understanding. They failed to note Wittgenstein's profound antipathy to the thought that the only understanding of what is problematic is scientific understanding.

Schlick made contact with Wittgenstein, and although Wittgenstein refused to take part in the weekly meetings of the Circle, he agreed to meet a select few of its members for regular philosophical discussions. The *Tractatus* and the discussions with Wittgenstein, relayed to the Circle by Schlick and Waismann, were formative influences upon the development of logical positivism in the interwar years. The famous Principle of Verifiability came directly from conversations with Wittgenstein. It is noteworthy that much contemporary analytic philosophy, especially in philosophy of language, traces its ancestry back to logical positivism *as modified by members of the Circle themselves*, especially Carnap and Quine. To that extent, contemporary endeavours in the construction of a theory of meaning for a natural language flow from the springs of the *Tractatus* – springs which Wittgenstein came to see as irremediably tainted.

Wittgenstein's interest in philosophy revived, and in early 1929 he returned to Cambridge to see whether he still had something left to say. Fortunately, the experience proved fruitful. First as a research student again, then as research fellow, and from 1939 to 1947 as professor, Wittgenstein spent the whole of his teaching career in Cambridge. Although his surviving notebooks from this period reveal that to start with he was concerned to elaborate in greater detail some of the lines of thought which he had sketched in the *Tractatus*, it is evident that he rapidly became convinced that substantial rethinking was necessary. Over the next three years, as he dismantled most of the central supporting pillars of his first philosophy, his thought underwent a complete revolution. What gradually emerged was a wholly new philosophical picture of the nature of thought, language and logic, of the nature of the mind and of mathematics, and a new methodology. These he attempted to convey to his students in the legendary classes which he held each term in Cambridge. Many of the students who attended these classes were to become leading philosophers of the next generation. Though he published nothing, his influence spread far and wide through his pupils and through the circulation of his occasional dictations. In particular, the philosophical movement known as 'Ordinary language philosophy', whose home was Oxford, was much influenced by the reverberations which spread from Cambridge.

Throughout the 1930s, Wittgenstein struggled to find an adequate formulation and form of presentation of his new ideas. Though he wrote a vast amount, leaving behind him a *Nachlass* of some 20,000 pages, he had great difficulty in finding a satisfactory expression for his ideas. He made numerous attempts, throughout the 1930s and early 1940s, to weld his ideas into a form that would satisfy him. The best he could do was in some sense still incomplete when he died in Cambridge in 1951. Entitled *Philosophical Investigations*, it was published in 1953, and is the philosophical masterpiece of the twentieth century. Its impact profoundly affected philosophy for the next quarter of a century.

Wittgenstein is unique in the history of philosophy in having constructed two fundamentally different original philosophical outlooks, each of which is complete in itself, immensely powerful and highly influential, and the second of which undermines the first. Wittgenstein's later work ranges over five central philosophical domains: (1) language, (2) logic, (3) mathematics, (4) philosophical psychology, (5) the clarification of the nature of philosophy itself. In each of these Wittgenstein ploughed up the field of European philosophy. His vision was of stunning originality. He had an unparalleled ability to bring to light the most fundamental presuppositions of received philosophical reflection and to subject them to critical scrutiny, presuppositions that lie so deep that they are seldom even noticed, but rather taken for granted prior to philosophical argument. Consequently, such presuppositions inform both sides of traditional controversies, e.g. between Realists and Idealists in metaphysics, or between Mentalism and Behaviourism in philosophical psychology, or between Platonism and Formalism in the philosophy of mathematics. In effect they constitute the framework within which the debates were conducted. It is characteristic of Wittgenstein's later work that he did not directly address his predecessors. In his later writings one will find hardly any mention of previous philosophers. One reason for this is doubtless the realisation that attacking a deep philosophical theory at its outer bastions – the philosophical theses it presents to view – is futile. Any philosopher worth his salt can always beat a tactical retreat, and erect a further curtain wall. What Wittgenstein did was to search for the concealed presuppositions of received philosophical doctrines. By bringing them into view and challenging them, he endeavoured to transform the philosophical landscape. That is why one cannot locate his views within the traditional parameters of debate. He was neither an empiricist nor a rationalist; he eschewed both realism and idealism; he was not a Cartesian dualist or a behaviourist nor yet a physicalist; he was not a Platonist or logicist in mathematics nor yet a formalist or intuitionist. He did not mean to add yet another philosophical theory to the existing ones, but rather to break through the constraints of the received presuppositions, and to show how traditional philosophical theories go wrong before battle is even joined.

It is impossible, in the compass of a single chapter, to compare and contrast Wittgenstein's early and later views, or even to sketch out his later contribution to the five main subjects upon which he worked. I shall confine myself to two of them, his later philosophy of language and his philosophy of mind, and try to indicate the direction of his thought. I shall then conclude with a few remarks upon his revolutionary conception of philosophy.

It is no coincidence that the *Investigations* opens with a quotation from St Augustine – and not from his philosophical writings but from the *Confessions*, in which Augustine spells out how he conceives of himself as having learnt to speak. In this autobiographical fragment, Wittgenstein found a natural picture of language, which, he thought, unselfconsciously exposed the presuppositions of much philosophical reflection about language, meaning and understanding. These are that words are names; they have a meaning in virtue of standing for things, and are correlated with the things they stand for by ostension. Words are combined to form sentences which represent how things are – describe states of affairs. So the essential functions of language are naming and describing, and it belongs to the essence of language to be linked to the reality which it describes by means of word–world connections.

These seemingly innocuous presuppositions underpin a multitude of divergent philosophical theories of language, although they are surrounded by a plethora of refinements and qualifications. While it may seem plausible to suppose that word-meaning is essentially a matter of correlating words with things, i.e. linking language with reality, there is ample room for different views on the mode of connection. According to some thinkers words are connected to the things they stand for by association, according to others by ostension and according to yet others by behavioural stimulus and response. One may qualify the claim that all words are names connected to objects in reality by a name-relation: one may distinguish between definables and indefinables, and hold that definables are analysable into their simple indefinable constituents, while indefinables connect the net of language to reality. And one may hold, as many philosophers have done, that definables must be analysable into necessary and sufficient conditions for their application, in the belief that the laws of logic will not apply to a language unless all expressions have a sharply determined meaning. The claim that the function of sentences is to describe leaves latitude for different philosophical views. So, for example, it is generally accepted that empirical sentences describe how things are in the empirical world, even though idealists hold that words stand for ideas in the mind while realists hold them to stand for independently existing objects. Among empirical sentences are first- and third-person psychological ones. These too are naturally thought of as descriptions of how things are – third-person psychological sentences describe the mental states of others, first-person ones describe how things are with the speaker (although, of course, the former describe mental states on the basis of outer behaviour, whereas the latter describe mental states from the inside, as it were, on the basis of introspection). It is equally natural to suppose that mathematical sentences are descriptions. Geometrical sentences describe the properties of ideal geometrical figures, and arithmetical ones describe how things are in the abstract domain of numbers and their relations. A sentence is composed of words, which have meanings, and it has seemed plausible to many to suppose that the meaning of a sentence is composed of, or a function of, the meanings of its parts. The combination of words into a sentence describes a state of affairs. The sentence (or the proposition which it expresses) is true if it corresponds with the facts.

Wittgenstein's genius lay in disregarding the disagreements

between opposing factions and focusing upon the agreed presuppositions. He criticised the idea that for a word to have a meaning is for it to stand for something. One can vacuously say that every word stands for something, e.g. that the proper name 'N.N.' stands for N.N., that the common noun 'man' stands for a man or for the concept Man (as Frege would have it), that the adjective 'red' stands for the property of being red, that the conjunction 'and' stands for a binary logical relation, and so on. But this says no more than that we can vacuously squeeze every word of the language into the straitjacket of 'the word "W" stands for W'. But nothing is achieved thereby save for an empty form of representation. If we wish to understand the roles which different words, different parts of speech, have in a language, we must scrutinise their uses, examine how words that can occupy similar positions in a sentence nevertheless fulfil very different roles, admit of altogether distinct forms of grammatical transformation and combinatorial possibilities, and are explained in different ways.

Correspondingly, it is futile to conceive of all words as names, or, with greater sophistication, to suggest that all *fully analysed* expressions consist of names in combination. And it is misguided to think that there is any such thing as *the* name-relation which connects a word to an entity in reality. There are as many 'name-relations' as there are different ways of explaining the meanings of words, and such explanations are poorly conceived of as establishing *a relation*, let alone a relation between word and world. For even in the favoured case of explaining the use of a word by ostensive definition, as when we explain that the word 'red' means this ↗ colour (pointing at a sample of red), the red patch at which one points is not the meaning of the word. Rather the ostensive definition gives a rule for the use of the word, namely that anything which is this ↗ colour can be said to be red. The ostensive definition does not forge a 'connection between language and reality', but rather uses a patch of red as a paradigmatic sample which guides the application of the word in subsequent cases. The sample pointed at is part of the *means of representation*, and is best viewed as an instrument of the language and not as something represented. The very picture of language as a network, logically isomorphic with the essential structure of the world, and connected to reality by indefinables, is misconceived. What metaphysicians (including the author of the *Tractatus*) conceived of as the logical structure of the world, the unalterable essence of things, is no more than the shadow cast upon reality by the structure of language. The essence of things is determined by grammar – by the rules for the use of words.

It is, Wittgenstein argued, mistaken to suppose that so-called 'analysable' or 'definable' expressions must be sharply defined, as if the only acceptable form of explanation were an analytic definition giving necessary and sufficient conditions for the application of a word. Many words, in particular many philosophically problematic ones such as 'language', 'proposition', 'number', are vague. There are no necessary and sufficient conditions for their application, and they do not have a defining essence. What binds together the various cases that fall under such a concept is a multitude of partially overlapping similarities (like the fibres in a rope), rather than a set of common properties – a family resemblance rather than a common essence. And we explain what such a word means, for example the word 'game', not by a definition specifying a common essence, but by a series of examples together with a similarity rider.

Truth is not a relation between proposition and fact. Facts are not *in* the world (or anywhere else). To say that a proposition is true is not to say anything about the relation between a proposition and reality, but to emphasise or reaffirm the proposition. 'The proposition that p is true if and only if it is a fact that p' seems to assert a correspondence between words and world. In fact it is (in a loose sense) a tautology based on the equivalence of 'the proposition that p' and 'the proposition made true by the fact that p', both phrases being different ways of referring to one and the same proposition. Trivially, a proposition is true if things are as it says they are, i.e. it is true that p if and only if p.

Any attempt to clarify the nature of language must correlate three pivotal concepts – meaning, explanation of meaning, and understanding. A linguistic expression represents what it does because it has the meaning it has. The meaning of an expression is what is spelt out in explanations of what it means. So too, it is what we understand when we understand the expression. Understanding an expression (knowing what it means) is not a mental state or event of, for example, having a mental image of an object or state of affairs (as the empiricists supposed), or of 'grasping' a proposition, conceived as an abstract entity (as Frege supposed). Nor is it a mental process of deriving the meaning of a sentence from the known meanings of its constituents and their mode of combination, as if in speaking or understanding what is spoken, we were operating a calculus of meaning-rules (as contemporary theorists of language, e.g. Chomsky, have supposed). It is rather akin to an ability – the mastery of the techniques of using words. Whether and to what degree an ability is possessed and what its nature is, is to be seen in, and is determined by, its exercise. The understanding of a linguistic expression is manifest in three ways: first, how the person uses it; second, how he responds to its use by others; third, how he explains what it means, or what he means by it, when asked. What a person understands by an expression is what he explains in his explanations of its meaning.

Our explanation of the meanings of expressions are very diverse; we explain word-meanings by analytic definitions, ostensive definitions, exemplifications, by a series of examples, clausal paraphrases, etc. These explanations are not connections between word and world, as if the words of language are interconnected by a network of logico-syntactical relations and are then given content by being pinned onto entities in reality by a mechanism of correlation. Rather, they are rules for the use of words, standards for their correct application. We explain sentence-meaning by paraphrase or contrastive paraphrase, by analogy or example, etc. We explain interrogative sentences or imperative sentences quite differently from the way we explain declarative ones. Nothing but the strait-jacket of a dogma demands that we think even of every declarative sentence as a description of a state of affairs. It is common to recognise that there are many different kinds of proposition, e.g. ordinary empirical propositions, first- and other-person psychological ones, logical and mathematical propositions. Taking for granted that the fundamental role of the proposition is to describe, philosophers are prone to explain the differences in kind of proposition by reference to differences in the kinds of thing described, i.e. in the kinds of things named by the constituents of the proposition. But this is wrong. The differences noted are logical, and they are differences in the role or function of the proposition in question. This becomes evident when we examine first-person psychological propositions, which are typically *expressions* rather than descriptions, or the propositions of logic, which are empty tautologies that say nothing, or the propositions of mathematics, which are rules for the transformation of empirical propositions about quantities or magnitudes of things.

Our ordinarily accepted explanations of meaning are not defective or incomplete. They are not provisional standbys which we tolerate until linguistic scientists come up with the real article, delivered by a theory of meaning. The meaning of an expression does not transcend the explanations of its meaning which we give and recognise in our *practices of explanation* – otherwise it would be conceivable that we might use expressions correctly, but be unable to say what they mean or what we mean by them. An explanation of meaning provides a standard for the correct use of the expression. This normative role depends upon the use to which the explanation is put. We accept certain explanations as correct and reject others as faulty or incomplete. We appeal to explanations to criticise or justify a given use of an expression, and we consult explanations to guide us in the use of expressions. This normative role of explanation is pivotal to our practices of linguistic use. Explanations of meaning are not theoretical constructions, but rules. They specify under what conditions it is correct to use an expression. And an explanation is adequate if it fulfils its role of providing guidance in using the word as it is generally used – if learners, once given the explanation, can generally go on to apply the word correctly.

The interrelated concepts of meaning, explanation and understanding converge upon the notion of use. The meaning of an expression is not an entity of any kind, neither an idea in the mind nor an object in the empirical world, neither an abstract object of some kind nor the contribution an expression makes to the determination of the truth-conditions of any sentence in which it may occur. In so far as it can be said to be anything, it is the use of the expression – the way the expression is used in accord with the accepted rules for its application. While sentences are composed of words, which have meanings, a use, the meaning of a sentence is not composed of the meanings of its constituent words or of anything else.

Expressions with similar forms often have altogether different kinds of uses, fulfil different kinds of roles in speech. And if there is philosophical puzzlement about their meaning, as there is in the case of expressions like 'mind', 'body', 'number', 'proposition', 'time', etc., one should investigate their use – how they are applied, in what circumstances and against what background presuppositions. One should enquire what counts as an appropriate response to their use in an utterance, how one would explain what they mean, and how one would judge someone to have understood the explanation. It would be misleading to say that the meaning of an expression is its use, since the phrase 'the meaning of . . . ' is not used in exactly the same way as the phrase 'the use of . . . ', but one may well say that the meaning of an expression is determined by its use. And one should add that it is unintelligible to suppose that the meaning of an expression should transcend its use, or indeed the explanations of its meaning that constitute roles for its correct use.

I have given a mere thumbnail sketch. But I hope that it suffices to indicate that Wittgenstein's philosophy of language is at odds with mainstream twentieth-century reflection (much of which flows, wittingly or unwittingly, from the *Tractatus*). If he is right, then contemporary endeavours in the philosophy of language (the programme for the construction of a theory of meaning for a natural language) and in theoretical linguistics (especially those inspired by Chomsky) are misguided.

Wittgenstein's reflections in the philosophy of mind were no less radical than in the philosophy of language. He tried to break the hold of a philosophical picture of the mind, of self-knowledge and knowledge of the mental states of others which had held philosophers in thrall for centuries. It might be dubbed the 'Inner/Outer Picture of the Mind'. Like the conception of language and its relation to the reality it is used to describe, the roots of the Inner/Outer Picture lie in proto-philosophical reflection. From those roots a multitude of conflicting philosophical theories grow, but, again, it was characteristic of Wittgenstein not to attack those theories head on, but to dig down to, and to extirpate, their roots.

It is natural to suppose that, parallel to our perceptual access to the public world, each of us enjoys access to a private realm of our own minds. Our inner life consists of the thoughts, feelings, desires and intentions that we have. We readily conceive of these as properties of our mind. The realm of the mind seems to be populated with objects, events, states and processes, just like the outer realm of the physical world. Our access to it seems privileged – nobody else can have my pains, we are inclined to say, and nobody else can know what they feel like. I know what I am thinking, but others can only do so if I tell them. The denizens of the inner realm are inalienably their owner's, and he can know of them in a way in which no one else can. For he stands in a relationship to what goes on in his mind which is unique – they are *his experiences*, and he can observe them by introspection. This faculty seems extraordinary, for in certain cases all possibility of error is excluded. Can I be mistaken about whether I have a pain or not? Can I be wrong when I say that I am thinking – might I have mistaken thinking for wanting a drink? Is it intelligible to suppose that I might err in saying that I am expecting N.N. for tea – could I have confused expecting with remembering? If this is impossible, is it not because my access to the contents of my own mind is not merely privileged, but also remarkably reliable? Indeed, looked at thus, it seems as if the Inner is better known than the Outer, that the mind is better known than the physical world. For after all, our perceptual judgements are not thus immune to error.

If we are prone to think thus about ourselves, then we cannot but think of the inner life of others as essentially hidden from our view. What we know of it we have to glean not by observing their minds, which only they can do, but by observing their behaviour, and inferring what is going on in their minds from the evidence of what they do and say. But this outer evidence seems shaky, and it is tempting to think that our grounds for making judgements about the experiences of others are insufficient to justify a knowledge claim at all. For the behavioural evidence for the Inner is not inductive – we cannot correlate the pain-behaviour of others with their pains, and conclude that they always go together. We can never know about the inner life of another in the way we know about our own, and, it seems, we can never have the certainty about what is going on in the mind of another which we have in our own case.

From these roots grows a large variety of philosophical theories about the nature of the mind, of the relation between the mind and the body, of the character of self-knowledge and of knowledge of others. In all cases, the Inner/Outer picture is at work. Sometimes one element or another of it is repudiated, but other elements are retained. Yet, as Wittgenstein showed, this picture is flawed through and through – and needs to be rejected in its totality. It is a fallacy to suppose that behaviourism escapes from the errors of dualism, for it retains a distorted conception of behaviour. Physicalism, which identifies the mind with the brain, typically replaces classical dualism by brain/body dualism. It retains the same distorted structures characteristic of dualism, merely substituting grey matter for an ethereal substance and misguidedly attributing properties to the brain which it only makes sense to attribute to a human being as a whole.

Wittgenstein aimed to overturn the picture. In almost every respect it is misconceived, resting on misconstrued metaphors and misunderstood conceptual articulations. The conception of the Inner is altogether wrong. We do not *observe* our sensations, feelings, thoughts and desires – we have them. Introspection is not a faculty of inner sense. It is a form of reflective thought and recollection, whereby we come to realise, for example, the nature of our motives, the pattern of our feelings and inclinations. It is true that anyone can say what they feel or think, but not because they observe their pains, watch their emotions or see their own thoughts. There is no such thing as *perceiving* what is going on in one, and one's ability to say what one is feeling or thinking does not rest upon a form of inner observation. To say 'I have a pain' is not to describe anything, but *to give expression* to a sensation – it is best viewed as a learnt extension of the primitive behaviour of groaning in pain. Indeed, we teach children how to use the word 'pain' by teaching them to replace their crying and moaning with the utterances 'It hurts' or 'I have a pain'. To say 'I think such-and-such' is not a report on an inner state; to say 'I believe Father is in the garden' is not a piece of autobiography; and to say 'I remember cutting down the tree' is not a description of a current process, but if anything a description of a past one. These are typically *expressions* of thought, belief and memory. In general, these propositional verbs are learnt not for the purpose of reporting upon something known only to the speaker by observation of what is going on within his mind, but as refined qualifications, for various purposes, upon the utterance of the constituent propositions.

It is a confusion to suppose that the mental is a form of meta-physically private property. To have a pain is not to own anything, and what one has another can have too, if he is unfortunate enough to have the same malady. I may have thoughts which I don't share, i.e. which I keep to myself. But that does not mean that someone else cannot have exactly the same thoughts. My memories are tautologically the ones I have, but that does not mean that someone else may not remember exactly the same thing, if he too was witness to it. If the 'private ownership' of the mental is a confusion, no less so is the thought that knowledge of it is intrinsically private. Indeed, it is senseless to say 'I know I have a pain' if that is construed as a cognitive claim, akin to 'I know I have a penny' or 'I know he has a pain'. For it only makes sense to speak of knowing where *it makes sense* to speak of ignorance, of doubt, of learning that things are so, of wondering whether they are but being unsure, of things seeming to be so but not really being so. But this makes no sense over a large range of first-person present tense psychological verbs. It is nonsense to say 'I do not know whether I have a pain, let's find out', or 'Maybe I have a dreadful pain, but I'm not sure', as it is to say 'I wonder whether what I am doing now is thinking'. It is senseless to say 'Either I believe that *p* or I do not, but I don't know which'. There is a use for the form of words 'I'm not sure whether I believe that *p*', but it is an expression of indecision not of ignorance. And to become sure what I need is not further scrutiny within, as it were, but another look at the evidence for *p*. The truth of the matter is not that I *know* that I have a pain when I have one, or that I am *certain* that I intend going to London tomorrow, rather it makes no sense, in many of these cases, to talk of either knowledge or of ignorance, of either certainty or of doubt.

If the picture of the 'Inner', of the subjective, is sorely awry, the picture of the 'Outer' is even more askew. To say that we know of the states of of mind of others *only* from their behaviour, that their inner life is hidden, is misleading. First, it intimates that there is some better way of knowing, from which we are debarred, i.e. the way the subject knows. But that is mistaken – the subject does not know, though he isn't ignorant either. Secondly, it misrepresents what we call hiding something from view. It is true that people can sometimes conceal their thoughts and feelings, and that they can deceive and dissimulate. It does not follow that they can always do so – if someone falls into the flames and screams, it would be absurd to suggest that maybe he is dissimulating. Nor does it follow that when he is not concealing his thoughts or keeping his feelings to himself, that anything is hidden. I can conceal my thoughts by writing them down in code, and I can hide my feelings by keeping a poker face. But when I tell you what I think, when I chortle with glee or weep with grief, what is hidden from view? True, some people, sometimes, are an enigma to us, but others are like an open book. And it is not as if the

subject of experience always or even usually, in matters of importance, understands himself. Self-knowledge is a hard won prize, which
is not exemplified in saying that one has a pain, or that one thinks
such-and-such. Thirdly, it distorts the character of observable
behaviour, and of the complex relations between what we call 'inner'
and 'outer'. In so far as it is true that we observe the behaviour of
others, it is also true that we often observe their pain and joy. Human
behaviour does not consist of 'bare bodily movements' from which
the inner is inferred. On the contrary, we describe the behaviour *in*
the terminology of the Inner and could often not describe it otherwise.
For we can discriminate between a polite smile and a friendly one, a
cruel smile and an ironic one, although the differences between them
may be a millimetric change in the curvature of the lips – which we
could not describe. We describe a person's mien as proud or dejected,
his demeanour as friendly or cold, but couldn't for a moment say
what it is in his posture, described in terms of mere movement and
stance, that makes his demeanour thus. It is a dire confusion to
suppose that the 'inner' is hidden *behind* the behaviour that manifests
it – rather it *infuses* it. Can we not see sorrow and joy personified on
a person's face? Can we not hear the eager anticipation or excitement
in a person's voice? Is happiness or depression not exhibited to view
in a person's demeanour? The forms of behaviour that we call
'manifestations of the Inner' – pain behaviour, behaviour of joy and
sorrow, of anger or anxiety – are partly constitutive of these very
concepts.

Wittgenstein's contribution to philosophy of mind is second to
none, and is of profound significance for the sciences of mind and
brain. It is dramatically at odds with our intellectual tradition and
with current modes of reflection. Obsessed as we are with the
progress made in neuro-psychology and with our gadgets (computers) on which we now model our theoretical understanding of
ourselves, the current generation finds it more and more difficult to
grasp Wittgenstein's ideas. But if he is right – and his arguments have
great power – then much contemporary reflection in this domain is
lost in a desert in pursuit of an intellectual mirage.

Wittgenstein wrote more, and more deeply, about the nature of
philosophy than any philosopher save Kant. His conception is radical
and unprecedented. Contrary to the whole tradition of Western

philosophy, he denied that it is a cognitive discipline. The aim of philosophy is not to add to the sum of human knowledge. It is neither continuous with the sciences which investigate empirical truths, nor does it have a special domain of its own – that of metaphysical truths. The so-called truths of metaphysics are either nonsense or disguised rules for the use of words. There can be no theories in philosophy, for theory-construction and hypothetico-deductive explanation belong to the province of the sciences. There are no philosophical propositions and no philosophical knowledge. If there were these in philosophy, everyone would agree with them, for they would be mere grammatical truisms (e.g. that we know that another is in pain by his behaviour). Philosophical problems stem from entanglement in grammar. Their roots lie in our language. The task of philosophy is to disentangle conceptual confusion. Its methods are purely descriptive. It describes the use of words with a view to dissolving philosophical problems. By reminding us of the way we use expressions, it shows how philosophical puzzlement arises when the use of one expression is illegitimately projected onto another (as when we construe the use of the word 'mind' on the model of the use of the word 'body', the expressions 'pain' and 'I have a pain' on the model of 'pin' and 'I have a pin'); when demands are placed upon the explanation of one type of expression which are licit only for expressions of a different type (as when we wonder what remembering or thinking *consist in*, on the model of what being a triangle consists in); when the form of an expression deludes us into thinking that its role is akin to that of a wholly different type of expression with a similar form (as when we think that 'red is darker than pink' is a description like 'blackberries are darker than raspberries' – whereas the former is a rule for the use of its constituent expressions, not a description at all). There is nothing new to find out in philosophy – all the information needed to resolve philosophical problems is already available, lying open to view in the familiar uses of words. The resolution of philosophical problems does not involve new discoveries, but a rearrangement of the rules for the use of words which we all know – a rearrangement that will make perspicuous how the questions we ask are typically confused, or how we typically misconstrue them, and how received answers traverse the bounds of sense. Philosophy does not seek fresh information, but insight into old information. It aims not at constructing new theories about anything but at clarity about what is already known. Its goal is not knowledge but understanding. It is a cure for diseases of the intellect – for the hallucinations of metaphysics and the illusions of the pseudo-scientific theories we are prone to erect when we try to answer philosophical questions on the model of scientific ones. Its product is intellectual health and the capacity to avoid the intellectual infections that arise when we are plagued by the grammar of our language. This is, to be sure a picture of philosophy fallen from grace. It is no longer the queen of the sciences. But it is not their under-labourer either, let alone their conceptual scullery maid. Rather it is the tribunal of sense.

Wittgenstein's revolutionary ideas fit ill with the mainspring of late twentieth-century culture. Mesmerised by scientific method as the route to, and by science as the repository of, both knowledge *and understanding*, contemporary philosophy has turned away from Wittgenstein's insights. It has embraced what he would, I believe, have thought of as scientism, namely a pseudo-scientific mythology of language and its use, and a pseudo-scientific theory of mental-cum-neural processes. This is both sad and deplorable, for Wittgenstein's arguments – often directed against his own earlier philosophy from which much contemporary thinking on these matters stems – have not been refuted. Indeed, they have by and large not been understood by the philosophical avant-garde.

Over the past four centuries, science has replaced religion as a source and authority of truth. Yet every source of truth must, in the nature of things, be not only a source of falsehoods too, against which it must itself struggle, but also a source of mythology, against which it is typically powerless. One great and barely recognised such source in our age is science itself. The unmasking of scientific mythology, of scientism both within and without philosophy, is one of the great tasks of philosophy, precisely because it is the tribunal of sense. Its rewards lie not in furthering our knowledge, but rather in restraining us from nonsense and in giving us a proper understanding of what we know.

CHAPTER 12

'Brains in their fingertips': physics at the Cavendish Laboratory, 1880–1940

JEFFREY HUGHES

The Cavendish Laboratory is probably one of the most famous scientific institutions in the world. The home of Cambridge University's Department of Physics, it attained in the late nineteenth century, and has retained throughout the twentieth, an international reputation for excellence in physics teaching and research. It has produced some of the most consequential and innovative scientific work of the last hundred years – including the disclosures of the electron (1897), the proton (1920) and the neutron (1932), the isotopes of the light elements (1919), the artificial splitting of the atom (1932), the elucidation of the structure of DNA (deoxyribonucleic acid) (1953) and the discovery of pulsars (1967). Since the foundation of the awards in 1901, over twenty Cavendish and Cavendish-trained physicists have won the Nobel Prize for Physics or Chemistry, among them J. J. Thomson in 1906, Ernest Rutherford in 1908, W. L. Bragg in 1915, F. W. Aston in 1922, James Chadwick in 1935, E. V. Appleton in 1947, P. M. S. Blackett in 1948, Crick and Watson in 1962, Hewish and Ryle in 1974, and Peter Kapitza in 1978. Indeed, such is the Laboratory's fame and prestige that it has sometimes been described as a 'nursery of genius'.[1] The Cavendish Laboratory occupies a special place in both the history of physics and in the lore of Cambridge science.

What, though, are the reasons for that fame? There is clearly more to the work (and to the success) of the Cavendish Laboratory than intellectual genius alone, for physics is a discipline with both practical and conceptual dimensions. In the early years of the twentieth century, it was in the field of *experimental* physics that the Cavendish excelled, and in which it largely established its reputation and its pre-eminence. Through the craft skills of the researchers who worked there and the new scientific instruments they developed, deployed and disseminated, the Cavendish became widely known as a centre of practical expertise, as well as a leader in the development of scientific theory. As we shall see, it was for good reason that Cavendish researchers were jokingly reputed to have 'brains in their fingertips'! Only by looking at some of the experimental work carried out at the Cavendish in the late nineteenth and early twentieth centuries and its significance in historical context, therefore, can we begin to understand the factors underlying its place in the culture of Cambridge science, and the reasons why the Cavendish Laboratory and Cambridge physics have come to be so famous.

THE BEGINNINGS: ESTABLISHING THE CAVENDISH LABORATORY

In the late twentieth century, we are all familiar with the idea of scientific research. We are all used to the idea of universities having physics departments and, through the cultural visibility of the products of technical and scientific research, be they particle accelerators, nuclear weapons or well-known bits of science like the equation '$E = mc^2$', we all have some idea about the kinds of things that physicists do. In other words, all of us today take for granted the idea of physics and the social identity of the physicist. But imagine the scientific Cambridge of a hundred years ago, and things become much less self-evident. In the late nineteenth century, very few people knew what 'physicists' (then a relatively recent term) were or what they did. There were no state grants and there was no such thing as a publicly funded physics laboratory – indeed, the very idea of a physics laboratory was itself a new thing. This was the context in which the Cavendish Laboratory was established.

In mid to late nineteenth-century Cambridge, what we now recognise as physics found its home in the University's prestigious Mathematical Tripos, a course of training 'intended to select young men for high office in Britain and the British Empire'.[2] Teaching in the Mathematical Tripos was consistent with the moral principles of a 'liberal' education. Students were taught to reproduce mathematical proofs and theorems and to solve problems quickly and accurately, and there was no such thing as 'research', since most of the graduates of the Tripos were destined to become clergymen, lawyers, civil servants or school teachers. During the 1870s and 1880s, as Britain began to compete economically and intellectually with France and Germany, however, there was an increasing emphasis on research throughout the University. New professorships and lectureships were set up, and with them a new laboratory – the Cavendish Laboratory. Established in 1871, at a time when Cambridge University was being reformed by Parliament, the Cavendish Laboratory initially met with stiff resistance from those who sought to maintain the prestige and reputation of the Mathematical Tripos. Against the critics' objections that the University lacked the funds to undertake such a revolutionary scheme, the Chancellor of the University, William Cavendish, the Duke of Devonshire – a landowner and industrialist – put up the money for the project himself, on condition that the University agree to fund a new professorship in *experimental* physics. Construction work began soon after, and in 1874 the new laboratory, named in honour of Cavendish, opened its doors to members of the University.

Seeking a director for the new laboratory, the University tried to attract the engineer and industrialist William Thomson, later Lord Kelvin, whose Glasgow physical laboratory was widely regarded as a model of its kind. But Thomson declined to come to Cambridge, so the University approached the leading German laboratory manager, Hermann von Helmholtz. He, too, turned down the offer. Cambridge finally turned to James Clerk Maxwell. Maxwell had been through the Mathematical Tripos in the 1850s, and had then established himself as a leader among the few researchers in electromagnetism and heat theory. He was persuaded to accept the Professorship, and began to make arrangements for teaching and research in the new laboratory. As the First Cavendish Professor of Experimental Physics, Maxwell quickly established a research programme based on the determination of electrical units and standards, especially the unit of electrical resistance, the ohm. Because of the rapid and widespread development of telegraphy in the 1850s and 1860s, it became an issue of national importance to establish reliable electrical units and international standards. Against competition from Imperial Germany, Maxwell's Cavendish was in the business of producing such a standard.

When Maxwell died in 1879, he was succeeded by another Cambridge man, Lord Rayleigh, who continued and extended Maxwell's programme of research on electrical standards. Rayleigh, a landowner and agriculturalist, also set up a more comprehensive system of training in experimental physics, catering to the beginner rather than the advanced student, so that in the 1880s, the number of students attending lectures and demonstrations in the new 'physics' option of the Natural Science Tripos increased rapidly. And as the number of students trained in the intricate (and to them strange) techniques of exact measurement increased, so in turn did the number of researchers. New kinds of research began to be carried out, including work in optics, spectroscopy and gravitation. By the mid-1880s, the Cavendish Laboratory had already established itself through the electrical standards programme and through its comprehensive training regime as one of Europe's leading physical laboratories.

CAMBRIDGE PHYSICS AND PHYSICAL CHEMISTRY: THE J. J. THOMSON ERA

In 1884, after only five years as Cavendish Professor, Lord Rayleigh retired to his country estate at Terling in Essex. There was considerable debate over who should succeed him. Many senior members of the University were uncomfortable with the distinctly industrial atmosphere surrounding the new laboratory and its work on electrical standards and the factory-like training programme fostered by Maxwell and Rayleigh. Even so, it was to the surprise of many (and against several better-qualified candidates) that a 28-year-old recent graduate of the Mathematical Tripos with little apparent interest or ability in experimental work was chosen to succeed Rayleigh.

Despite his youth, Joseph John Thomson, known affectionately to generations of physicists as 'J.J.', had already made quite a reputation for himself in Cambridge as a skilled mathematical physicist. He had also been one of the small group of young men who used to go to the Cavendish to help Lord Rayleigh with his electrical standards measurements. During the first few years of his Professorship, Thomson made more improvements to the teaching system and oversaw a continued increase in the numbers of students passing through the Cavendish, and a further broadening of the kinds of research carried out there. In particular, the 1880s and 1890s saw the emergence of an entirely new way of thinking about matter which broke down the established boundaries between physics and chemistry. From studies of the way matter behaved under certain conditions, it became possible to think of it as consisting of positively and negatively charged particles called *ions*. Because they were electrically charged, these particles could be detected and measured by their behaviour in electric and magnetic fields. J.J. found useful resources in this 'ionist' doctrine (which formed the basis of the new discipline of physical chemistry), and much of his subsequent work was directed towards elucidating the connections between these 'ions' and the phenomena of electricity.

In the late 1880s, J.J. began to develop a new line of experimental research based on the discharge of electricity through a gas in a sealed tube. By passing a spark or an electric current through a gas at low pressure, it was possible to produce strange and fantastic shapes and colours in the evacuated glass tube (a technology familiar to us today in the more domesticated form of the neon lamp). The eerie, etherial glow of an electrified gas fascinated Victorian scientists like J.J. If the pressure of the gas in the tube was made very low, mysterious rays were found to emanate from the electrodes, and these, too, absorbed the attention of experimental physicists all over Europe. In common with researchers in France and Germany, J.J. began to investigate the peculiar rays emanated by the negatively charged electrode – the 'cathode rays' – in an attempt to characterise them. This exciting new research programme demanded new kinds of apparatus and new kinds of skills. It also redefined the character of Cavendish physics. Where researchers in Maxwell's Cavendish had needed the tools of engineering and the skills of precision measurement, delicate gas discharge tubes, high vacua and the creation of high electrical potentials became the new, state-of-the-art experimental technologies in Thomson's Cavendish. Glass-blowing became the main skill now required by researchers and lab assistants.

This new emphasis on the material technology of gas discharges yielded rich dividends later in the 1890s, when the sensational discovery of X-rays by the German experimentalist Wilhelm Conrad Röntgen suddenly brought the cathode ray tube to the very centre of modern experimental physics. Like Thomson, Röntgen had been carrying out experiments on gas discharges, and had noticed that the discharge tube produced a strange and very penetrating radiation – so strange that Röntgen designated it 'X' for 'unknown'. Researchers at the Cavendish immediately began attempts to replicate Röntgen's work, and it was out of one of the following series of experiments that Thomson was led in 1897 to propose the corpuscular and ionic character of the cathode rays. By deflecting the cathode rays in electric and magnetic fields of known strengths, it was possible to show that the rays were streams of negatively charged, sub-atomic particles or corpuscles of small mass – what would later come to be called *electrons*. It followed from this that there existed particles of matter smaller than atoms, and that the atom must therefore have some kind of structure. For the next forty years, up to the Second World War, much of the work of the Cavendish would be devoted to elucidating that structure.

WRITING THE CONSTITUTION OF MATTER: THE CAVENDISH
LABORATORY AND ATOMIC STRUCTURE

Thomson's discovery of the electron came at a time of remarkable, even revolutionary change in the physical and chemical sciences. The disclosure of X-rays in 1895, of radioactivity in 1896, and of Thomson's corpuscle of negative electricity in 1897 all shook the foundations of experimental physics to the core. These developments were followed only a few years later by the development of Max Planck's quantum theory of radiation with its challenge to the conceptual foundations of energy physics. These challenges to the cherished conventions and orthodoxies of science came at a time when laboratories all over Europe were beginning to become interested in these questions, and equipped to attack them. The Cavendish was among the first to take up the new developments, and quickly assumed a leading position in the field. But it was also in the 1890s that one of the most crucial changes responsible for the success of the Cavendish took place. Until 1895, only graduates of Cambridge University had been allowed to undertake work in the Cavendish Laboratory. But in that year, a change of University regulations allowed the admission of scholars – 'research students' – from elsewhere for the first time. The new regulations led to a rapid influx of talented young experimenters from Britain and from overseas, among them the Frenchman Paul Langevin and, famously, the New Zealander Ernest Rutherford.

Many of those who subsequently came to Cambridge to work with Thomson, now increasingly recognised as an authority on gas discharges and ionic physics, did so with the aid of Science Research Scholarships funded from the profits of the Great Exhibition of 1851. Such Scholarships were available to researchers from the countries of the British Empire, putting the Cavendish at the centre of an extensive Imperial network of physics laboratories. And many of those who came to work at the Cavendish returned in due course to their country of origin to take up teaching jobs, through which they would then send students of their own to Cambridge and the Cavendish. It was a perfect, self-reproducing, self-perpetuating system, which enormously increased both the influence of the Cavendish and the dissemination of the work done there.

But the new regulations of 1895 brought more than research students to the Cavendish They also brought a change of status relative to other kinds of physics. As Cavendish experimental physics flourished, the fortunes of the *other* Cambridge physics – the physics of the Mathematics Tripos – went into decline. The numbers of students plummeted as undergraduates flocked to the Cavendish and experimental physics. By the early years of the twentieth century, the once élite Mathematical Tripos was in a state of crisis. It was completely reformed in 1907, effectively leaving the Cavendish as the sole representative of Cambridge physics. Even by 1900, a distinctive Cambridge 'school' of physics was widely recognised. The Cavendish Laboratory had started to become the main centre of physics teaching and especially research certainly in the British Empire, and perhaps in the world.

The successes of the cosmopolitan 'Cambridge school of experimental physics' continued to be led by J.J.'s own research. After his success with cathode rays and the 'discovery of the electron', J.J. began to work on positive electricity in an attempt to discover whether that, too, could be accounted for by the existence of fundamental particles analogous to the electron but positively (rather than negatively) charged. Using the same gas discharge technology and combinations of electric and magnetic fields that he had used for the earlier experiments, Thomson tried to find these positive particles, but failed miserably, even after several years of trying. His efforts improved considerably after 1910 when he was joined by a new assistant. Francis Aston had studied physics and chemistry at Birmingham, and was a self-taught (but expert) glass-blower. He had done independent research on X-rays soon after Röntgen's discovery in the 1890s, and had become an accomplished experimenter, knowledgeable in vacuum technique and skilled in the manipulation of the delicate and temperamental discharge tubes. He took charge of J.J.'s experiments, and soon managed to produce the kinds of results that J.J. was looking for. Between them, Aston and J.J. were able to show that any gas in the discharge tube produced a characteristic photographic trace dependent on the chemical weight of its constituents – so that if an unknown gas were placed in the tube, it should be possible to identify it by finding its weight from its characteristic positive rays. This meant that the technique could be used as a method of chemical analysis, and therefore for the discovery of new elements – an intriguing possibility. As Aston put it:

> We need not be surprised to find . . . lines [in our photographs] corresponding to molecules found neither in the heavens above nor in the earth beneath; nor need those of us who are chemists hold up our heads in horror at such unnatural and grotesque monsters of the world of molecules as [may be found]. Rather we should look forward to this line of investigation as an extremely hopeful field in which to study the actual mechanism of dissociation, ionisation and chemical interaction.[3]

Excited by the prospects of the new technique, and encouraged by the exemplary discovery of the rare gas argon by William Ramsay and Lord Rayleigh in the 1890s, Aston and J.J. embarked upon a systematic analysis of all the gases available to them, hoping to make significant new discoveries. They were in luck. When they put the inert gas neon (a member of the argon family) into their machine, they found not the expected single photographic line corresponding to neon, but two lines – one corresponding to neon, the other to some previously unknown gas. They named the new gas *meta-neon*, and Aston began an investigation of its properties. Through 1913, he tried to separate the new substance from neon, but found it very difficult to separate the two gases, even by the use of long and complicated separation procedures.

Aston was about to embark upon a more comprehensive series of experiments aimed at separating the new gas when disaster struck. War broke out. The Cavendish was turned over to the military in 1914, and used for the production of radio valves and other devices. Many of the Cavendish researchers went away to war, either to serve in the army or to undertake research for the government. Aston, for example, spent the four years of the Great War testing materials for aircraft wings for the newly formed Royal Air Force – just as well, for his diffusion apparatus was shut down for the duration of the war owing to lack of space in the laboratory. By the time Aston returned to Cambridge in 1919, there had been great changes. J.J. had been elected Master of Trinity College, and had resigned as director of the Cavendish. The man appointed to succeed him was his most illustrious pupil: Ernest Rutherford.

EXPLORING THE NUCLEUS: RADIOACTIVITY AND RUTHERFORD'S CAVENDISH

A New Zealander by birth, Rutherford had been one of the very first research students to come to the Cavendish to work with J.J. under the new regulations of 1895. Not long after he arrived, the sensational discovery of X-rays was announced, and Rutherford joined J.J. in an investigation of the process by which X-rays cause a gas to become a conductor of electricity. After Becquerel's discovery of radioactivity in 1896, Rutherford switched topics, and began to work on the properties of uranium and other radioactive elements. In 1898, he was appointed to the Professorship of Physics at McGill University in Montreal, where he quickly established himself as one of the world's foremost authorities on the emerging new science of radioactivity. It was in Montreal that he and the chemist Frederick Soddy put forward the novel disintegration theory of radioactivity, in which an unstable radioactive element was seen as decaying gradually into a more stable one. Although this theory was greeted with contempt by many chemists, it provided a new way of looking at the evolution of the elements, and one closely related to the physicists' electrical theory of matter. In 1907, Rutherford returned to England to become Professor of Physics at the University of Manchester. At Manchester, he established a large and influential group of researchers in radioactivity, and made his laboratory one of the chief centres for radioactivity research in Europe. By 1919, his repute was such that he had become the obvious heir to Thomson.

Coming to Cambridge after the war, Rutherford brought with him a new programme of research and a change of direction for the Cavendish Laboratory. His work over the previous ten years had led him to propose the nuclear model of the atom, in which the bulk of an atom's mass is concentrated in a tiny, dense core, or *nucleus*. This nucleus would then be surrounded by the atom's complement of electrons, making the whole structure electrically neutral. During his years at Manchester, Rutherford had gradually accumulated evidence for this model. But the real proof (as he saw it) came just at the end of the war. Rutherford was doing some experiments in which the energetic particles emitted by radioactive substances were used as projectiles to bombard the atoms of a variety of light elements. During these investigations, Rutherford obtained what he considered to be evidence that he had split – or disintegrated – the nucleus of a nitrogen atom, releasing an atom of hydrogen (what he would soon call a *proton*). Not only was this decisive proof for the existence of the nucleus, it also showed that the nucleus was itself composed of still smaller particles. The new programme of research for the Cavendish Laboratory was to study the structure of the nucleus.

In order to carry out this programme, Rutherford needed to enrol the help of a large number of research students and other collaborators who could be assigned different parts of the investigation. He therefore inaugurated and routinised a system of training for new research students, based on a system he had developed at Manchester. All new researchers were required to spend a month or so following a course designed to teach them the rudiments of radioactivity technique. With other reformers, Rutherford also argued successfully for the introduction of the Ph.D. degree at Cambridge, so that many of those who would have gone to Germany to obtain their doctorate could now come to the Cavendish. As in Thomson's day, the Cavendish would continue to train most of the men who would become professors of physics in the Imperial and Commonwealth universities – a point Rutherford was keen to stress in 1919 in an attempt to raise money for the Laboratory in the precarious post-war economic climate:

While the Cavendish Laboratory had, from the beginning, been a focus of research in physics, the beginning of a definite research school dates from the year 1895 when the university opened its doors wide to advanced students from other Universities. This new step led to a rapid increase in the research students in the Cavendish Laboratory . . . The output of important work in physics grew rapidly and the laboratory was soon recognised as the chief centre for research activity in physics . . . It may safely be said that a large proportion of physicists now holding important scientific positions in the country and in our Dominions have at one time worked in the Cavendish Laboratory.[4]

As Rutherford recognised, its imperial role was a crucial element in the laboratory's success. And like his predecessor, Rutherford took advantage of grants, fellowships and the 1851 Scholarships to ensure that the Cavendish remained at the centre of the extensive network of Imperial physics laboratories. Rutherford's colleagues in Canada, Australia and elsewhere (some of whom had themselves been students at J.J.'s Cavendish, and some of whom had been students of Rutherford himself) sent the brightest and best of their students to Cambridge to work with the new professor in his investigations on the structure of the atom. Through its deliberate emphasis on visitation and return, and with its unique system of training and research, the Cavendish Laboratory was a powerful machine for social, geographical and professional mobility.

With a steady supply of skilled young experimenters and its regime of training in radioactivity, Rutherford's Cavendish embarked upon an investigation of the innermost constitution of matter – the structure of the nucleus. Using a variety of techniques, Rutherford and his collaborators began to determine which of the elements could be disintegrated, and thereby to deduce something of their innermost structure. At first, they used a technique known as scintillation counting, in which tiny flashes of light (scintillations) had to be counted through a microscope in a darkened room. This technique was very difficult to duplicate elsewhere, though, as shown in the mid-1920s when the Cavendish became involved in a bitter controversy with a laboratory in Vienna concerning the results of such experiments. The difficult, time-consuming and tiring scintillation method was eventually replaced by another method of counting atomic particles: the Geiger counter.

In the nuclear age, we all somehow know that the clicking Geiger counter is a direct and transparent indicator of radioactivity – and therefore of danger. The Geiger–Müller counter is one of the most familiar and black-boxed instruments in modern radiation science. Sixty years ago in the Cavendish Laboratory, though, the Geiger counter was a new, untested and often unreliable instrument. It depended upon the operation of the radio valves just becoming available from the booming radio industry of the 1920s. Just as it could detect a wireless signal and turn it into broadcast sound, a valve (or vacuum tube) could also detect the passage of a charged particle of the kind found in Cavendish experiments, and turn it into a click, which could then be counted through headphones. The new technology allowed experimenters to perform new kinds of experiments. Using a valve amplifier, for example, Rutherford's deputy James Chadwick carried out a series of experiments in 1932 which led him to the discovery of the *neutron*, the third elementary particle to be discovered and one of the most significant achievements of Rutherford's Cavendish.

As the example of the Geiger counter illustrates, instrumentation played a crucially important part in the work and success of the Laboratory, for it was only through instruments that new phenomena like the neutron could be elicited and made accessible to experiment. Rutherford's Cavendish, no less than Rayleigh's or Thomson's, took pride in the development of new instruments and techniques, many of which opened up completely new possibilities for the investigation of the structure of matter. Continuing his work on neon and meta-neon, for example, Aston devised a machine using the old gas discharge bulb and a new arrangement of electric and magnetic fields, with which he was able to show that 'meta-neon' was in fact an *isotope* of neon. The new device, which he called a mass-spectrograph, also showed that most of the other chemical elements consisted of two or more isotopes. Aston's discovery, for which he won the Nobel Chemistry Prize in 1922 (that year's Physics Prize being won by Niels Bohr), was crucial to the success of Rutherford's own research programme. And the mass-spectrograph continued to churn out data on the isotopes of the elements throughout the 1920s and well into the 1930s. Aston's first machine was superseded by a larger, more powerful device in 1927, and by a third, still more powerful machine ten years later. Later on, as the mass-spectrometer, the instrument became extremely important in the oil industry, where it could be used to analyse the content of oils and gases. Today, the mass-spectrometer is a tool found in every chemical laboratory.

Aston's mass-spectrograph was by no means the only technical development central to the work of the Cavendish in the 1920s. Another was the cloud chamber, which had originally been invented at the Cavendish by C. T. R. Wilson in the 1890s in an attempt to understand atmospheric phenomena by making artificial clouds in the laboratory – hence 'cloud' chamber. As with the mass-spectrograph, however, the cloud chamber was an instrument developed in one context which quickly found its main application in another. In 1910, Wilson had put a small piece of radium inside the chamber, and had produced a series of impressive photographs clearly showing the radiations emitted by the radioactive matter as thin particle tracks. In the 1920s, this property of the cloud chamber was used to look for evidence of atomic disintegration, and pictures of atomic trails featured prominently in scientific books and journals. Because of its utility, the device was manufactured and sold by the Cambridge Scientific Instrument Company, which had been associated with the Cavendish since Rayleigh's day. Dozens of cloud chambers were sold to universities, colleges and schools. In the 1920s and 1930s, the cloud chamber became a key tool in nuclear research. According to Sir Arthur Eddington (author of the best-selling book *The Expanding Universe*), for example, the cloud chamber had 'become to the atomic physicist what the telescope is to the astronomer' – praise indeed!

FROM RADIOACTIVITY TO NUCLEAR PHYSICS: THE CAVENDISH LABORATORY IN THE 1930S

Instruments like the cloud chamber and the mass-spectrograph belonged to the tradition of bench-top experimentation familiar since Maxwell's times. But the 1920s and 1930s saw the emergence of entirely new kinds of experiment on a scale hitherto unknown, including the development of huge machines to make very intense magnetic fields and very high voltages. Peter Kapitza, a Russian engineer, arrived in England as part of a trade delegation in 1921, and began work at the Cavendish Laboratory soon afterwards.

Rutherford first set Kapitza to work on problems connected with the cloud chamber. Before long, however, Kapitza had begun to apply his engineering expertise to some of the problems facing Rutherford and other Cambridge researchers. He devised a method for producing very intense magnetic fields, so that the behaviour of atomic particles could be studied under extreme conditions. Kapitza also founded a famous discussion group, the Kapitza Club, which met at regular intervals to discuss recent developments in physics. His intellectual influence on many younger members of the Cavendish was profound. During the 1920s, Kapitza continued to work on magnetic fields; he also began to devise methods of producing extremely low temperatures, again to study the behaviour of matter under extreme conditions. In 1933, a special new Royal Society laboratory was opened for Kapitza, bringing to Cambridge and the Cavendish science on an unprecedented scale. One visitor joked that '[a]t Prof. Kapitza's laboratory, you [have] to ring to be admitted by a "flunkey" and [are] confronted not with men working in their shirt sleeves, but with Prof. Kapitza seated at a table, like the arch criminal in a detective story, only having to press a button to do a gigantic experiment'.[5]

The same change of scale was evident in the experiments on atomic disintegration, where electrical engineering methods became important in the 1930s. A new kind of experiment developed, in which particles like protons and electrons were accelerated through high voltages at enormous speed, then smashed into target atoms in order to produce disintegration fragments, whose identity could then be determined. In 1932, Cockcroft and Walton succeeded in splitting an atom of lithium using this method – the first disintegration of the atom using artificially accelerated projectiles. During the 1930s, larger and larger accelerators were built in an attempt to produce smaller and smaller disintegration particles. Eddington, always a perceptive commentator, remarked that 'in a contest between the sun and the Cavendish Laboratory as to which could do the most violence to a single atom, I would back the Cavendish Laboratory'.[6] But the new machines had profound consequences for the idea of research and for the future of the laboratory. As particle accelerators became increasingly important in nuclear physics, the old style of Cavendish research began to disappear. Particle accelerators quickly became laboratories in their own right.

One no longer needed to be a glass-blower to be a good experimenter. The successful physicist now needed to be an electrical engineer, or an expert photographer, or even an administrator. Rutherford noted, evidently with a tinge of regret, that '[a]t Cambridge, a great hall contains massive and elaborate machines rising tier on tier', reminding him of 'a photograph in the film of H. G. Wells' "The Shape of Things to Come"'.[7] Ironically, these machines were exactly the shape of things to come, for particle accelerators like this were among the forerunners of the huge machines we use today to study the structure of matter. In large part, the sorts of experiments carried out in today's particle accelerators at CERN and elsewhere have their origins here, in the Cambridge of the 1930s.

Rutherford, who became Lord Rutherford of Nelson in 1931, was often accused of concentrating the Cavendish Laboratory on radioactivity and nuclear physics research to the exclusion of other important kinds of work. Such a charge is unfair, though, because Rutherford was keen to foster research in wireless and atmospheric physics under E. V. Appleton and J. A. Ratcliffe, and a group working on X-ray crystallography under J. D. Bernal. In the late 1920s, the Cavendish also housed a very important group of theoretical physicists, including R. H. Fowler and Paul Dirac. Through their frequent visits to Niels Bohr's Institute for Theoretical Physics in Copenhagen and their contact with influential theoreticians like Werner Heisenberg, Erwin Schrödinger and George Gamow, Fowler and Dirac were closely associated with the development of the new quantum or wave mechanics. This new way of thinking about matter and energy in terms of waves as well as particles opened up many new problems to scientific investigation, and initiated another profound change in the way physicists thought about matter. Theoretical physics became important once again in the work of the Cavendish, although practical skills remained paramount – according to Blackett, for example, the experimental physicist of the 1930s had to be 'enough of a theorist to know what experiments are worth doing and enough of a craftsman to be able to do them'.[8]

In October 1937, just as the Cavendish Laboratory was beginning to adapt fully to the new development in 'atom-smashing' with the construction of a new high-voltage laboratory and the installation of a cyclotron (a form of particle accelerator devised by E. O. Lawrence at Berkeley in the USA), Rutherford died after a short illness. The choice of his successor was not obvious, several of his most promising students having recently moved to professorial appointments of their own elsewhere. Eventually, W. L. Bragg, who had succeeded Rutherford at Manchester in 1919, was appointed as the fifth Cavendish Professor of Experimental Physics. Like his predecessors, he brought with him his own programme of research and his own ideas about the future direction to be taken by the laboratory. The dark clouds of war were once more looming over Europe, however, and within two years, Cavendish physicists would again find themselves working for the government – this time on the technical development of radar and the atomic bomb. Their work had consequences which have shaped our lives and our culture.

CONCLUSION

Between 1880 and 1940, the kind of research carried out at the Cavendish Laboratory, and the wider scientific context in which it played a part, both changed in important respects. From electrical standards to the innermost structure of matter, the experimental research of the Cavendish both reflected the wider scientific milieu and impacted on it in significant ways. In the process, the Laboratory itself was transformed. In 1880, the Cavendish housed a dozen or so researchers, enthusiasts who came to help with Rayleigh's programme to establish electrical standards. There were no grants, and no career structure for the would-be physicist. By 1940, research was an accepted part of a university's function. There were forty or more researchers in the Cavendish, state grants and other rewards for them, and a career ladder they could look forward to climbing. After the Second World War, during which they played prominent parts in the organisation of military scientific research, several of Rutherford's students, including Blackett, Chadwick and Cockcroft, achieved great distinction as physicists and as administrators and managers of British science – testament to the deep and enduring influence of the Cavendish, both within Cambridge and in the shaping of wider twentieth-century scientific culture.

NOTES

1 E. Larsen, *The Cavendish Laboratory. Nursery of Genius*, London: Edmund Ward 1962.

2 A. Warwick, 'The worlds of Cambridge physics', in *The Physics of Empire*, ed. R. Staley, Cambridge: Whipple Museum for the History of Science 1993.

3 F. W. Aston, 'Sir J. J. Thomson's new method of chemical analysis', *Science Progress* 7 (1912), 48–65, p. 65.

4 D. Wilson, *Rutherford. Simple Genius*. London: Hodder and Stoughton 1983.

5 The Cavendish Laboratory archives.

6 A. Eddington, *New Pathways in Science*, Cambridge: Cambridge University Press 1935, p. 144.

7 A. Wood, *The Cavendish Laboratory*, Cambridge: Cambridge University Press 1946, p. 48.

8 P. M. S. Blackett, 'The craft of experimental physics', in *University Studies: Cambridge 1933*, ed. H. Wright, London: Ivor Nicholson and Watson 1933, 67–96, p. 67.

CHAPTER 13

J. N. Figgis and the history of political thought in Cambridge

MARK GOLDIE

'What is justice?' asked Socrates in Plato's *Republic*. When Thrasymachus defined justice as a trick played by the strong upon the weak, Socrates embarked upon the demanding task of showing that he was mistaken. Over the centuries philosophers have continued to debate the fundamental questions of politics. What is the best form of government? Is obedience to the state grounded in consent, nature, tradition, utility, or God's will? Is there a right of resistance against tyrants? Is law the command of the ruler, or the custom of the community? Is private property legitimate? The books which offer compelling answers make up the canon of texts in the history of political thought. They include those of Plato and Aristotle in the ancient world, Augustine and Thomas Aquinas in the Christian middle ages, Machiavelli and Thomas More in the Renaissance, Thomas Hobbes and John Locke in revolutionary England, Rousseau and Adam Smith during the Enlightenment, and Hegel, Marx and John Stuart Mill in the nineteenth century.

The study of these philosophers is well established in universities across the world. Yet the subject often has an uneasy relationship with the disciplines within which it falls: history, politics and philosophy. The historian seeks to know when and why a book was written; the philosopher asks whether its arguments are coherent. Whilst it is possible to allow each question its proper sphere in the academic division of labour, it is arguably the case that the meaning of a text cannot properly be assessed independently of its historical context.

This chapter examines the relationship between history and political philosophy by showing how one doctrine fundamental to the modern state, the idea of sovereignty, can be explored in its historical setting. John Neville Figgis, an early and distinguished practitioner of the history of political thought, devoted his career to investigating the origins of the concept of sovereignty – and, as a political theorist, to deploring it as a malign influence in his own time. It was a preoccupation shaped by his association with the Cambridge History Faculty, which had, from its foundation, given a special place to the history of political thought in its curriculum and research programme.

Today the 'Cambridge School' is internationally recognised in the three disciplines I have mentioned as a distinctive and influential approach to the history of political thought. That approach is characterised by the insistence that philosophical ideas are best understood by placing them in the wider context of the discourse or mentality of their time. Rather than expounding the great texts in isolation, the aim is to survey the prevailing ideologies and conventional languages of public debate. It follows that a wider range of texts, beyond the canonical classics, must be investigated. The programme of the present Cambridge School dates from the 1960s, but the study of the history of political thought in Cambridge is exactly one century old, and is rooted in the unusual nature of the Historical Tripos created in the late nineteenth century.

There are few Victorian books which can still safely be placed on student reading lists. One of them is Figgis's *The Divine Right of Kings*. The brilliant product of a young man who had graduated just three years previously, it was written as a prize essay in 1892 and published in 1896. Its limpid, epigrammatic style makes it eminently readable. Its sweep across the centuries and openness to the disciplines of law, social science and philosophy broaden the historian's horizons. As an exercise in exploring a climate of ideas, beyond the classic texts, and in reconstructing the political mentality of the past, Figgis's book is itself a classic. It was the first significant product of the distinctive character lent to the early Historical Tripos by John Seeley and Henry Sidgwick, for they entrenched the study of political science, historically conceived, as a permanent feature of the course.

Figgis's name is not well known today. Yet early in the century his influence was considerable, not only in historical scholarship, but also in public debate in Britain, for he became a theorist and moralist in his own right. By the time he died, in 1919, aged 52, he had been awarded an honorary degree by Glasgow University and an honorary fellowship by his Cambridge College. The son of an evangelical minister, he became a student at St Catharine's College and achieved first class honours in history in 1889. A man of powerful intelligence who acquired a remarkable erudition at an early age, his brilliance as a teacher and conversationalist, and later as a mordant preacher of jeremiads won him a devoted following.

There were two phases in his career. During the 1890s he was an energetic tutor, single-handedly putting the fledgeling Historical Tripos on a sound footing in his college, whilst researching and writing the books and essays which are still valuable today. Then, in 1902, having been ordained a minister in the Church of England, he became rector of a parish, and, in 1907, joined an Anglican monastery, the Community of the Resurrection at Mirfield in Yorkshire. There he remained, though frequently emerging to lecture and preach. When he was crossing the Atlantic in 1918 on his third visit to the United States his ship was torpedoed; he never recovered from the trauma.

Figgis combined a radical outlook in politics with an Anglo-Catholic conservatism in religion. His later writing consisted mainly of sermons and theology. His was a career partly in the traditional mould of the college tutor turned parish clergyman, and partly in the new pattern, forged after the transformation of Cambridge in the 1860s, which saw the emergence of the modern professional researcher and teacher. Some historians, in particular the non-believers among them, have not forgiven Figgis for turning to the church, and it is true that his full potential as a historian was not fulfilled.

The Historical Tripos had achieved independent existence in 1873. Like most new disciplines it struggled to find respectability. Hitherto, classics and mathematics predominated, and Figgis himself graduated in mathematics before turning to history. History was open to the suspicion that it only told stories and demanded nothing more intellectually strenuous than a good memory. In 1868 a University committee judged that 'history could hardly be said to constitute a science'. The term 'science' was crucial, for this period saw the high tide of the aspiration to turn the human studies into inductive sciences on the model of the natural sciences.

It was Seeley's inaugural lecture as Regius Professor of History in 1870 which infused new purpose into the discipline. He conferred upon history the dignity of a science and announced its mission to provide a school of statesmanship for civil servants and imperial administrators. Students should understand the development of political institutions and the relationship between the state and society. What they needed was 'the suggestive treatment of large phenomena, rather than microscopic investigation of details'. For this reason, the Historical Tripos after 1873 is striking for its emphasis on politics. There were papers in political philosophy, jurisprudence, political economy, constitutional law and international law. This was an emphasis enhanced by Lord Acton, who succeeded Seeley in 1895, and laid his own foundations for the study of political ideas in Cambridge – in his ambition to write the history of freedom, his inclusion of the history of political thought in the multi-volume *Cambridge Modern History*, and through his vast collection of rare books now housed in the University Library.

However, the emphasis on political science became a matter of controversy. Another breed of historian was emerging, influenced by the German historical schools – the inventors of the Ph.D. – and keen to train historians in the disciplines of archival research. The trumpet was sounded by Mandell Creighton in his inaugural lecture as Professor of Ecclesiastical History in 1885. History must be document-based and provide a systematic apprenticeship in critical methods. The existing Tripos was not properly historical, and its emphasis on political philosophy encouraged superficiality and undisciplined speculation. As one critic put it, political philosophy was 'useless and even harmful', for it 'encouraged a pernicious taste for vague disquisition'. A towering figure in the same cause was F. W. Maitland, the Professor of Law at Downing College. A barrister by origin and a professor in the German mould, Maitland insisted that the understanding of legal institutions was the key to historical study. The history of freedom was, he believed, grounded not in rights but in writs.

These two rival approaches made for dramatic quarrels over the reform of the Tripos. In 1885 a compromise was reached: a compulsory source-based special subject was introduced, but compulsory political science remained. It is easy to caricature the quarrel by way of stereotypes: the claims of a liberal education versus a training in research; the broad sweep of ideas versus the close analysis of documents; or, more crudely, Seeley's 'thought without facts' against Creighton's 'facts without thought'. Yet it is false to assume a sharp dichotomy. All the protagonists were anxious to ground theory in research and to put history on a scientific footing, thereby rescuing it from the romantic and the littérateur. Seeley produced a jingle intended to capture the proper balance between history and politics: 'history without political science has no fruit; political science without history has no root'.

Figgis was indebted to both schools. He often quoted from Sidgwick's *Elements of Politics*, and it was Seeley who suggested he wrote about the Divine Right of Kings. He revered Acton, the philosopher-historian (whose essays and lectures he edited for publication), but equally he praised Creighton, the bishop-historian, and Maitland, the lawyer-historian. His *Divine Right of Kings* learnt from them all.

The theory of the Divine Right of Kings is chiefly known today as an object of ridicule. Figgis set himself the formidable task of rendering explicable one of the most unsympathetic of political doctrines, and yet one which was ingrained in European attitudes between the Reformation and the Enlightenment. The historian's task, Figgis insisted, was not to act as judge and jury, but to understand the mind of those for whom a strange doctrine 'seemed natural, and to set it in relation to the conditions which produced it'. To the modern mind the Divine Right of Kings was absurd, but 'the modern standpoint is not the only one'. Figgis's target was Lord Macaulay's *History of England* (1848), a rousing tirade against the despotism of the Stuart monarchs, full of contempt for the sycophants and doctrinaires of the royal Court, and which sang the praises of the Glorious Revolution of 1688 for putting an end to Stuart absolutism.

The central thesis of Figgis's book is that the Divine Right of Kings was in fact the doctrine of sovereignty dressed up in theological language. It is true that writers in early-modern Europe constantly invoked scripture and pronounced that kingship was God-given. They exhorted absolute obedience as a duty laid down by St Paul's Epistle to the Romans: 'the powers that be are ordained of

God'. It is also true that English and French monarchs continued to exercise miraculous powers to cure disease by 'touching for the king's evil'.

Yet it is mistaken to see Divine Right as a mystical or magical idea of kingship. The theorists of the age were lawyers and theologians who hammered home one simple, hard-headed legal point. A state cannot exist without sovereignty. All laws must be the will of the sovereign, and sovereignty can safely lie only in the person of the king. Consequently, other ideas, those of Parliamentarians and Whigs, about the 'mixed and balanced constitution' and the independent rights of parliament, were muddle-headed recipes for anarchy. A divided sovereignty was a dangerous nonsense. Given the historical supremacy of English monarchs, it was indeed difficult for Parliamentarians in the Civil War of the 1640s, and Whigs a generation later, to grope their way towards a satisfactory theory to justify war and revolution against their king.

The idea of sovereignty did not disappear when Stuart absolutism was defeated. It remained a dominant doctrine of Figgis's own time, and ours – in the form of the sovereignty of parliament. In Victorian England the textbook version of the pure theory of sovereignty was provided by John Austin's *Province of Jurisprudence Determined* (1832). Every state, he argued, must have a single, unchallengeable source of law, and all law is the command of the sovereign. The mistake of the seventeenth-century Royalists was to fail to see that sovereignty could lie just as well with a parliament as with a king. After the Glorious Revolution the English had come to recognise that fact, and thus liberty was secured.

Figgis agreed with this view of English history, but did not like the upshot. What was wrong with the modern British state was that after 1688 parliament had inherited the absolute powers of Stuart monarchs. The Royalists had grasped the essence of the doctrine of sovereignty and had used it to defend kingship, but had thereby forged an ideological instrument which others inherited on behalf of parliaments and peoples. They learnt it from Jean Bodin, the absolutist of the French Wars of Religion; they flinched but fundamentally agreed when Hobbes's *Leviathan* put the doctrine in its starkest form; they applauded when Sir Robert Filmer's *Patriarcha* added a paternalist warmth to it; and they delivered it to posterity. What Hobbes and Filmer asserted on behalf of King Charles I,

Austin echoed on behalf of the modern parliament. And, more dramatically, the same idea was reworked by Rousseau in eighteenth-century France, in creating the doctrine of the sovereignty of the people.

The idea of sovereignty therefore dated from at least Reformation times, but could it be traced earlier? Figgis, following Maitland, judged that the concept of sovereignty as an attribute of territorial states could not be found in medieval thought. In medieval society custom rather than legislation was the governing principle, and a multiplicity of overlapping jurisdictions – of local lords and manors, and especially of the church – existed alongside that of the monarch. How, then, had the idea of sovereignty emerged?

The answer lay, Figgis argued, in the history of religion, and specifically the history of Catholicism. He showed that the Divine Right of Kings was invented not to combat Parliamentarians and Whigs, but to refute the claims of Rome. Only the divinity of kingship could match papal pretensions to divine authority. The papacy, in its most ambitious period, had claimed to be *dominus mundi*, lord of the world, a temporal as well as spiritual emperor over all earthly kingdoms. The pope's defenders in turn derived their idea of papal *imperium* from Roman Law, the system of the Roman Empire. The Roman imperial claim that the emperor was *legibus solutus*, the sole lawgiver, had been taken over by the popes. So, Figgis concluded, the idea of sovereignty did after all exist in the middle ages, but in the hands of the church.

In order to defy the exorbitant claims of the church it was necessary for the defenders of city-states and nation-states to offer a formidable alternative, the idea of the *imperium* or sovereignty of earthly, territorial rulers. Figgis sketched the arguments of the early defenders of this stance: Dante, Marsilius of Padua, William of Ockham and John Wycliffe. He showed that the political essence of the English Reformation lay in Henry VIII's Acts of Appeals of 1533, which declared that 'this realm of England is an empire', wherein the pope had no jurisdiction. The ideal of the Godly Prince as both spiritual and temporal leader was soon fashioned for Protestant monarchies. Thus, Figgis believed, the Divine Right of Kings had its '*raison d'être* as a contradiction and a counter-theory to that of papal supremacy'. It was the 'indispensable handmaid of national Reformation', for 'the omnicompetence of the state' had to be asserted against Rome. Only later was the doctrine mobilised against internal opposition to the crown.

Figgis had identified a long tradition of theorising about *imperium*, within which the Divine Right of Kings was but one phase. Divine Right was a doctrine appropriate for its time, for it allowed the state to assert its right of existence against Catholic theocracy. But, as we shall see, Figgis believed that it left an evil legacy. He came to identify Romanism, the imperial idea of law as sovereign command, as Europe's inner demon. It had descended from the law codes of the Emperor Justinian, to the canon lawyers of the medieval papacy, to the absolutism of Renaissance monarchies, and finally, after 1688 in England and 1789 in France, to those who proclaimed the unimpeachable majesty of parliaments and peoples.

After *The Divine Right of Kings* Figgis turned his attention to a rival theme in European thought. His other major historical work was *Political Thought from Gerson to Grotius, 1414–1625* (1907). Here he explored the idea of constitutionalism, grounded in the autonomous rights of human communities to self-government. The book opens with the decree against papal monarchy issued in 1415 by the church council meeting at Constance. It was a challenge provoked by the need to settle the schism in the church which had produced two, and finally three, rival popes. To depose a pope was an awesome thing. It was the French theologian Jean Gerson who provided the justification by arguing that the church's representative body, congregated in the council, was superior to the pope. The church was a self-governing corporation and not merely the servant of the papacy.

Conciliarism does not ordinarily figure in histories of political thought, but Figgis saw it as pivotal. He claimed that early modern secular constitutionalism, such as the Parliamentarianism of seventeenth-century England, took its root in conciliar theory. The council's challenge against the pope was a model for parliament's against the king. For this reason the decree of Constance was 'probably the most revolutionary official document in the history of the world . . . the watershed between the medieval and the modern world'. Conciliarism had, however, been only temporarily successful, since it had been defeated by a triumphant papal monarchy in the fifteenth century. This, thought Figgis, was a disaster, for it made necessary a Protestant revolt in a form which involved the assertion of the absolute rights of the secular state. The spectre of absolutism, now national rather than papal, would have to be laid again, and that was the task, most signally, of the seventeenth-century revolution in England. It was possible, therefore, to trace 'a road from Constance to 1688', and to see in John Locke's vindication of the English revolution an inheritance from Gerson. Figgis thus insisted on the importance of religious debate as a backdrop to secular political thought, and on the need to see the connections between medieval and modern political theories. 'Our politics', he wrote, 'are largely due to ecclesiastical differences we are apt to despise, or to theological animosities which we ignore.'

Figgis's perspective had a significant impact upon his selection of texts for discussion. He drew attention to writings outside the acknowledged classics. He dwelt, for example, on Philippe Mornay's *Vindiciae Contra Tyrannos* (1579), a plea for defensive arms by a French Protestant against Catholic persecutors, which laid a groundwork for Locke's inheritance of the 'Calvinist theory of revolution'. He showed the unexpected debts owed by Protestant natural law theorists to Catholics, particularly to the Spanish Jesuit Francisco Suárez. He touched on the neglected theorists of the Dutch Revolt and on the Scottish 'monarchomachi' or 'king-killers'. This broadening of the terms of reference of the history of political thought, by including wider streams of ideology, is the central achievement of his book, and set the agenda for future scholarship.

In later work, Figgis became less of a historian and more self-consciously a theorist for his own time, though his ideas grew naturally out of his historical work. In castigating the 'idol' of sovereignty he proposed in its stead the political theory of pluralism. Here his most influential book was *Churches in the Modern State* (1913), a tract profoundly hostile to the monolithic modern state. Figgis feared that parliamentary sovereignty was producing a new leviathan. He wrote at a time when many intellectuals became alarmed at the new turn in favour of state action designed to curb the excesses of free market capitalism, an advocacy for the state which emerged from the 1880s both in the New Liberalism and among Fabian socialists. As early as 1905 A. V. Dicey's *Law and Public Opinion in England*, which Figgis cited, identified British history after 1865 as a period of 'collectivism'. Liberty would fall victim to paternalist state autocracy and socialist utilitarianism. Fear of the new leviathan was not confined to the conservative Right, for on the Left there grew up a movement called 'guild socialism', which sought a more pluralist and less state-centred vision of socialist fellowship. Figgis was close to the latter, and indeed once called himself a syndicalist. His pluralist doctrine had two complementary aspects: a critique of sovereignty, and a theory about the autonomous sphere of human associations.

As we have seen, the idea of sovereignty supposes that in every state there must be a single source of unimpeachable law. Law is here construed as a command, so that it is meaningless to speak of law as a custom, norm, or axiom, unless it is anchored in the positive utterance of whoever has authority in the state. Thus, on the one hand, one cannot satisfactorily speak of 'international law', except as an expression of pious hopes, for there is no international sovereign with power to command and to enforce obedience. And, on the other hand, it is unhelpful to speak of the common or customary law of communities within the state, except in so far as such self-governing groups are licensed by the state. Consequently, it is difficult for communities within the state, such as trade unions, city corporations, or churches, to have any meaningful autonomy as independent bodies. In totalitarian states scarcely any such associations exist except under the control of the state: what is called 'civil society' is absorbed into the organs of state and so dissolved. In democracies the state bows towards the plurality of civic life, but even here the notion of 'concession' prevails: the life of a sub-community is often not recognised as inherent to it, but made to depend upon the state's permission. Thus the 'mandate' of a democratic vote may produce state power as arbitrary as in other systems, and in Britain a cry against 'elective despotism' is often heard. In short, the doctrine of sovereignty is unfriendly to communities and associations both within and beyond the state.

The great theorists of sovereignty wrote as if the only relevant political actors were the state and the individual. Figgis referred to the famous frontispiece of Hobbes's *Leviathan* (1651), with its image of numerous subjects making up the body of the sovereign. Historically, those who evolved the theory of sovereignty were actively hostile to associations which rivalled the state, particularly the churches, which they saw as threatening social peace through godly militancy. Stability was impossible unless competing authorities bowed to the state. In Figgis's view, whatever the historical necessity of the idea of sovereignty in disciplining barons and churches, it had resulted in an intellectual juggernaut which threatened to create autocracy in the modern world. Two contemporary issues specifically preoccupied Figgis: the rights of trade unions, seriously threatened by the judges in the Taff Vale case of 1906, and the rights of churches, at a time of increasing secularism, as signified by liberalised divorce laws, agnostic politicians in government, and conflicts over the autonomy and funding of church schools.

In place of the new leviathan, Figgis and other pluralists argued that the fundamental social fact was that individuals come to have their civic identity through the communities and associations of which they are members.

> [We are] trying to set down the actual features of civil society. What do we find as a fact? Not, surely, a sand-heap of individuals, all equal and undifferentiated, unrelated except to the state, but an ascending hierarchy of groups, family, school, town, county, union, church, etc. etc. All these groups (or many of them) live with a real life; they act towards one another with a unity of will and mind as though they were single persons; they all need to be allowed reasonable freedom . . . ; they are all means by which the individual comes to himself . . . In the real world, the isolated individual does not exist; he begins always as a member of something, and . . . his personality can develop only in society, and in some way or other he always embodies some social institution.

The pluralists argued that associations have an organic life and a collective will. Such groups do not exist merely as agencies of the state, for the public sphere is autonomous, having inherent rights of self-government. The 'real question of freedom in our day', Figgis wrote, was not the rights of individuals but 'the freedom of smaller unions to live within the whole'.

Figgis recast this position in juridical terms. Associations have a legal, corporate existence, and function as if they were persons: they have a legal personality. We know that a business or a college may sue and be sued. The question, however, was 'Are corporate societies to be conceived as real personalities or as fictitious ones?' By 'real personality' he meant that associations have a legal personality intrinsic to their very existence. Consequently, the state should, in its law-making, recognise those real personalities, rather than act as if it arbitrarily creates a series of legal fictions.

Figgis's doctrine of real personality was borrowed from the great German legal historian Otto Gierke, whose book *Das Deutsche Genossenschaftrecht* (1868) Maitland regarded as the greatest book he had ever read. Maitland gave currency to Gierke in England by publishing a translation of part of it. Figgis never tired of praising Gierke and Maitland for 'inculcating a more real view of the nature of the corporate life'. Often he borrowed Gierke's distinction between *Herrschaftsverband* – sovereignty, lordship, hegemony, *dominium* – and *Genossenschaft* – fellowship, community, association. Figgis believed that the idea of sovereignty was impoverishing and dangerous, for law and the state should come to terms with the autonomy of civil society, the federation of autonomous associations. Gierke, like the philosopher Hegel before him, continued a characteristically German tradition of pluralism, in a society where a multiplicity of particular jurisdictions, especially the ancient urban and artisanal guilds, continued far longer than elsewhere. Figgis enthused about 'merchant and craft guilds, with borough charters, guild liberties, the baronial honours, with courts Christian, courts royal, and courts manor, all functioning, with special laws and customs recognised for fairs and markets and universities'. He sometimes called it a 'federalist' vision of law and society.

This vision was carried over into Edwardian England, where we can trace in Figgis's generation a strain of nostalgic medievalism, a celebration of the small town guild with its ethic of mutual self-help, in contrast to the exploitation and anonymity of modern industrial society. Figgis wrote of the 'horror' or the 'economic and industrial oppression which is the distinctive gift of modern capitalism to history'. Yet he had too secure a grasp of modernity to be convicted of gothic sentimentalism, and he was too legally minded to veer towards a mystical and emotional approach to group personality, which led some towards fascism. Figgis did, however, inherit from Gierke a tendency to see a permanent struggle for the soul of Europe between Romanist and Germanist conceptions. On the eve of the Great War he put his faith in the German idea of freedom, in what he called the 'more vital Teutonic notions' – 'the federalism and independent life of the Teuton fellowship world'.

Figgis's legacy was twofold, in the public arena of political debate and the academic arena of the history of political thought. In both, his influence was at first short-lived, but has revived in recent years. In public discussion of contemporary politics his name regularly cropped up during the 1920s, when ideas of pluralism and federalism remained strong. He powerfully influenced the prominent publicist of the Left, Harold Laski, professor at the London School of Economics and chairman of the Labour Party, and he influenced the social teaching of Archbishop William Temple. But by the 1940s Figgis's name had faded. The national consensus had shifted towards faith in state action. The Depression, the Keynesian revolution, the popularity of Marxism, and the experience of the wartime command economy, brought a renewed trust in the wisdom of central planning and state welfarism. Symptomatic of this was Laski's abandonment of Figgisian pluralism in favour of a Marxist commitment to national-isation of the economy.

However, with the collapse of the post-war consensus in the 1970s there has been renewed interest in Figgis as a political theorist. In 1989 essays by Figgis and the early Laski were reprinted in a collection entitled *The Pluralist Theory of the State*, edited by Paul Hirst, a scholar hitherto in the Marxist tradition who now found himself pitting the Anglican clergyman Figgis against Margaret Thatcher. In Hirst's view, the pluralists have 'a vital and missing contribution' to make to current debates about democracy. In the face of Conservative legislation in the 1980s Figgis would 'turn in his grave'. Thus Hirst returned to the point, sixty years before, when Laski applauded Figgis before turning towards Marxism. For many, the intervening years increasingly look like a giant wrong turning by the Left, dominated by Marxian class analysis and faith in the state as the solution to the cruelties of capitalism. Figgis, by contrast, had encouraged a view of the state not as providing all the instruments and agents of social improvement, but as the handmaiden and enabler of all those fellowships, communities and associations which flourish within the state.

Thatcher's government brought home to liberals and socialists alike the vulnerability of British civil society under a system of parliamentary sovereignty, in circumstances where parliamentary supremacy was wielded more ruthlessly than hitherto – though, in the twentieth century, it is the Prime Minister, rather than parlia-ment, who is heir to the powers of Stuart monarchs. The inroads made upon the autonomy of trade unions, city governments, the professions and universities, were unprecedented. Simultaneously, the reaffirmation of market economics, the demise of communist command economies, and the limitations of the Welfare State, leave the Left increasingly doubtful about the old nostrums of national-isation and state paternalism, which, in Britain, had been no less dependent upon the dogma of winning unchallengeable power through parliamentary supremacy. To this tally, we may finally add the forces which are rapidly eroding the concept of British national sovereignty – the ceding of authority to the European Community, and the federalist demands of the Scots, Welsh and Irish.

In these circumstances, liberals and socialists are rediscovering traditions of pluralism which pre-dated the collectivist and centralist faith of the past half-century. The term 'civil society', for that federation of autonomous public associations which flourish inde-pendently of sovereign fiat – a term loosely inherited from the Hegelian tradition – has become fashionable. The revival of interest in Figgis is a small indicator of these broad changes in contemporary political sensibilities.

I return finally to the local context of the University. The type of history of political thought which Figgis sponsored soon ran into the sands. He himself became too preoccupied with theology and preaching to undertake serious scholarly work. And he died young. The fate of his historical project came to lie with the holders of the Chair of Political Science created in Cambridge in 1926. To endow a chair in such a subject at that time was audacious – a simultaneous proposal for a chair in sociology was rejected, and not until 1969 did Cambridge acquire one. In 1926 the new chair was allocated to the Faculty of History and not to Economics and Politics, still less to Social and Political Sciences since no such thing then existed. It thus continued the tradition of Seeley and Sidgwick in placing political science in intimate relation to history.

The first holder, Sir Ernest Barker, was an exceptionally productive historian of political thought. His inaugural lecture acknowledged a debt to Figgis, amid a recitation of the apostolic succession – Sidgwick, Seeley, Maitland, Acton:

> No influence has been more profound in this place than that of Acton;
> and I would commemorate among those who felt and propagated that
> influence the name of Neville Figgis, whom I was proud to call a

friend; who adorned with incisive wit and industrious scholarship all the themes of political theory which he touched; who loved and prophesied the cause of liberty, both political and religious . . . and who, if he had lived, would have been an occupant as proud as he would have been worthy of the chair to which, in his stead, I am called.

After Barker's retirement, however, the Figgisian tradition was not continued. For forty years the Chair was held by two men whose intellectual commitments lay elsewhere. Then, in 1978, Quentin Skinner was appointed. Since the 1960s he had pioneered a new approach to the methodology and practice of the history of ideas, work which culminated in the publication of his two-volume study, *The Foundations of Modern Political Thought* (1978). His colleagues and students, working in universities throughout the world, belong to that 'Cambridge School' to which I referred at the outset.

In 1980 Skinner's book was reviewed by a Renaissance scholar, Denys Hay. Hay was struck by the parallels with Figgis's *From Gerson to Grotius*, published seventy years before. He remembered being made to read Figgis at school, and it had made him

> very excited about political theory as a central field of historical enquiry . . . In some sense I have been living on Figgis ever since; my feeling even survived the cursory political thought paper in my Oxford course which rests only on Aristotle, Hobbes and Rousseau. I still think of Figgis's book as one of the finest ever written on political speculation.

There are, indeed, three distinctive ways in which the parallel between Figgis and Skinner may be drawn. First, both aimed to survey the broad main stream of early modern ideologies, rather than offer a series of hermetic analyses of a few classic texts. In so doing, a galaxy of lesser names among past controversialists came to acquire their due significance. The story was not only of Machiavelli and More, but also of Gerson, Marsilius, Mornay, Buchanan and Suárez. The alabaster busts of the 'great philosophers' were dislodged from their pedestals so that we may reach the bookshelves and see those philosophers' works standing, where they belong, alongside the tracts and treatises of their contemporaries. This aspiration to make better known a wider range of past political treatises currently finds expression in an ambitious publishing project, amounting to over one hundred editions – Cambridge Texts in the History of Political

Thought. As well as the traditional canon, the series includes Nicholas of Cusa, Gerson's fellow conciliarist, and J. B. Bossuet, the French absolutist about whom Figgis wrote a book which was lost when his ship was sunk. It also includes those whom Figgis did not think to rescue from obscurity, the female political writers, Christine de Pisan, Mary Astell and Mary Wollstonecraft.

The second shared ambition of Figgis and Skinner was to show that, whilst political thinking arises from practical needs and interests, it remains equally true that political action is always the embodiment of ideas. Drawing on contemporary philosophy, Skinner has, furthermore, argued that the writing of a text itself constitutes a 'speech act', so that the historian must grasp that 'words are deeds' and that 'the pen is a mighty sword'. Figgis was not given to methodological speculation, but he made essentially the same point: 'If ideas in politics more than elsewhere are the children of practical needs, none the less is it true, that the actual world is the result of men's thoughts. The existing arrangement of political forces is dependent at least as much upon ideas, as it is upon men's perceptions of their interests'.

The third parallel ambition of Figgis and Skinner was to offer a history of the concept of the state, as it emerged in the period of the Renaissance and Reformation. Figgis's guiding idea of sovereignty is restated in Skinner's definition (echoing Max Weber) of the modern state, as that which claims to be 'the sole source of law and legitimate force within its own territory, and the sole appropriate object of its citizens' allegiances'. For both historians a crucial purpose in writing their histories was to show that a doctrine that claims to be a universal truth turns out to be a contingent historical phenomenon. To show that the idea of the state, and specifically of sovereignty, became normative within a particular context and vocabulary is implicitly to question its general applicability. The practice of history, therefore, can help to exorcise the ruling doctrines of our time, and enable us to see that there are alternative possibilities in our political thinking.

CHAPTER 14

Molecular biology in Cambridge

M. F. PERUTZ

In 1936, I left my home town, Vienna, for Cambridge, to seek the Great Sage. He was an Irish Catholic converted to Communism, a mineralogist who had turned to X-ray crystallography: J. D. Bernal. I asked the Great Sage: 'How can I solve the secret of Life?' and he replied: 'The secret of life is in the structure of proteins, and there is only one way of solving it and that is X-ray crystallography.' So I became an X-ray crystallographer. We called him the Sage because he knew everything from history to physics. His conversation was the most fascinating of anyone I have ever come across. Actually, what had attracted me to Cambridge was not the Sage. It was the lectures of a young organic chemist in Vienna who told me of the work being done in the biochemistry laboratory headed by Gowland Hopkins, one of the founders of biochemistry.

Hopkins had shown that all chemical reactions in living cells are speeded up by enzymes. They are *catalysed*, chemists say. And he showed that all enzymes are proteins. The remarkable thing in the living cell is that chemical reactions go on at room temperature, in water, at near neutral pH. When chemists make these reactions happen, they need strong solvents or high pressures, or a vacuum, or strong acids and alkalis. In the living cell they take place without any of this, because there is a special protein that speeds up each particular reaction – and speeds it up by a fantastic amount. For instance, hydrogenperoxide is stable at room temperature, but there is an enzyme which decomposes it at the rate of half a million molecules per second. So, the great question was: how do these proteins work? We had no idea. Proteins were black boxes. All we knew about them was roughly their chemical composition.

Genes were also believed to be made of protein. There was another great man at Cambridge: J. B. S. Haldane, one of the most imaginative scientists of this century. He had shown that enzymes are controlled by genes, but he believed that genes – which, we already knew, lie in chromosomes – are also made of protein. This is why the Sage said that the secret of life lies in the structure of proteins. They were regarded as the most important molecules of the living cell, and very little was known about them.

We did know that proteins are made of polypeptide chains. They in turn are made of amino acids, and each amino acid is made of atoms of oxygen, carbon, nitrogen and hydrogen. Two of them also contain sulphur. It was known that there are approximately twenty different amino acids, but the exact number was not known until much later – not until Watson and Crick guessed it right in the mid-1950s. The important thing is that amino acids can be joined together – it is as if they contained press-studs with male and female parts. One amino acid can join another with the elimination of a molecule of water, leaving male and female press-studs free at either end. In this way many amino acids can join together to form long chains. Along those chains the different amino acids were thought to be arranged in some sort of order, but nobody had any idea what it was.

Emil Fischer, one of the great classic German chemists, first showed proteins to be made up of chains of amino acids, some longer and some shorter. Today, we know that there can be enormously long ones. For instance, it has just been discovered this year that the protein responsible for Huntington's Disease, a terrible neurological disease, has over 3,100 amino acids joined together in one long chain. There are other proteins, like insulin, with only twenty-one joined together in a chain. So proteins were known to be of different size. They were generally regarded as colloids, molecules of indefinite structure. People's idea was that the chains were just coiled up in some random fashion. But this seemed odd, because, if their structure was so random, how could each of the proteins catalyse (speed up) a specific chemical reaction? It was all very mysterious.

In the late 1920s, James B. Sumner in Canada succeeded in crystallising an enzyme – urease – and a little later, in the 1930s, John

H. Northrop, at the Rockefeller Institute for Medical Research in Princeton, crystallised the enzymes that are responsible for digestion. He crystallised pepsin, which is in the stomach, and trypsin and chymotrypsin, the enzymes which digest proteins in the intestine.

Crystallising these enzymes meant that they must be made of molecules which are all structurally identical. However, the idea was still looked at with great scepticism until, in 1934, two years before I arrived in Cambridge, Bernal did a crucial experiment with his research assistant, Dorothy Crowford. (She later married Thomas Hodgkin and became famous for discovering the structure of Vitamin B_{12}, for which she got the Nobel Prize. She is one of the great English scientists; but then she was just a very attractive young girl.) They placed a crystal of pepsin, which they got from a biochemist in Sweden, in a glass capillary, in front of an X-ray beam, with a photographic film behind it. What they got on the film was a pattern of spots. So what? That pattern had great significance. The crystals would give a sharp pattern of spots only if the molecules of pepsin had an exact, specific structure and if every molecule of pepsin in the crystal was the exact counterpart of every other. This experiment showed for the first time that an enzyme really has a specific structure such that every atom occupies a specific place, and is in the right place. *And* it meant that, in principle, X-ray analysis could solve that structure – it could find out how the atoms are arranged in a protein molecule.

I didn't know about this result when I started off from Vienna, but I heard about it in Cambridge and obviously I wanted to work on the structure of proteins. But when I got there, Bernal had no protein crystals. At first, I messed around with various projects and had no proper subject for my Ph.D.; but in the following autumn, in 1937, a Cambridge physiologist, Gilbert Adair, gave me some crystals of horse haemoglobin. Adair was another great Cambridge scientist, because he was the first to determine the molecular weight of a protein correctly. That was haemoglobin. Up to then, nobody even knew how big proteins were. Adair developed a method to determine the molecular weights of very large molecules by using osmotic pressure. From the osmotic pressure of a haemoglobin solution he was able to work out that its molecular weight was 67,000 times the weight of a hydrogen atom – that was a great advance. He also crystallised haemoglobin, and when he heard that I was interested, he gave me some of his crystals. I put them in front of an X-ray beam and got a beautifully sharp pattern of spots, proudly showed it to all my friends and said: 'Look what a marvellous X-ray diffraction pattern I got from my crystals!' Then they would ask me, 'But, what does it mean?' and I would be embarrassed and change the subject because I had no idea.

What is worse, at that time I had no idea of how to find out what the diffraction pattern meant, because in the 1930s X-ray crystallographers had not yet solved even the simple structure of ordinary sugar. The other graduate students in the lab thought it was absolutely crazy to try and solve the structure of a molecule with 10,000 atoms because X-ray crystallography had not yet advanced to the stage of solving the structure of a sugar molecule with only 55 atoms. But I was young and optimistic and I thought the great thing about difficult problems was to have a go at them. Then a terrible thing happened. Austria, my home country, was overrun by Hitler, overrun by the Nazis, and overnight I was turned from a guest to a refugee. (Imagine, if you have come here from abroad, if someone should come up to you and say, 'Your country has been conquered by a foreign power'; and because your grandparents had the wrong religion – my grandparents were Jewish – you could not go back there, because if you did you would be locked up in a concentration camp and might be killed. Imagine what you would feel when you heard this news.) I was shattered, but there were also some disastrous practical consequences for me, because up to then my father had supported my research here. (People nowadays always ask me, 'What sort of a fellowship did you have when you came to Cambridge? In those days, in the 1930s, there were no fellowships. If I hadn't had a fairly wealthy father I couldn't have come here.) My parents became refugees and my money ran out and I thought I would have to give up science and find some other job.

Luckily for me, W. L. Bragg had just become Cavendish Professor of Physics. As a young man, he had come here from Australia and had graduated in physics at Cambridge. In the summer of 1912, his father told him that a German – Max von Laue – had discovered that crystals produce X-ray diffraction patterns, but had not been able to discover their meaning. Young Bragg – he was 22 then – took an X-ray diffraction picture of a crystal of common salt and worked out how the atoms of sodium and chlorine are arranged. That was the first time that anybody had found out how atoms are arranged in crystals. After that, he worked out how the carbon atoms are arranged in a crystal of a diamond, and how the zinc and the sulphur atoms are arranged in a crystal of zincblende, and that was the beginning of X-ray crystallography. Some of this later work he did in collaboration with his father. He and his father got the Nobel Prize for Physics in 1915. Young Bragg got it at the age of 25, which is a record that has never been broken. He was the father of X-ray analysis, and I was lucky that he came to Cambridge as the head of the physics laboratory. When I went to him and showed him my X-ray diffraction pictures of haemoglobin, he was fascinated by the challenge of extending his method of X-ray analysis to the molecules of the living cell. He got a grant from the Rockefeller Foundation in New York which enabled me to carry on my work. This was marvellous for me, because Bragg was the most ingenious and most experienced of people in that subject, and I thought that, with his help, surely I would be able to solve the problem of protein structure.

In 1949, after various interruptions due to the war, I thought I really had solved the structure of haemoglobin. I thought it was a cylinder, and in the cylinder the protein chains were arranged in a simple zigzag, all in parallel. I thought I had solved the problem – but then my little team was enlarged, and Francis Crick came to join me as my graduate student, to help me with the work on haemoglobin. And the first thing he did was to show that this model, which I was so proud of, was completely wrong. (This can only happen in England. You could not imagine that in Japan or Germany a graduate student would tell his professor that his model is completely wrong. In England, graduate students are really independent, which is a good thing.)

I therefore had to start all over again; and for some years I was deadlocked. I tried all kinds of methods of solving the problem, but I got nowhere. In the meantime, the problem of protein structure was being attacked by another young man: Fred Sanger. He was a graduate student in the biochemistry department here, and he thought he would try and find out how the twenty or so different amino acids are arranged along a protein chain, and for this purpose he invented new methods of chemistry. (He still lives near Cambridge – a great chemical inventor.) Let me explain what the problem was, and how he tried to solve it. Sanger thought he would try the smallest protein he could find – insulin – and he invented a method of sticking a dye on to the amino acid at the end of the chain and then splitting it off, and identifying its nature. Having done that, he did the same again – he stuck a dye on to the end of the next amino acid, split it off and identified it. But he couldn't repeat this process right along a long chain, because chemical complications set in. He could only do it with short chains. However, he could split the insulin chains at random, into various fragments, by boiling the protein in acid: then he fished out the individual fragments, separated them by chromatography and applied his method step by step to each of them. When he had isolated a fragment, he could attach a dye to the first amino acid, split it off, then attach the dye to the next amino acid, split it off, and so on, and determine the sequence of amino acids along this fragment. Having done this, how did he know how all the different fragments should be put together? The splitting gave him a great many different fragments, partially overlapping, so that he was able to tell by the overlaps how they fitted together.

After doing this immensely laborious research – it sounds simple but he took years to do it – he was able to write down the complete sequence of the twenty-one amino acids along the first of insulin's two chains: insulin contains a second chain with thirty amino acids, and finally there are sulphur atoms that form bridges between the chains. After many years' work, Sanger was able to determine the complete chemical formula of insulin. That was the first time the chemical formula of any protein had been determined. It caused a sensation, because it proved for the first time that protein had a specific arrangement of amino acids along its chain. By determining the sequence of the different amino acids in the insulin molecules of different animals, Sanger was able to show that the sequence is genetically determined. It was a fantastic breakthrough and earned him the Nobel Prize for Chemistry in 1958. Sanger was a great inspiration to us, because before that, even if we had solved a protein structure by X-ray crystallography, we wouldn't have had the chemical knowledge to build an atomic model, but now we knew that in principle, at any rate, this was possible.

I was still struggling with the problem of interpreting my X-ray diffraction pictures of proteins when another young man arrived. One day in 1951, the door of my lab opened and a man with a crew-cut and bulging eyes popped his head in, without so much as a 'hello', and said, 'Can I come and work here?' I did some quick thinking and remembered that my colleague John Kendrew had had a letter from an American biologist, Salvador Luria, telling him that young Jim Watson wanted to come and join us in Cambridge, and this was he. In his famous best-seller, *The Double Helix*, Watson describes himself as a kind of western cowboy entering our genteel circle in Cambridge. In fact his arrival had an electrifying effect on us, because he told us that more important even than the structure of proteins was that of DNA, because genes are not made of protein, but of deoxyribonucleic acid, or DNA. That discovery had been made at the Rockefeller Institute for Medical Research in New York by Avery, Macleod and McCarty, and published in 1944. We knew about it, but somehow its tremendous importance hadn't sunk in. The great riddle was, if genes are made up of DNA, how is the genetic information laid down, how is it copied and transmitted from one generation to the next? Watson persuaded Crick to drop his work on haemoglobin and instead help him to determine the structure of DNA.

DNA consists of a chain of sugar molecules, five-membered rings made up of carbon, oxygen and hydrogen. Successive sugars are linked together by phosphate groups which form bridges between them. Just as the amino acids have different side-chains, so do nucleic acids. The side-chains are bases made up of rings of carbon and nitrogen and they are of four different kinds. We can think of them as single letters: T, G, C and A. They form the genetic alphabet – the code in which the genetic language is written.

Watson and Crick attacked the problem by trying to build an atomic model. They knew what the X-ray diffraction pictures of DNA looked like; Maurice Wilkins and Rosalind Franklin at King's College in London had taken X-ray diffraction photographs of fibres of DNA which gave some indication of the kind of geometry the DNA molecule has. By ingenious reasoning about the properties of long chain molecules and the nature of the X-ray diffraction pattern, Watson and Crick were able to guess the correct atomic model. One Monday morning they called me into their room, which was next to mine, to show it to me.

It looked like nothing on earth. They had fixed it to retort-stands reaching from floor to ceiling. They had represented the bases by aluminium plates, and the sugar rings and phosphates by rods of brass, all held together with retort clamps. Two nucleic acid chains were coiled around each other in a double helix, looking like a spiral staircase in which the phosphate–sugar chains form the banisters and the four different bases the steps. The sequence of bases in the two helices had to be complementary, so that A was always joined to T, and G to C. This was the model's most vital feature.

What did it mean? The marvellous thing about it was that it told us what the genetic information consists of and suggested a way in which that information might be replicated every time a cell divides, so that it is transmitted accurately from parent to daughter cell.

The model suggested that when a cell divides, the two chains of the double helix separate and each becomes a template for the growth of the complementary chain along it. In this way, one double helix with a specific complementary sequence of bases is replicated to form two daughter double helices, each with the same complementary sequence of bases as the parent double helix, thus transmitting the genetic information from parent to daughter cells. This simple idea forms the secret of almost all life – not quite *all* life because some viruses carry another kind of nucleic acid, RNA – but the genetic language which specifies how these viruses are made is the same. All the information which specifies *us*, the information which specifies a human being, is laid down in 46 chromosomes, which together contain a length of DNA of about 1 metre. This one metre contains about 3 billion bases, the equivalent of a library of about 5,000 volumes, all packed together into a single cell. Because the DNA is of atomic dimensions, that information is packed so tightly that it can fit into a single sperm or a single egg.

Watson and Crick's was a fantastic discovery. It was made in March 1953. This was a wonderful year, because in July of that same year, at last, I discovered a way of solving the riddle of the X-ray diffraction patterns of haemoglobin. We attached two atoms of mercury to each haemoglobin molecule. I then compared the X-ray diffraction pattern of this mercury-haemoglobin crystal with that of another crystal that was naked, mercury-free. In principle, this trick solved the problem that had preoccupied me for sixteen years, but there were still a lot of technical complications to be overcome before I solved it in practice.

I have not mentioned John Kendrew yet. He joined me after the war. He had been in operational research in Sri Lanka and there he had come across Bernal who enthused him about proteins and made him decide to switch from physical chemistry to X-ray crystallography. When the war ended, Kendrew came to Cambridge and joined me to work on the structure of proteins. He thought that haemoglobin was too big a molecule and decided to work on the simpler molecule of myoglobin, which is the haemoglobin of muscle. (Your steak is red not because it contains blood but because it contains myoglobin.) It is a molecule a quarter the size of haemoglobin and it also binds oxygen. After my experiment with mercurihaemoglobin, Kendrew and his collaborators attached heavy atoms to myoglobin, which turned out to be easier than attaching them to haemoglobin. In 1957, Kendrew built the first rough model of myoglobin. It was a horrible, visceral-looking object, because Kendrew had used a long sausage of plasticine to represent the protein chain, bent it round as in myoglobin, and fixed it on to wooden sticks from a children's building kit. The sausage mapped out the course of the protein chain. Kendrew's discovery was sensational, because it showed for the first time that X-ray crystallography can really deliver the goods, that it can solve protein structures, which only very few people had believed.

Two years later, Kendrew built the first atomic model of myoglobin. He built a forest of ⅛" steel rods; on to the rods he fixed meccano clips in a colour code that indicated density. At points of high density he placed atoms, and the sequence of atoms marked out the amino acids of the protein chain.

That model was the result of an enormously long calculation – a calculation that could not possibly have been done by hand; but by very good luck we had here in Cambridge one of the first two digital electronic computers. (You may think that IBM in the United States were the first to build one, but that was not so. The first working digital electronic computers were the one built here in Cambridge and another in Manchester.) Thanks to that pioneering work of the Cambridge University Mathematics Laboratory, Kendrew and I had the computing capacity to solve the first protein structures. The computer had electronic valves, and its output took the form of punched tape. There was a huge room in the Mathematics Laboratory which was filled with cabinet after cabinet of hundreds of thermionic valves producing an enormous amount of heat; great fans were necessary to extract it. (Nowadays, a computer of the same power is about the size of my briefcase.) This computer had to work all night, or rather the two men who helped Kendrew – Bror Strandberg from Sweden and Dick Dickerson from America – worked all night. In the morning we saw the output of the computer on miles of punched tape. The output was then plotted on paper. It took the form of contour maps specifying the atomic density in the myoglobin molecule in a series of sections, like the microtome sections through a tissue, but on a thousand times smaller scale. These maps allowed Kendrew to build the model. At the same time, I got a rough model of haemoglobin which showed four chains of high density all coiled in a similar way to the single chain of myoglobin.

I have not yet told you why I worked on haemoglobin, and what it does. It is the protein of the red blood cell. It carries oxygen from the lungs to the tissues and helps the return transport of carbon dioxide to the lungs. It is a protein that evolved at the same time as large animals, because without this oxygen-transport molecule, the life of the higher animals would not be possible. So it's a crucial protein. If you are anaemic you are short of haemoglobin, you don't get enough oxygen and feel weak. There are 250,000,000 red cells in one small drop of blood, and inside every red cell there's the same number – about 250,000,000 – of haemoglobin molecules. Haemoglobin contains four atoms of iron embedded in a dye – a pigment – called haem; this is what makes blood red. The four haems in the haemo-globin molecule are arranged in separate pockets on its surface.

Discovering its structure was wonderful. You must imagine the time when proteins were black boxes. Nobody knew what they looked like. There I was, having worked on this vital problem for twenty-two years, trying to find out what this molecule looked like, and eventually to discover how it worked. When the result emerged from the computer one night and we suddenly saw it, it was like reaching the top of a difficult mountain after a hard climb and falling in love at the same time. It was an incredible feeling to see this molecule for the first time and to realise that my work had not been in vain: because at many stages during those long years I feared that I was wasting my life on a problem that would never be solved. It was marvellous that it came out, but that was only the first stage, when we saw how the four chains were coiled. The real thing was to find how the atoms were arranged and how the molecule works. Another exciting thing was that the way in which the chain was coiled in haemoglobin turned out to be the same as in myoglobin. We soon realised that the fold is universal in nature, and is the way all haemoglobins are built. Haemoglobin is not just an oxygen tank: it is a molecular lung. It changes its structure every time it takes up and releases oxygen. You can hear your heart going 'thump, thump, thump', but in your blood the haemoglobin molecules go 'click, click, click' all the time – but you can't hear that!

CHAPTER 15

James Frazer and Cambridge anthropology

ERNEST GELLNER

James Frazer is probably the most famous anthropologist – certainly the most famous British anthropologist, and quite probably the most famous anthropologist altogether.

His dates were 1854 to 1941. It was a very long life, a life that began deep in the Victorian Age, but lasting right into the Second World War. The dates are significant. To the outside world, he is still perhaps *the* anthropologist. Within the anthropological profession, his position is somewhat different. He is King Harold – the last king of the old regime – slain by the Conqueror. The Conqueror, in the case of the British social anthropological tradition, is a Pole: Bronislaw Malinowski. There is indeed a marked similarity between the Harold-to-William relationship, and that of James Frazer to Bronislaw Malinowski.

Before that particular great leap, we find quite a different kind of history. Real history, with a kind of *continuous* regime, where you can say what happened and who influenced whom, with a sustained interaction – a kind of continuous moral climate – and a continuous set of institutions – all that only visibly begins with Malinowski. Before him, it was all like a kind of Chinese painting, where the background is missing, and where you only get isolated images. There are indeed various figures which most people might have heard of: Tylor and Morgan, McLennan and Marrett, Maine and Robertson Smith. But precisely what the relationship between them is is not all that clear. It is only known to specialists. It is not part of a *lived* history. It is all rather like English History before Harold, with funny names like Ethelred and half-mythical figures like Arthur and Alfred, with the blanks between them and with no *continuous* history, no *continuous* context.

The history of anthropology is rather like that. Frazer himself does have a clear image, because he was indeed the last of the old lot – and before him, not exactly darkness, but no cumulative story: at least no familiar, immediately recognised, clear and familiar story. After him, the continuous story does begin: and this is not an accident, because the changeover from the ideas of Frazer to the ideas of Malinowski is itself of the essence. Malinowski engendered a shared style, practised by an entire professional community, and thus made continuity and comparability possible. It acquires a kind of dense quality: those within the anthropological community *know* the history, as part of their living environment.

Naturally, the Battle of Hastings in this case was very slow and, of course, not physical. The relationship between Harold and William – or rather in this case between James Frazer and Bronislaw Malinowski – was complicated, intimate and ambivalent. In a physical sense, this Harold lived on for a very long time. James Frazer only died in 1941. Bronislaw Malinowski, his successor as Number One Anthropologist, died a year later. So he only just had time to make a posthumous appreciation of his predecessor, in which he said Frazer was the greatest of the old school, leaving it quite clear – without having to say – whom he considered to be the greatest of the new school. So he commented on the great revolution in which he succeeded Frazer, and, implicitly, on the irony of the relationship, which many people have noticed. As the paradigmatic anthropologist Frazer was killed and replaced by Malinowski during the inter-war period.

The central starting-point of Frazer's famous, great book – great in both a physical and an evaluative sense – *The Golden Bough* – is the sacred grove at Nemi, the place where there was a curious rule of succession: the priest at Nemi was succeeded by whoever slayed him. So it was not exactly a job which gave its possessor the best possible life expectancy. Frazer presents *The Golden Bough* as an attempt to explain this strange – strange even by classical standards – and brutal and exceptional rule; and by the end of *The Golden Bough* you are supposed to understand why it had to be so. That at any rate was the pretext; the real underlying theme is more complicated. However, this *is* the nominal topic: it takes thirteen volumes to explain why that strange custom prevailed in that grove some twenty or so miles south east of Rome. The relationship between Frazer and Bronislaw Malinowski was similar. Malinowski 'slayed' Frazer, intellectually speaking, and so became king of the Sacred Grove of Anthropology. This is the central and obvious irony of their relationship.

A few more general observations about Frazer: he is the last of the great anthropologists – at any rate, in Britain – in the sense of offering an overall picture of the human mind and of human history. After him – and this was part of the Malinowski revolution – anthropologists were meant to look at individual societies. Theorising about man and society at large, whilst not excluded, was no longer at the centre of the subject. For instance, you cannot get a Ph.D. for it and enter the profession: a field monograph is required for that. On the whole it became the kind of thing people do in their retirement, or when asked to give the Reith Lectures.

The one anthropologist since Frazer who has had similar impact, and who has become a world figure with an enormous impact on literature, and who offers a comprehensive picture, is Claude Lévi-Strauss. There is moreover a certain similarity between the two men. In each case you can sum them up in the following formula: a powerful, unifying, philosophical insight, plus a vast amount of ethnography, a vast amount of detail concerning diverse, usually exotic and strange customs or myths. The insight gives unity to the mass of material, the mass of material, presented in a lively and vigorous way, give substance to the insight.

Naturally the insight is not the same in the two cases.

In the case of Frazer, the insight is associationist psychology or – to put it another way – the image of the human mind which you find, above all, in David Hume, and which continues to be the kind of picture of mind and man offered by British Empiricists from their beginnings in the seventeenth century to Russell. The model sees the mind as a kind of snowball of sensations: a kind of accumulation of data provided by the senses. The *association of ideas* is the key notion used to explain how the human mind works and also – in the case of Frazer, by extension – of how human society works. Frazer is an intellectualist twice over: not only does he think that man is primarily a theoretician, but he also supposes that society is a reflection of human ideas. One way of summarising Frazer is:

suppose that Hume's theory of mind is correct, and suppose that you tried to make sense of all the ethnographic reports that have come in from the diversity of human culture – if you try to make sense of that mass of data in the light of the Humeian model of the mind, the result will be *The Golden Bough*.

In the case of Lévi-Strauss the basic insight is something different, a notion that in a way is the inverse of Hume's picture. It is not that the mind and its content is built up from the data, but the data themselves are made possible by a pre-existing structure system of polarities or of extremes. The best way to illustrate is the difference in the two insights – the Hume insight which underlies Frazer, and the structuralist insight which underlies Lévi-Strauss – is to do it in the terms of something Hume himself raised, namely, *the missing patch of blue*. Hume's central doctrine is that all our ideas are but a kind of aftertaste of our experiences; you have an experience of a given patch of blue, the aftertaste stays with you, and that *is* your idea of blue. It is a general theory of ideas – the opposite of Plato's theory, which would make things and impressions into faint echoes of abstract Ideas.

But then Hume, who was a very honest man, thought of one counter-example to his own principle. His own principle was that there are no ideas without previous perceptions – you cannot have an *after*taste without the *initial* taste. Any aftertaste presupposes a previous experience. That, in Hume, is the general law according to which the human mind is constructed. No ideas without impressions. But then, being an honest man, he notices an interesting counter-example: imagine a kind of scale of shades of blue as you might have, say, in a shop which sells wallpapers. You can choose your preferred shades of blue, and on a kind of scale you are offered all the shades of blue from very very dark blue to very very light blue. But, for some reason, one particular shade is missing. Well, says Hume, if you had the whole scale you would notice the gap, for suddenly at this point the jump from one shade to the next is a bit greater than usual. So you can *imagine* that particular missing shade of blue, even though you had never previously experienced it. You *can* fill the gap. Hume noticed this contradiction of his general principle that all ideas are but aftertastes of previous experiences. He notes it, but then just goes on to live in a sort of peaceful coexistence with the counter example to his own theory, and does not worry about it any further.

The way you could sum up the difference between the implicit picture which underlies Frazer and the structural picture which underlies Lévi-Strauss is that what Hume considers an *exception*, for a structuralist like Lévi-Strauss is, on the contrary, the *norm*. You would not be able to perceive and conceptualise different shades of the blue unless your mind were already endowed with the polarity between extremes, into which various shades could *then* be placed. In other words, the spectrum of polarities *precedes* the contents of the mind. I am never quite clear whether Lévi-Strauss wants one universal mind for all mankind, or one mind per culture. But the polarities of sensibility or conceptualisation are there already to receive the various shades. Anyway, Frazer's anthropology is based on Hume's model, and Lévi-Strauss's on the generalisation of the *exception* which Hume acknowledged.

One further point about Frazer's position in history: I have described his position in the history of anthropology, but in the wider history of thought he can usefully be compared to Bertrand Russell. Once again, one can offer a kind of formula for the main position of Russell. He changed his mind a great deal, but the main kind of position with which he is associated is: *David Hume plus modern logic*. He restated the basic philosophy of Hume at a time which possessed a new and more complicated logical machinery, which he used in an attempt to answer the question of how mathematics works. This is the simplest formula for the general position of Bertrand Russell. Similarly, Frazer is Hume's philosophy, Hume's theory of mind, plus a preoccupation with the diversity of human cultures. So, in both cases, you get a kind of Augustan eighteenth-century attitude, adapted to the latter part of the nineteenth century and the first half of the twentieth. Both exemplify a kind of updated Cambridge reformulation of an Enlightenment view of mind. In both cases we find somewhat similar values.

Frazer was an Augustan in at least two senses. This emerges when one turns to the layers of theory which are to be found in *The Golden Bough*, and in the work of Frazer generally.

The top layer – the official doctrine, which is in effect the main theme of *The Golden Bough*, behind the pretence that it is all aimed at explaining the murders at Nemi – is a combination of Hume's associationism – the snowball theory of mind – with evolutionism in the sociological sense, i.e. the notion that the main fact about human society in history is a progression from lower to higher forms. In brief, associationism plus evolutionism. The basic idea is the adaptation of associationism to the problem of diversity in human culture. And the answer is – there is indeed an enormous variety, but do not be deceived – there is also an underlying unity, and the underlying pattern is progress from the lower forms of thought to the higher ones. This is Frazer's main and official theory.

The further crucial feature of his particular version of evolution-ism – of seeing an overall pattern of development and improvement – is a three-stage theory. The famous three stages, offered by Frazer, of the development of the human mind are: *magic, religion, science*. That is the overall *official* theory of *The Golden Bough*. The human mind begins with magic, proceeds to religion and ends with science. He does not believe that any of these elements are ever present *alone*. It is rather that magic predominates at the beginning, and science predominates at the end and religion predominated in between. But the other elements are also ever-present; it is a matter of relative dominance.

Robert Fraser's *The Making of the Golden Bough* demonstrates in great detail something which has always been obvious to me, namely that Frazer's theory of magic is a direct adaptation of associationist principles developed by Hume. His terms, like 'sympathetic magic', have passed into common speech. That sort of magic is based upon the idea that the connection between *things* resembles the connections by which we associate *ideas* – we associate A with B either through resemblance or because they happen to have appeared together. One thing reminds us of the other. And similarly magic – or magical connections – are based on the application of this principle. The underlying notion of magic is that nature can be manipulated by employing connections which we can identify by this natural operation of the human mind, by finding links between things through associated connections, similarity or contiguity.

Magic doesn't work, and Frazer's theory is that, because it failed to work, mankind proceeded to religion. This conception of religion is basically animistic: it is based on the existence of spirits behind things. Whilst the magician manipulates nature, the priest appeases the spirits behind nature, who are assumed to be responsible for what happens. That does not work either, and then mankind proceeds to science, the essence of which is looking very carefully at what *really* causes what, instead of being misled by accidental associations.

We sort out the real connections by the experimental method. This, for Frazer, is the basic pattern of human history. There were various things wrong with this. Magic fits the model of the human mind as specified by David Hume very well, religion not nearly so well. Animism is not based on some kind of association. It is the postulation of a new explanatory principle of an event. You can perhaps fit it in if you try hard enough; you can say that the individual mind experiences, in its own individual psyche, the connection between consciousness and will and experience, and some similar association can then also be projected on to nature. But it does not fit nearly so well as magic. It is really the invention of a radically different hypothesis. Secondly, it is all a bit absurd. The idea of mankind progressing from magic to religion because magic failed to work, would seem to presuppose that at some point, say, in the first millennium BC, when the shift occurred from the simpler religions to the more theoretical world religions – the so-called Axial Age – there was some sort of world congress of shamans, at which they read papers to each other, and said 'Well, we've been keeping records of this here magic lark, and the failure rate is appallingly high. It really does not work. We really must think of something else. How about animism?' This is not very plausible. People do not keep such records, and most societies are simply not bothered by the failure rate of their magical practices. There are always ways around this, and, moreover, they do not compare notes. It never happened like that.

You might think that the intellectualist account of the next transition is a bit more compatible with Frazer's vision. Something like this did happen in the seventeenth and eighteenth centuries. In the seventeenth century scientific theories were developed which seemed to fit facts rather better. With the coming of Copernicus and Galileo, there came the success of theories based on theorising and observation, as opposed to revelation. This was then echoed in the eighteenth century by philosophers who thought about this success and developed a theory of scientific method. They advertised the success and their explanation of it, and converted much of mankind to it. So Frazer's model might fit that particular transition, possibly. Perhaps you could fit the scientific revolution, and its philosophical echoes, into his model. But the first transition doesn't fit at all, and it is absurd to try and make it fit.

But to return to the layers in Frazer's thought. The top layer is evolutionist/associationist theory – using the associationist's theory of mind to produce an evolutionary pattern of different kinds of thought, engendering the variety of human cultures. The second layer is rather different. This is the second layer in which, once again, Frazer was very Augustan, very much a kind of throwback to Hume, and this incidentally is relevant to the tangled topic of Frazer's relationship to religion. But this layer manifests a different aspect of his Augustan attitude, and one questionably compatible with his evolutionism/associationism. If you look at his passages about the influence of Oriental religion in Europe, you find a kind of throwback to the attitudes of the Augustans, Edward Gibbon, for example. You can find this approach in the famous chapter on the expansion of Christianity in Gibbon's *Decline and Fall*, or in another work of David Hume, *The Natural History of Religion*. There is, on this view, a crucial contrast between the religion of classical antiquity and the scripturalist monotheism which replaced it. As in the case of Hume and Gibbon, Frazer's sympathies are clearly with classical antiquity, and not with Christianity or the world religions. The contrast is the following: ancient religion was basically a civic cult; it inculcated civic virtues of living or dying for your city, a kind of ethic of social cohesion and obligation. By contrast, what replaces it is other-worldly and egotistical – it teaches men to be concerned with the salvation of their own individual souls, and not to be concerned with the world, except incidentally, at most as a kind of moral gymnasium, where they prove their worthiness for another life. It is a transition from civic this-worldliness to egotistic other-worldliness. Well, this is a perfectly possible attitude. Note, however, that it doesn't fit with the top layer of Frazer's thought, which assumes that what people do when they practise magic or take part in the religious rituals, or subscribe to religion, is the same as that which people later do when they practise science. They are, on that view, basically intellectuals, *theorising* about the world. Magic has one theory about the world; when it doesn't work it is replaced by the second one, and when that doesn't work either, it is replaced by the third one. It is assumed that man down the ages was a kind of scholar, a don sitting in his study, shifting from one theory to another, as his thought progressed. Well, of course, this is nonsense: theorising about the world, and about nature, is one activity amongst others, and for most people and at most times, *not* the dominant one. When people take part in ritual they are not theorising; they are expressing their participation in a social order. The intellectualism of the main theory is one of its weaknesses, but the paradox is that in the second layer of Frazer's thought – when he concretely compares the religions of the classical Mediterranean with the world monotheisms which replaced it, warmly favouring the former – he is not talking as an intellectualist at all, but as a kind of comparative sociologist, interested in social structures and social cultures, religion as *ethos* or social cement, not religion as bad scientific theory. Frazer's second layer sees religion as the expression of a social order, and is not compatible with the first layer. So there is a tension between the two layers – though both are very Augustan, they still contradict each other.

Finally, there is the third layer, what you might call the *Waste Land* layer. Of course, Frazer – because of the richness of the material, its cohesion, and the vividness of his prose – had a very great impact on literature. His presence is very vivid in T. S. Eliot's *The Waste Land*. But Eliot's use of Frazer is totally contrary to the spirit of Frazer himself. When Frazer was presented with *The Waste Land*, he found it unintelligible. One may suspect that had he understood it, he would have found it distasteful. T. S. Eliot was *not* Augustan.

Now the point is this: the literary – and, I think, the most common use of Frazer – is what you might call a *Jungian* use. Frazer assembles all his rich material about bizarre beliefs and practices from all over the world, he groups it together, and he finds a great deal of similarity of pattern. There is a great deal which is in common. The solution to his main formal problem about the rule of succession to Nemi in the end is that it is not so bizarre after all – something like it is found all over the world. There are *many* other examples of succession by murder or the killing of the priest or the king. And the theme of *The Waste Land* is just that: the land is waste because of the lack of vigour of the monarch. So Eliot does borrow the main theme from Frazer.

But, if there is a similarity in the myths and the rituals of mankind, what *is* the explanation? Frazer did have an answer – the laws of mental association, as laid bare by Hume and the British empiricists. But there is another explanation, put forward in its simplest form by the psychologist Jung: namely, that all these patterns are dredged up from a kind of store, a shared collective unconscious. There is a common reservoir of symbols or archetypes (or whatever you wish to call them) and these then reappear all over the world. Claude Lévi-Strauss had quite a different answer later – the similar underlying *structure* of the human mind, not a shared content, would engender the same patterns of mythology all over the place. The Jungian explanation proved more persuasive to the literary kind than associationism. So the way in which Frazer has assembled his material lends itself to this Jungian interpretation. It is in this form that Frazer has possibly made his most influential contribution. I don't think this was his most meritorious contribution, but this is the form in which he has made his greatest impact. People evidently like dredging *The Golden Bough* and the assembled material for an account of the rich shared imagery and symbolism of the human mind. This was hardly Frazer's intention, but the way he arranged the material lends itself to it.

What more is wrong with Frazer? Some of it has already been stressed: the intellectualism, the assumption that early man was primarily a theorist rather than a practitioner, and all that goes with it: the lack of social context – the lack of the notion of culture as a unity. It is here that the new regime set up by Malinowski reacted against Frazer. Its main principle was insistence on *context*, and the seeing of the whole set of cultural features and institutions rather than tearing individual bits and fitting them into a collage. This avoided the magpie method which was so very characteristic of Frazer.

But over and above the intellectualism, the contextlessness, another further crucial weakness in Frazer: he did put enormous weight on the association of ideas. The presupposed theory really is very bizarre. Let's take him at face value and present the doctrine the way he put it in *The Golden Bough*. It begins with this bloody, macabre ritual – a rule of succession, rather – with the priest prowling in the sacred grove near the lake at Nemi – knowing that sooner or later he will be killed by someone who wants to be his successor. Why? Why does he put up with it? Why did he get himself into such an unenviable situation? And why on earth does his successor risk his life only to secure a post which is not exactly a sinecure, a job where you're going to be done in by the next successor, and so on? Why do they do it? Answer: That's how the human mind works, you see – by the association of ideas and, in this particular case, the association of ideas of prosperity of the land and the vigour of the king/priest. This mistake in association makes for the acceptance of an invidious rule. In reality, the potency of the ruler/priest and the productivity of the land are not connected, as scientific agronomy will tell you; but the plausibility of magical association makes it seem so. So people become victims of the association of ideas. A strange theory. It really credits association with a hold over human behaviour which is truly astonishing. I for one am not going to get myself killed for the association of ideas. I can associate anything with anything, but draw a line when it gets me into danger.

If you fail to be convinced by this criticism, it can be strengthened. The trouble about association is that almost anything *can* be associated with anything. The expression *free association* is really a pleonasm. Hume himself began by distinguishing various kinds of association. Similarity is one of them, but then so is contrariety. You associate A with B because they are *close* to each other but A with Z precisely because they are *distant*: you can (and do) play it either way. By the time you invoke the various principles of association you can go from anything to anything whatever, as indeed, in the course of free association, people do, and are meant to do. Now this is not a criticism of Frazer alone, but of the entire empiricist tradition, of which he is a distinctive part, in so far as it tries to give an account of the actual working of the human mind. If the human mind really worked by association, we should all be suffering from a kind of semantic cancer – a kind of rapid growth of association in all directions, which would bring us from anything to anything. I have my private association because my life is what it is. So if I say a given word, that word would mean something to me because it had come to me in a context of certain experiences. But *your* life is different, and when you hear me saying the same word, it would bring up completely different associations. So, because your associations are yours and mine are mine, there is virtually no chance of our really communicating. If associationism explained the way the human mind really worked, there would be total semantic chaos.

Now the interesting thing is that there is no chaos. The surprising thing is that, semantically and verbally, people are dreadfully well behaved. People generally speak proper – they don't *behave* proper but they do *talk* proper. People generally observe the phonetics and syntax of their subculture. The orderliness of conceptual behaviour is very remarkable in any one society. Associationism fails to explain that order, and this links up with the other criticism I mentioned: it doesn't explain moral order, either. Why do people have strong moral compulsions and strong taboos – why did the priest observe that strange rule? Association is simply too undisciplined and too weak to explain all this. Associations are born free, but are everywhere in chains.

This problem of compulsiveness and order lay at the heart of the thought of another man who worked at the same time, and who did get the question right, and who was far more influential than Frazer on the actual thinking of later anthropologists: Emile Durkheim. For Durkheim, the question of the enforcement of conceptual and moral order – the extraordinary discipline which people display in their thinking and conduct, and the discipline in any one society – *was* problematic, and he worked out an answer. This may or may not be correct but it is ingenious and powerful – namely: ritual. Whether valid or not, his answer underscores the problem, whilst Frazer's obscures it.

Ritual is a way of instilling conceptual order in people. Durkheim was willing to leave animals to David Hume, so to speak – associationism worked for them, the animal mind is just an accumulation of associations – but what makes humans human is religion. At the heart of religion is ritual: it is the undergoing of the same intense ritual experience which stamps the same compulsions on people. This then makes society possible twice over: by enabling people to communicate, and by engendering those shared compulsions, those inhibitions, which make social and moral order possible. Now Frazer didn't fully see the problem. He really thought associationism could do the trick – and it can't. Associationism is too chaotic to account for the order which he had himself so painstakingly noted and assembled. The similarity of patterns he had found can be explained in a facile way by some kind of Jungian theory: they all come out from a great collective store, an enormous attic of shared furniture, dredged up by various groups in diverse ways, but still drawing on the same store. The orderliness which can (in a facile way) be explained by Jung cannot be explained by Frazer at all. Associationism simply cannot do the job.

So, what is it that Frazer really did? I think his whole enterprise was back to front. He mistook the empiricist theory of the human mind – brought to its highest point by Hume, and restated in our century by Russell – for an actual account of how the human mind really works. But it doesn't work that way. What the empiricists *really* did was to codify, not how the mind actually does work but how it *should* work. They set up a kind of model, a kind of prescriptive, normative model of how science works, of how we test theories: we break up everything into parts that are as small as possible, so as to prohibit and exclude the maintenance of circular belief systems. Having broken it up we then experiment, and see which connections really hold. It is a kind of summary of the rules of scientific method. But, projecting this norm backward on to the whole of humanity as a fact, and trying to fit in the changes associated with a transition from magic to religion and religion to science, we end with Frazer's theory.

His vision is also mistaken in assimilating ancient liberties – the kind of tolerance found in the religion of an ancient city, arising from the fact that the religion is danced out and told out in stories but not codified in a theology, so there's no orthodoxy and hence no heresy-hunting – to modern ones. Hume expressed his admiration for ancient liberties by greatly commending the reply of the Delphic oracle in response to the man who asked which rites are to be observed. The oracle answered: in each city the rites of their city. The recipe was relativistic, tolerant, civic as well as being this-worldly.

Now the assumption that this is similar to modern liberties is deeply misguided, and people began to notice that in the nineteenth century. Hume had failed to notice it, and Frazer didn't do so either. Nor did he notice that the kind of pressures in an internally organised and heavily ritualised society would be intolerable for moderns. Modern liberty assumes not merely the absence of the tyrant, but also the absence of excessive social pressures – the freedom to choose one's kind of associations, the freedom not to take part in ritual. Nor did Frazer notice the conflict between the social theory of religion which he implicitly assumes when he compares the ancient to the moderns, and the highly intellectualist, non-social theory which he assumes in his main theory of the evolution of the human mind.

These are his weaknesses. In professional anthropology he was replaced by Malinowski, who overturned him at both the crucial points: Malinowski rejected the contextlessness, and he rejected the evolutionism, not by saying evolution did not occur, but by saying it does not concern us when we explain specific social structures and cultures. It is not our job to indulge in speculative history about the evolution of the human mind and human society in general; it's our job to compare, describe and analyse societies as totalities, along with the interdependence of their institutions and their cultures. There was still some room for theory after that. It wasn't quite clear what it was going to be, but it clearly was not going to be evolutionist.

Frazer's central ideas were overturned, but he remains as a kind of marvellous monument to the attempt to carry them out. Like Russell, he exemplified a Cambridge attempt to make Enlightenment ideas work for the data and problems of a later age. In anthropology, he was not followed, either in Cambridge or elsewhere. (And at least one Cambridge anthropologist, Edmund Leach, had a strong distaste for him.) Still, as a literary figure, and as King Harold in the history of anthropological thought, as the man who worked out fully and with great elegance the implications of a single vision, he will continue to live.

FURTHER READING

Robert Ackerman, *J. G. Frazer, his Life and Work*, Cambridge: Cambridge University Press 1987.

R. A. Downie, *James George Frazer: The Portrait of a Scholar*, London: Watts 1940.

Frazer and the Golden Bough, London: Gollancz 1970.

Robert Fraser, *The Making of the Golden Bough: The Origins and Growth of an Argument*, London: Macmillan 1990.

(ed.), *Sir James Frazer and the Literary Imagination*, London: Macmillan 1990.

Ian Jarvie, *Revolutions in Anthropology*, London: Routledge and Kegan Paul 1964.

Bronislaw Malinowski, *A Scientific Theory of Culture and Other Essays*, Oxford: Oxford University Press 1944.

George Stocking, *Victorian Anthropology*, New York: Free Press 1987.

CHAPTER 16

Michael Oakeshott

ROBERT GRANT

The political philosopher Michael Oakeshott died in December 1990, a few days after his eighty-ninth birthday. He had enjoyed a fair if controversial reputation in his lifetime among his colleagues, but he never became a global guru in the manner of (say) Gunnar Myrdal, J. K. Galbraith, F. A. Hayek, Milton Friedman, or his own pre-decessor in the Chair of Political Science at the London School of Economics, Harold Laski. (It is perhaps worth noting, as a sign of the times, how many of these eminences are or were economists.)

Oakeshott's death, and the almost universally glowing obituaries which followed it, sparked off a veritable explosion of interest in his work. There were, I believe, several reasons for Oakeshott's low public profile during his lifetime. The first is purely personal. He was a modest, unassuming man, with a deep aversion to the limelight. By modern academic standards he published little. I always supposed that he had been passed over for public honours, but it now appears he had more than once declined them, on the grounds (one obituarist quoted him as saying) that public honours should be reserved for public people.

Secondly, throughout most of Oakeshott's life the prevailing intellectual atmosphere was contrary to both the spirit and the substance of his work. In a word, it was socialist or at least sympathetic to socialism, and, though Oakeshott's precise location on the political map is a matter for debate, no one will claim that it was anywhere in the socialist quarter. Oakeshott called himself a conservative, and, whether or not he was strictly right to do so, it has to be admitted that to be, or claim to be, a conservative was until very recently virtually to exclude oneself from serious intellectual consideration. (Unless like Aristotle, Hobbes, Hume, Johnson, Burke, Hegel, Coleridge, Newman and Eliot, you happened to be safely dead.) Also, Oakeshott had little enthusiasm for politics in its everyday sense, and next to no respect for modern politicians (though, perhaps surprisingly, he made something of an exception for Mrs Thatcher). In other words, he could look to no advancement from that quarter. When asked, long before Mrs Thatcher's time, why he supported the Conservative Party (so far as he actually did, which was unenthusiastically at best), he is supposed to have replied, 'Because they do the least harm.' (Those were the days.) Oakeshott was a romantic in many respects, but emphatically never in politics.

Thirdly, Oakeshott's thought is peculiarly elusive. It cannot be condensed into a slogan, inscribed on a banner, or readily incorporated into anyone's political programme. In short, it does not lend itself to formulation. Not that there is anything mystical about it (contrary to what some of Oakeshott's critics have alleged); in respect of being unformulable, it is simply of a piece with the traditional, experience-based practices and procedures which it offers to justify as being uniquely appropriate to morals and politics, and which have their familiar equivalents in every sphere of human activity (riding a bicycle, for example, a skill which no knowledge of mechanics could ever suffice to impart). All of which is to say that Oakeshott's thought has little partisan appeal. It promises no short cuts to wisdom or right action, let alone to moral salvation. It is hardly too much to say that its appeal (or at least, its political appeal) is largely negative.

George Orwell said of Dickens that 'it is not so much a series of books, it is more like a world'. Something similar is true of Oakeshott. His works are really a kind of imaginative vision: one, I should say, of great scope, depth and, in its undramatic way, power. (I do not mean, of course, that they are visionary; if anything they are rather the reverse. What I do mean is that they represent a settled, harmonious, compelling and consistent way of looking at the world; this world, that is, not another and better one.) Oakeshott's world, because it contains few dragons, is apt to prove a disappointment to the dragon-slayer. But that will not worry those who have given up knight-errantry; who are inclined first to hear what life has to say on its own behalf, before offering their views as to whether and what respects it might be improved.[1]

There is a long-standing myth which it will be as well to debunk at the outset. In a famous essay, 'Rationalism in politics', widely construed at the time as an attack on the post-war Attlee government, Oakeshott voiced a distrust of the democratic *arriviste*, who lacks the instinctive 'feel' for government of a long-established political class. As if this were not bad enough, he gave as an analogy the house-guest who is out of his *social* class, and the well-known ability of butlers and housemaids to spot his embarrassment. On the strength of all this it was decided that Oakeshott must be too much of a toff, or 'Tory dandy' (as Professor Bernard Crick put it), to be taken seriously. (It will doubtless not have helped that Oakeshott had also written a book with the sub-title 'How to Pick the Derby Winner'.)

In fact, Oakeshott's origins, like his subsequent life style and aspirations, were modest. His mother, a nurse, was the daughter of the Rector of Islington; his father, the son of a Newcastle postmaster, left school at 16 and worked all his life in the Inland Revenue at Somerset House, where he eventually rose to the rank of Principal. (His father's professional world, Oakeshott told me, was straight out of Trollope's *Three Clerks*.) The family were, or had become, about as 'upper' in the 'middle-middle' class as it is possible to be: that is to say, unaffluent but liberally educated professionals. They were also, in the manner of their kind, notably public-spirited: Oakeshott's mother took a lifelong interest in charitable work (she had met her husband through it, at the Hoxton Settlement), while his father, a founder-member of the Fabian Society, was a friend of George Bernard Shaw and the author of a Fabian leaflet on the Reform of the Poor Law. Such things apart, the Oakeshott parents devoted themselves almost wholly to the education of their three children (all boys), moving house several times to be within reach of their schools.

Oakeshott was sent to a new and for those days unusually 'progressive' experimental school, St George's, Harpenden. It was co-educational; the founder and Headmaster, Cecil Grant, was an Anglican clergyman, socialist, art-lover and friend of the educational reformer Maria Montessori (who twice visited the school). Some pupils complained in later life that Grant had tried to indoctrinate them with his enthusiasms, and that they had been left in consequence with an abiding prejudice against religion and socialism. Oakeshott, however, appears to have been very happy. (Indeed, he denied, when questioned on this point, that his later opinions were a reaction against either his schooling or his upbringing.) In a revealing memoir of 1967, Oakeshott wrote as follows:

> I do not think that my happiness depended upon . . . the immense amount of freedom we were allowed – or what it really was at times, being neglected and allowed to roam. It did depend, however, on the huge range of quite informal opportunities. St George's was a place surrounded by a thick, firm hedge, and inside this hedge was a world of beckoning activities and interests. Many of them emanated from Grant himself, many of them were the private enterprise of members of staff, some one made for oneself. There was a great deal of laughter and fun; there was a great deal of seriousness.

Here Oakeshott's fundamental creed is expressed in a simple metaphor. Freedom, choice, invention and individuality (all things he prized) are impossible without security, the 'thick, firm hedge'. For Aristotle, such security was conferred upon the cultivated or leisure classes, physically by the labour of slaves and artisans, and politically (upon all) by law. For Oscar Wilde, as for Marx, it would be provided by a socialist system of production, upon the abundance of whose output the edifice of freedom and individuality would subsequently be raised. But for Oakeshott, as for one of his masters, Hobbes, the security which counts is neither material nor existential, but is simply such as law can provide. If freedom, pluralism and individuality follow, they do so spontaneously. They cannot be actively engineered by government, nor delivered in any other way than by guaranteeing, through law, the necessary conditions for their emergence.

The tiny passage I have just quoted may be likened to the famous thirteenth chapter of *Leviathan*, in which Hobbes compares the benefits of authority (which, as he later makes clear, can only mean government according to law) with the unspeakable misery of anarchy. Without authoritative government, says Hobbes,

> there is no place for industry; because the fruit thereof is uncertain: and consequently no culture of the earth; no navigation, nor use of the commodities which may be imported by sea; no commodious building; no instruments of moving, and removing, such things as require much

force; no knowledge of the face of the earth; no account of time; no
arts; no letters; no society; and which is worst of all, continual fear, and
danger of violent death; and the life of man, solitary, poor, nasty,
brutish, and short.

What are those goods of which, according to Hobbes, anarchy
deprives us, but a macrocosmic version of the 'world of beckoning
activities and interests' which Oakeshott discovered in his school-
days, and spent the rest of his life defending?

Oakeshott was just too young to serve in the Great War, an event
which impressed him greatly by so swiftly claiming the lives of many
of his senior schoolfellows. In 1919 he went up to Gonville and Caius
College, Cambridge, to read history, taking the political thought
option in both parts of the Tripos. He graduated in 1923, and was
elected to a Fellowship at Caius in 1925. He had spent both the
intervening summer vacations at the German universities of
Tübingen and Marburg in order to pursue his twin interests at the
time, theology and German literature. While there he went tramping
off with the *Wandervögel*, an informal student movement dedicated to
nature-worship, camping out, and (according to D. H. Lawrence, of
whom Oakeshott thought highly)[2] 'free love'. Though very much of
its time and place (Weimar Germany), the movement also embodied
a traditional vein of German romanticism, harmless enough and even
valuable in itself, which the Nazis were later to exploit. Its main
legacy to Oakeshott, however, was his lifelong taste for solitude and
the simple life. Typically of him, however, this in no way precluded a
love of company, conversation and all the sophisticated artifice of a
mature liberal civilisation of which, incurable bohemian though he
was, Oakeshott was a stern and loyal defender.

Heidegger was lecturing at Marburg when Oakeshott was there,
and it seems likely that Oakeshott heard him, though as far as I have
been able to discover he cited Heidegger only once in his works. I
mention Heidegger here simply to note the three-way link between
him, Oakeshott, and the Oxford philosopher Gilbert Ryle, one of
the very few academic philosophers with whom Oakeshott maintained
a personal acquaintance. (Oakeshott never belonged to a university
department of philosophy. At Cambridge his official subject was
history; at LSE, politics.) In 1929 Ryle had scandalised the
analytically inclined readership of the journal *Mind* by favourably
reviewing Heidegger's *Being and Time*. This work, despite its vast

difference in point of lucidity from Ryle and Oakeshott, nevertheless has much in common with them, as it also has with the later Wittgenstein. It is characteristic of Oakeshott that, though he and Wittgenstein were in Cambridge together for twenty years, they never met. He also claimed never to have set eyes on F. R. Leavis, to whose literary journal *Scrutiny* he contributed three times in the 1930s. And yet Leavis was a lifelong Cambridge resident, who even as late as the 1960s (as I myself well recall) was a familiar figure about the place. Intellectually Oakeshott shunned schools, at least if they were contemporary with himself. His affinities with individual contemporaries such as those just mentioned seem not to have been generally remarked until lately.[3] He was in his way a natural loner, both behind his times and, given the propensity of intellectual fashions to rotate, ahead of them.

Oakeshott's first book, *Experience and its Modes*, appeared in 1933, when he was 31, and is the basis of all his subsequent thought. It received highly enthusiastic notices from R. G. Collingwood and T. M. Knox in Oxford, but was reviewed very sniffily in *Mind* by L. Susan Stebbing, who observed that 'those who have not been convinced by Bradley are unlikely to be converted by Mr Oakeshott'.[4] The fact was, quite simply, that the philosophical Idealism of Bradley, Collingwood and Oakeshott was out of date, and Logical Positivism had come into fashion. The first edition of *Experience and its Modes*, a mere 1,000 copies, took over thirty years to sell. It is noteworthy, however, that Oakeshott's return to serious philosophical consideration(e.g. by Richard Rorty, who brackets him with Heidegger and Wittgenstein)[5] has coincided with the recognition of the importance of Wittgenstein's later, so-called Idealist phase. *Experience and its Modes* has been reprinted three times since the 1960s.

The book is a work of systematic metaphysics, with no immediate application to politics. The fundamental idea behind it is Hegelian, to the effect that for all practical purposes the real is the same as the knowable, and that only that can be known which can in some sense be experienced; in short, there is nothing outside experience. To be real is simply to belong to experience, and every experience is an 'idea', i.e. a part or content of consciousness (whence the name Idealism). Furthermore, consciousness cannot ultimately be distinguished from its contents, since to be conscious is always (as Hume pointed out) to be conscious *of* something. It follows that if the

Idealists are right, then both the realist notion of there being an 'external' world, and the empiricist notion that our experience is distinct from it, must be wrong.

Obviously such matters, which have occupied philosophers for hundreds if not thousands of years, cannot be thrashed out here, so I must ask the reader for present purposes simply to accept the Idealist position as a postulate. One thing that must be said is that the real, though identical with experience, is not identical with immediate experience. The immediate is inevitably both incomplete and subjective; partial, one might say, in both senses of the word. Only experience as a whole is fully real, and, according to the young Oakeshott, only philosophy can give us access to it. Reality is what remains or subsists once all partial perspectives have been reconciled, all contradictions resolved or reduced, and the lot finally subsumed into and apprehended as the Whole.

All this is supposedly the business of philosophy which, being the experience of the Whole, is (implausibly) identical with it. Ordinary life, however, is entirely composed of partial perspectives and fragmentary experience. Your experience, for example, is different from mine. And there are also partial perspectives, distinct ways of experiencing or understanding the world, which (in principle) are common to all of us. Following Bradley, Oakeshott calls them 'modes' of experience. In our culture, three predominate: science, history and practice. (Oakeshott later added poetry, by which he meant aesthetic experience, whether of art or nature, to their number. In *Experience and its Modes* art, like religion, is part of practical experience.)

Oakeshott's predecessors Collingwood and Croce had seen such modes as constituting a hierarchy of Hegelian 'moments' – that is, successive steps or platforms – in the self-unfolding (which is also to say, self-understanding) of reality. Oakeshott, however, follows Bradley in making the modes autonomous and equal. None contains the truth about experience; but each participates equally in the whole, and is equally abstract, in the sense of literally being abstracted from it. In principle, that is, in the logical or philosophical overview, the modes neither overlap nor contradict each other, though in fact each model activity, when pursued unqualified by a simultaneous awareness of the existence of other kinds, has a natural propensity to invade its neighbours' territory.

The practical view of things is utterly different from the scientific and the historical. It sees the world under the aspect of desire and aversion, pleasure and pain, as also of good and bad. Morality, like religion, is a central feature of it. Science and history, however, are value-neutral. They seek not to manipulate the objects of their attention but to understand them. Science does so under the aspect of regularity and generality, so that every phenomenon appears as an instance of an all-covering law. History does so under the aspect of particularity, so that every historical event is perceived first and foremost as contributing to, and being determined by, some local, immediate and unique configuration of circumstances, and as being explicable not by any overarching, causal, pseudo-scientific law, but simply in terms of its own detailed internal structure and its contingent 'situatedness', that is, its place in a network of directly contiguous events (which are themselves contiguous with others, and so on outwards, in ever-widening circles).

The office of philosophy is not to supersede the modes. It can never finally deliver us from the Platonic Cave of modal experience. (Nor would it be a good thing if it could, at least so far as the practical mode is concerned, for the whole purpose of the practical mode is survival.) Philosophy is neither a necessary nor a universal activity; indeed, Oakeshott claims with Hegel that it is actually a symptom, in its way, of decadence, of innocence lost. What it can usefully do is police the modal boundaries. The greatest intellectual sin is to transgress them, for example by interpreting history in the light of one's own moral, religious or political principles (all of which are pertinent solely to present practice), by offering to establish morals and politics on a 'scientific' basis, or by forcing scientific theory (which then immediately ceases to be scientific) into an approved political mould.[6]

Oakeshott was unconcerned by the reception of *Experience and its Modes*. He knew who his friends were, and despite his subsequent eminence seems never to have been academically ambitious. Nor, in modern academic eyes, productive (as I have already noted). But every one of Oakeshott's later essays alone is worth a couple of hundred books in any contemporary academic publisher's catalogue, and represents as much real thought. Like Goethe, or any of the great Victorian intellectuals, he was a superlatively educated mind. By that I mean that not only was he a man of impressively wide and various learning, but he knew also how to deploy it. In his view, the cardinal intellectual virtue is relevance. We might inhabit many different universes of discourse, each governed by its own unique rules, norms and principles. Ignorance of what these are, the blundering habit of applying the assumptions of one discourse to the conduct of another, leads to moral barbarism, intellectual chaos, and, in politics, war.

Oakeshott's own experience of war clearly underlies his diagnosis of the political disease of modernity, which he famously calls Rationalism. In 1939 he compiled an anthology called *The Social and Political Doctrines of Contemporary Europe*. Despite its muddle and incoherence, he finds what he loosely calls Representative Democracy the least unattractive, because its central principle (which is also his own) is that 'the imposition of a universal plan of life on a society is at once stupid and immoral'.

Now such a universal plan is exactly what war makes imperative. Oakeshott had what is called a 'good' war. He joined the Army immediately on its outbreak, and eventually commanded a squadron of the GHQ Liaison Regiment (alias 'Phantom', a quasi-freelance battlefield intelligence force) in Holland. However, in sharp contrast with most post-war socialists (who, impressed by the nation's wartime singleness of purpose, would speak, e.g., of 'winning the peace' in the same spirit), Oakeshott thought war and military organisation the worst of all possible models for peacetime society.[7] In his view, not only does war necessitate collectivism (since the society has only one goal, to survive, and all resources and energies must be forcibly bent in that direction), but the reverse is also true. Like a society at war, a collectivist state is dedicated to a single end (the realisation of some overall scheme); and when, owing to its citizens' natural propensity to prefer their own ends, its goal proves impossible of achievement without massive coercion, such a state is driven to war in order to make its ideology and methods seem legitimate.

Oakeshott returned to Cambridge after the war, and in 1947 he and a few colleagues started a lively and wide-ranging humanities review, *The Cambridge Journal*. Before long Oakeshott had become its star turn and general editor. In a classic and striking series of essays, notable for their eloquence and literary grace, he set out the essentials of his ethics and politics. The theme of them all, in their different ways, was the absurdity, inappropriateness and hubris of all forms of comprehensive planning, when applied to social, ethical, political and economic life. They attracted a good deal of attention and a certain amount of outrage among the enlightened classes, who took them (as I have already said of one) for an attack on the ethos and methods of the Attlee government, which to some extent they were.

It is true that they are probably the nearest Oakeshott ever came to genuine political activity, and one detects in them both a whiff of satire and a certain barely suppressed exasperation But it would be wrong to regard them simply as a form of up-market pamphleteering. Oakeshott was not attacking socialism specifically, still less any particular items in the Labour administration's programme, but the whole post-Enlightenment style of thought to which socialism belongs. This Oakeshott calls Rationalism, and in his view it has also spread to socialism's political rivals.

According to Oakeshott, the Rationalist believes that there is only one kind of 'reason', and that it is external to, and valid independently of, the activities to which it is applied. Furthermore, his possession of it gives him both the power and the right to reorganise the world in accordance with its dictates. These dictates find articulation in an 'ideology'; that is, in some comprehensive and (usually) pseudo-scientific programme of action, the 'plan', together with its intellectual justification.

The planning mentality, of course, is not wrong in itself. Like all conceptions, it has its roots in practice. It would be perfectly appropriate, say, to an engineering project (which is why social planning is often pejoratively called 'social engineering'). What is wrong is the idea that 'planning' is the appropriate form of organis-ation for a *society*. For a society is not a machine, consisting of inert components whose interrelations are meaningful only in the light of the external force which impels them and the external purpose which they jointly serve. It is, rather, a living thing whose common life and fulfilment derive from the unforced convergence of its members' self-chosen purposes. In short, if society is not literally an organism (as Bradley claimed it was),[8] it at least resembles one. (Oakeshott, as a matter of fact, nowhere uses this familiar Romantic analogy.)

Oakeshott's objection was not so much that 'planning' is a threat to freedom (though it is that), as that the whole Rationalist approach is misconceived. Because it is, and even boasts of being, external to the activities it offers to supervise, it can never acquire full knowledge of them. The only relevant knowledge is contained in the unself-conscious traditions which have emerged from them, and which govern their constant evolution. The Rationalist's plans are bound in practice not only to fail (or to 'succeed' only by the constant application of force), but also to destroy both future activity and its spring. The pretended 'efficiency' of planning turns out to be a sham. So rationalism is actually irrational.

Oakeshott's inaugural lecture at LSE (1952), called 'Political education', though widely recognised as a distinguished utterance, provoked the same combination of puzzlement and outrage as his previous *Cambridge Journal* pieces had done. (His appointment to Laski's Chair in 1951, of course, had a certain symbolic quality, noted by the newspapers at the time, not least because it coincided with the end of the Attlee period.)[9] The burden of 'Political education' was that politics has no substantive goal, that history is unpredictable, that there is no infallible recipe for our collective happiness, salvation or even security, and that the least unsound of our guides is tradition, since it is the fruit of our continuing historic experience. 'In political activity,' Oakeshott announced, in words which have since become famous,

> men sail a boundless and bottomless sea; there is neither harbour for shelter nor floor for anchorage, neither starting-place or appointed destination. The enterprise is to keep afloat on an even keel; the sea is both friend and enemy; and the seamanship consists in using the resources of a traditional manner of behaviour in order to make a friend of every hostile occasion.

The message was ill received, and, as Oakeshott had predicted in the lecture itself, treated as at best a counsel of despair. He was accused of irrationalism, and even (as earlier noted) of mysticism. But his point had never been more than this: that every activity naturally generates its own kind of rationality (that is, the principles, articulate or otherwise, appropriate to its successful pursuit), and that it is foolish and futile to apply the techniques and assumptions appropriate to one kind of activity to others for which they were never designed and from which they never emerged. To do so, in Ryle's terminology, is essentially a 'category mistake'. (Oakeshott had recently given Ryle's *The Concept of Mind* an exceptionally favourable review.)

For Oakeshott tradition is not necessarily anything romantic, decorative, legendary, symbolic, changeless, or nostalgic. Doubtless tartans, May Day, Trooping the Colour, the Durham Miners' Gala, the apes of Gibraltar and opening doors (or not) for ladies are all traditions of greater or lesser venerability, but they are not the only sort. A tradition in itself is no more than a particular way of doing or conceiving things (including oneself and one's membership of a moral and political culture) which can only be learnt by immersing oneself in them. It is a form of embodied practical knowledge which, though concrete, is not amenable to rationalisation, but which can and (since there is no alternative) must be handed on through a process of induction and apprenticeship, in the manner of a physical skill.

In fact every practice, including even intellectual activities such as science and history, possesses this traditional character. In all, the core knowledge, however important the additional informational component (which Oakeshott somewhat misleadingly calls 'technical knowledge'), is of this tacit, irreducible kind, which Ryle would call 'knowing how' as opposed to 'knowing that'. The Rationalist's error is to imagine, first, that technical knowledge, which can be written down (notably in the form of rules and methods), is the only genuine sort; secondly, that those practices (especially of a scientific or technological kind) which depend upon a large stock of technical knowledge should furnish the model of all understanding, particularly in fields, such as morals and politics, which have traditionally been understood otherwise, through habit, experience, taste, flair and rule of thumb.

The Rationalist thinks that abstract intelligence, when suitably backed by the necessary technical or factual knowledge, is a superior substitute for wisdom or humane understanding. To him the latter are mere fancy titles for prejudice or inertia. And his delusion is such that he can never learn from his failures, since wherever the fault lies it cannot be in him, his approach being underwritten, so to speak, by the Universe itself. Rationalism, Oakeshott observes, is in some ways the relic of a belief in magic. Or to put it another way, it involves a fantasy of control, a dream of instrumental reason.

What, in contrast, are the proper relations between the various discourses which make up the human world? The ideal relationship, Oakeshott tells us in his writings of the late 1950s and thereafter, is 'conversational'. Conversation in its literal sense was something highly prized by Oakeshott, and he used it as an all-encompassing metaphor for the ideal structure of education, social life generally, politics and much else. The traditional liberal university, in which different disciplines are brought together, not in a common substantive enquiry, but in a common *spirit* of enquiry, which involves no sacrifice of any of their autonomy, is for Oakeshott another model of the conversational relationship, and very probably a further source of his later all-embracing pluralism.[10]

The whole essence or definitive ethos of conversation is anti-teleological. Argument, which presses forward to a conclusion, is the pattern of many single intellectual disciplines or undertakings, just as planned endeavour is of a business enterprise (or a Rationalist state). But universities, friendships, clubs, fraternities and the common life pursued within them are, like love and art, as pointless and inconclusive as conversation; which is only another way of saying, with Aristotle, that the most important things in life (to which all our material efforts are in the end directed) are simply ends in themselves, intrinsically or uninstrumentally valuable, literally useless.[11]

Once we read Oakeshott's conversational paradigm into politics we have what looks like a sophisticated version of liberalism. It is conservative only so far as it is seen to have emerged from a specific historical inheritance which is thought worth preserving. This is what Oakeshott presents us with in his last large-scale work (which in fact was only his third 'serious' book), *On Human Conduct* (1974). It is the densest of his longer works, and for the most part is devoid of his usual elegance. Curiously, its obscurity seems the result of a dogged effort not to be misunderstood, as though its author were issuing his final intellectual testament to the world. It is certainly the first of his books that can reasonably be expected to baffle, or even repel, the common reader. (For that reason I do not recommend it to the would-be student of Oakeshott; *Rationalism in Politics and Other Essays* is far and away the best from that point of view.)

On Human Conduct consists of three long, interconnected essays. In the first, Oakeshott reconsiders the world as apprehended in experience. He now divides it into two grand categories or 'orders', the realm of 'processes' and the realm of 'procedures'. The first is the domain of nature, which is inert, unconscious, mechanically ordered and open only to scientific understanding; the second is what Kant would call the domain of freedom, that is, the world of intelligent, self-conscious action, the specifically 'human' world. There seems to be no possibility of 'conversation' between the natural and the human orders, of the kind which allegedly took place between the modes. (Indeed, the neo-Kantian Dilthey, who was something of an influence on Oakeshott, allocated wholly different kinds of study to each, which he called the *Naturwissenschaften* and the *Geisteswissenschaften*, the natural and the cultural sciences.)

It follows that attempts, such as sociology and psychology, to treat the human world in a natural-scientific manner must simply be enormous category-mistakes; or would be, if that were nowadays actually what those disciplines tried to do. In fact most social scientists have taken serious note of criticisms in the Dilthey–Oakeshott vein, and would deny that they were in any sense seeking to reduce human conduct to a 'process'. To explain manifest regularities in the aggregate outcomes and unintended consequences of individual human decisions is to say nothing about those decisions in themselves.

All conduct is a form of utterance or (as Oakeshott calls it) performance. Every performance belongs to a practice (that is to say, mode, discourse, language-game or whatever) and is to be understood only by reference to its local rules and conventions. Performances are of two kinds. A self-disclosure simply announces that the self in question is open for business. Here it advertises its wants, invites co-operation in securing them, and either does or does not succeed in completing a transaction. Though subject to external moral considerations as to what kinds of transactions may be made, self-disclosure considered simply by itself is ethically insignificant. A self-enactment, on the other hand, is a revelation or even a deliberate display of character, and is subject to moral evaluation in point of its motive. The only moral consideration relevant to a self-disclosure is whether or not it is lawful. The kind of consideration relevant to a self-enactment is whether it is honourable or shameful. Oakeshott does not hesitate to assimilate virtue so understood (i.e. as compelled by considerations of honour, grace, generosity, appropriateness, etc.) to the aesthetic, to treat it as a kind of poetic utterance.

In the second essay Oakeshott expounds two ideal types of human association, which he calls enterprise and civil association. Enterprise association is purposive, voluntary, subject (like self-disclosure) to external moral considerations, and managerial, the management being deputed to act according to the association's general policy. It is the commonest form of association, and the only one adapted to the satisfaction of our material needs.

Civil association is association in terms not of specific wants or purposes, but (as in conversation) of generally acknowledged rules, that is to say, of law;[12] and though its features clearly derive from those of voluntary (but externally purposeless) associations, it belongs wholly to politics. A state constituted entirely in terms of civil association is almost unheard of, but if it existed it would be governed wholly by law and never by policy, except so much as was necessary for its survival. Its legislature and executive might be democratically elected or they might not. All that matters is that the citizen's wishes should find formal representation, and that the administration be accountable to its own laws. The bond of society will be nothing more substantial than the citizens' common acknowledgement of the authority of the laws; no further cement is required, in the shape (for example) of national, ethnic or tribal sentiment (though doubtless a degree of cultural homogeneity will help). The sentiment which really counts is the sentiment of civility, the disposition to respect others simply as fellow-members of the same legal community, even if one happens to dislike them personally or disapprove of their particular culture or life style.

Just how much in the way of morality such a society's laws should attempt to reinforce is doubtful. The more culturally plural the society, the more the bond of civility will be strained by either excessive moralism or excessive liberality, since both are likely to offend some substantial segment of society and tempt it into disobedience. A social bond as tenuous as civil association almost presupposes, and will certainly depend upon a homogeneous liberalism of sentiment among its subjects. It may therefore be put at risk by the very pluralism it appears to foster. The reason is that, among the diverse human types and cultures which civil association purports to accommodate side by side, there will always be some whose freedom to live as they desire is actually threatened by liberalism, as we can see from the acts and pronouncements of religious fundamentalists of every stripe worldwide. It is all very well for liberals to condemn such people, especially when they break the law or behave obnoxiously (to the liberal way of thinking) in defence of their values and convictions, but what is to be done about them? These are questions, I am afraid, to which Oakeshott, like liberalism, returns no answer.

The third essay in *On Human Conduct* illustrates the historical emergence, in European culture, of two different conceptions of the state, one corresponding to civil and the other to enterprise association. Much of the substance had appeared earlier, in an article entitled 'The masses in representative democracy'; it is by far the raciest, least technical, and most immediately intelligible part of the book. Oakeshott's fundamental contention is that when the state is construed as an enterprise association the outcome is something not far removed from slavery. For the state cannot be a true enterprise association, precisely because citizenship, in most important respects, is not a voluntary or optional condition. It is one thing to be obliged to acknowledge the authority of the state's laws, but quite another to be forced to participate in its projects. Needless to say, the great totalitarian experiments of modern times are attempts to turn the state into an enterprise association.

A civil association, however, is just what the state ought to be, and what only a state can be. What will life be like in the 'civil' state, and why should anyone prize it? We know already that it will be united by a sentiment of 'civility'. But it will lack the stifling intimacy of traditional societies, for which Oakeshott, traditionalist though he may be in some respects, expressed no affection whatever. It will also lack the 'solidarity' and 'fraternity' prized by socialists (though seldom if ever found in actual socialist states). In short, Oakeshott shares none of the communitarian sentiment of certain recent political thinkers on both left and right. His outlook is individualist, but without the abstract quality generally found in liberal thought. The freedom which he cherishes can exist only in society, and only under law. It is not a right, still less a natural right, but a collective historical accomplishment which the citizen comes to value and to cultivate both for its own sake and as the precondition of self-enactment. The free man or Oakeshottian individualist is not a lawless pirate, a neurotic rebel or a banal egoist, but rather a virtuous explorer of his moral, cultural and intellectual inheritance.

As people are now increasingly coming to realise, Oakeshott occupies a distinguished place in contemporary thought, even if it is a tricky one to specify. Superficially he belongs with that group of

post-war anti-totalitarian thinkers whose more celebrated representatives include his nearly exact contemporaries Popper and Hayek.
Purely as a political thinker, however, he seems to me superior. The
reason is that, unlike them, he endeavours to give a complete account
of human experience, and his conception of politics emerges both
from that wider understanding and from a detailed historical
awareness, neither of which is the case with the Austrians. For it
is undeniable that Hayek's politics are modelled primarily on
economics, with all the limitations that implies, as Popper's are on
the philosophy of science. It is not surprising that Oakeshott
regarded them both as crypto-Rationalists. ('A plan to resist all
planning', he wrote of Hayek's wartime tract *The Road to Serfdom*,
'may be better than its opposite, but it belongs to the same style of
politics.') And of course Oakeshott has nothing in common with
more recent liberal thinkers such as Rawls and Nozick, since the
Kantian thought-experiment on which Rawls bases his theory and
the confessedly dogmatic Lockean rights from which Nozick begins
are both quite frankly Rationalist, in that they view political questions
– which they reduce simply to the ethics of distribution – from an
Archimedean standpoint wholly removed from the day-to-day
realities of government and citizenship (though not from the day-to-
day concerns of the democratic politician competing for votes). It
would not be altogether unjust to describe their efforts as exactly the
sort of 'crib' or bluffer's guide to politics that Oakeshott once accused
Marxism of being.

On one thing, however, Marx and Oakeshott are agreed, namely
that theory is the shadow of practice. From what practice, then, does
Oakeshott's own thought derive, and must not its being thus
derivative diminish its claim to be taken seriously? The two questions
may be answered together: Oakeshott's thought derives from a
tradition of freedom and pluralism, and precisely for that reason
because (though conditional) it is not compelled but chosen, it
deserves to be treated with respect, on its own terms. Characterising
the political heritage he shared with his readers, Oakeshott wrote
that:

> Our need now is to recover the lost sense of a society whose freedom
> and organization spring, not from a superimposed plan, but from the
> integrating power of a vast and subtle body of rights and duties enjoyed
> between individuals (whose individuality, in fact, comes into being by

their enjoyment), not the gift of nature but the product of our own
experience and inventiveness; and to recover also the perception of our
law, not merely as a body of achieved rights and duties, the body of a
freedom in which mere political rights have a comparatively insignificant place, but as a living method of social integration, the most
civilized and the most effective method ever invented by mankind.

Those words were written in 1948. But they are not less relevant in
our own controversial and politically hyperactive times. For what
they point to is a cultural inheritance under which 'mere' politics was
once kept severely in its place, that place being primarily to protect
the cultural inheritance and ensure both its survival and its future
development. Whether the cultural inheritance of which Oakeshott
speaks can actually be recovered, and the role of politics accordingly
reduced, in the face of the fact that, notwithstanding the fall of
communism, nearly all modern states are still at least partly enterprise associations, are questions which Oakeshott does not consider,
and which one would have to be a considerable optimist to answer in
the affirmative.

How far Oakeshott can usefully be considered a 'Cambridge mind'
is doubtful. He himself acknowledges his debt to Bradley (an
Oxonian) in respect of his early Idealism; and his aesthetics, like those
of the Bloomsbury set, to which they bear a certain resemblance, also
have an Oxford flavour. (To my mind, Oakeshott's aesthetics, though
interesting, are the least satisfactory part of his philosophy.) On
the other hand, his reflections on the practice of history (which
Collingwood rightly called 'the high-water mark of English thought'
on the subject) are rooted in the patient, anti-teleological, scholarly
empiricism of the Cambridge historical school, as typified by such a
writer as Maitland. (Though 'empiricism' is perhaps a misleading
word here. The raw material of history is not immediate experience,
for that was never on record, but experience selectively rendered
into documentary form; and secondly, even so-called immediate
experience is the part-product of conceptual frameworks which are
themselves a deposit of both individual and collective experience.)[13]

If Oakeshott is undeniably 'Cambridge' at all, it is mostly in his
politics, which are both sceptical and pragmatic, and not at all 'high'
in the traditional Oxford manner. (To be sure, Wittgenstein too
was at Cambridge, but he was not in any sense a product of it.) But
how can one really categorise a mind which, despite the admitted

transparency of some of its affiliations, was at the same time both notably individual and notably independent?

NOTES

1 Oakeshott more than once quotes or alludes to Butler's *Hudibras*, the seventeenth-century satire on political and religious activism as personi-fied in the eponymous anti-hero, a ridiculous Presbyterian squire, moral crusader and general spoilsport, deliberately conceived as a latter-day Quixote. (Cervantes was one of Oakeshott's favourite authors.)

2 In his first book, *Experience and its Modes*, published only three years after Lawrence's death, Oakeshott cites him as a notable exponent (along with Kant and Hebbel) of the idea of 'the integrity and separateness of the self'. And in an essay of 1949, 'The universities', he unconsciously borrows the pejorative expression 'the plausible ethics of productivity' from Lawrence's *Women in Love*, where it is applied to the industrialist Gerald Crich.

3 See, e.g., Paul Franco, *The Political Philosophy of Michael Oakeshott*; Robert Grant, *Oakeshott* (both 1991). W. G. Greenleaf, however (*Oakeshott's Philosophical Politics*, 1966), usefully details Oakeshott's affinities with his more narrowly politico-economic contemporaries, such as Hayek, Jewkes, the Mont Pélerin Society and the Chicago school (relative to the last of which, see Oakeshott's 'The political economy of freedom', in *Rationalism in Politics and Other Essays*.)

4 In her own book, *Philosophy and the Physicists* (1937), there is much concerning the impossibility of reducing macrophysical systems to the microphysical systems of which they are notionally composed. Oddly enough, this echoes ideas found in *Experience and its Modes* and much later in *On Human Conduct*, where their debt to Dilthey is obvious.

5 In his *Philosophy and the Mirror of Nature* (1979).

6 To come to specifics, all the following would be examples of modal irrelevance, or as Oakeshott calls it in scholastic idiom, *ignoratio elenchi*: providential and so-called Whig history; Marxism, Benthamism, Nazi race theory; Lysenkoism; accusing a cabbage of theft (his own example).

7 Some wartime conscripts were not actually demobilised until 1949. And of course many controls (e.g. rationing) remained in force long after there was the slightest justification for them (a contrast, incidentally, with their early abandonment in post-war Germany by the Adenauer administration).

8 See F. H. Bradley, 'My station and its duties', in *Ethical Studies* (1876).

9 The extent and importance of Laski's influence at the time, especially on

the indigenous nationalist leadership of the British colonies then graduating to independence (notably India, independent in 1947), can scarcely be overestimated. It is only now fading, partly as a result of socialism's failure to deliver the desired benefits, partly as a consequence of the world-wide collapse of serious faith in socialism. (The two last-mentioned phenomena, though obviously interconnected, are also, I think, distinct. After all, socialism had always previously shown itself immune to anything suggestive of empirical refutation. And it may do so again as people discover that liberal capitalism, equally, does not come without its price tag.)

10 There are radical difficulties in Oakeshott's conversational paradigm. The most striking is perhaps this: since Oakeshott's whole central idea of relevance depends on the recognition and maintenance of modal boundaries, how can conversation be possible, since (a) nothing in it can be irrelevant, and (b) it postulates communication, or some community or subject-matter, between the modes? I have attempted to answer such questions in chapter 5 ('The conversation paradigm') of my book *Oakeshott* (see n. 3 above).

11 Oakeshott shows a marked hostility to the whole Western, so-called Faustian and (some might say) masculine ethos of 'achievement' (it seems to go along with his scepticism concerning 'progress' and the like). He had an amusing, tongue-in-cheek affectation, when out hill-walking with friends, of refusing to go the last few feet, protesting that it was 'vulgar' to get to the top.

12 Legal rules differ from moral rules, though the subject's obligation to observe them is (like any other) a moral one. Moral rules are sustained mainly by their subscribers' collective conviction. They are not formal, and though they change, they do so spontaneously, not in consequence of any deliberate decision. (For a start, there is no procedure for changing them.) The authority of a legal rule, however, is independent of the subject's moral approval. He obeys it, not because it is good or right in itself (nobody can morally approve of every single law to which he is subject), but because it is 'the law' (i.e. is formally authoritative), and because to obey 'the law' generically is the good and right thing to do.

13 I have written at length of Oakeshott's aesthetic and historiographical views in *Oakeshott*, chapter 7.